PORTRAITS OF POWER

PORTRAITS OF POWER

Compiled by Jeremy Murray-Brown

A
Jonathan-James
Book

NYT
Times
BOOKS

A Jonathan-James Book

Published by TIMES BOOKS, a division of
Quadrangle/The New York Times Book Co., Inc.
Three Park Avenue, New York, N.Y. 10016

Library of Congress Cataloging in Publication Data
Main entry under title:
Portraits of power.

   1.   Statesmen.   2.   Power (Social sciences) —
Case studies.   3.   History, Modern — 20th century.
I.   Murray-Brown, Jeremy, 1932–
D445.P65   920'.02   79 — 51439
ISBN 0-8129-0846-5

Editor: R. Carolyn King
Designer: Annette Tatchell
Picture Research: R. Carolyn King with Nancy Falconer

Jonathan-James Books
5 Sultan Street, Toronto, Ontario, Canada M5S 1L6

Manufactured in the United States of America

It is essential not to have faith in human nature.
Such faith is a recent heresy and a very disastrous one.

Professor Herbert Butterfield
Christianity and History

CONTENTS

PREFACE

And it was only when I lay there on rotting prison straw that I sensed within myself the first stirrings of good. Gradually it was disclosed to me that the line separating good and evil passes not through states, not between classes, nor between political parties either — but right through every human heart.

Alexander Solzhenitsyn

Caesar's Laurel Crown

by Jeremy Murray-Brown

Power, like nature, abhors a vacuum. Remove one source of power and a different one will immediately present itself. Cut off one hated head, and many others still more hateful will instantly spring up in its place. The greater the power structure, the more dreadful the repercussions of its fall. Like the fearful image in Nebuchadnezzar's dream, after the gold came the silver, and after the silver, the brass and the iron. Or as William Blake put it:

> *The hand of Vengeance found the Bed*
> *To which the Purple Tyrant fled;*
> *The iron hand crush'd the Tyrant's head*
> *And became a Tyrant in his stead.*

Power, in this sense, means political power. It is the power of rulers of all kinds: Kings and queens, presidents and politicians, pontiffs and mullahs, generals and general secretaries, the power of the assembly and the power of the mob. It is what Pascal called "carnal greatness," the power that is recognized with the eyes, as distinct from the power of the intellect or the power of the spirit. The greatness of geniuses and the greatness of saints belong to different orders of power from the greatness of "kings, rich men, captains."

The eighteen men and one woman portrayed in this book all belong to Pascal's first order of power. Whatever their differences in background or in method of operation, they have this in common: their relationship toward power is not an unwilling one but is a matter of choice.

No one, in other words, comes by power accidentally or holds it without a purpose. The point was well put by Adolf Hitler when he was defending himself for his part in his first attempt at a coup d'état in Munich in 1923, known as the Beerhall *putsch*. "The man who is born to be a dictator is not compelled; he wills it. He is not driven forward, but drives himself. There is nothing immodest about this . . . The man who feels called upon to govern a people has no right to say: If you want me or summon me, I will cooperate. No, it is his duty to step forward."

The principal characters featured here do not have to be dictators to fit Hitler's description of the road to power. Gandhi no less than Hitler offered himself as a leader. The Queen of England and the Emperor of Japan chose to associate themselves with actions performed in their name. Churchill, de Gaulle, Truman — fate may have helped them, but power was their lodestar. And so with all nineteen; in one way or other, they stepped forward from the society into which they were born to become seekers and holders of power.

Few people took Hitler or his words very seriously at the time; 10 years later when he became dictator of Germany they did not realize how seriously Hitler took himself, although few men spelled out so clearly what they intended to do with power and stuck so closely to their program. Another characteristic of power is that all who pursue it find very good reasons for doing so which for the most part they believe themselves. The more honest of them make no bones about it. "The great questions of the day," said Bismarck, "are not decided by speeches and majority votes, but by blood and iron." Others, especially in the West, resort to various ideological subterfuges. War, which is power in its most extreme form, accounts for some of the worst subterfuges, such as the pretence propagated by Roosevelt and Churchill that the alliance between the Western democracies and Stalin's Russia represented an agreement between people who had the same values and ideals.

This pretence, enshrined in the Yalta agreements, led to the great betrayals of the postwar era like the fate of the people of central Europe, especially Poland, and of those unfortunate Russians who trusted in British and American good faith only to find themselves forcibly repatriated to the Soviet Union in the most brutal manner. "In war," writes Professor Trevor-Roper, "one great aim obviously overrides others and gives, for the time, an absolute validity to the lesser decisions it entails."

Yalta was an extreme example, but the self-deceptions of power are found at all levels. In defending the abduction of Eichmann from Argentina by Israeli agents, Ben-Gurion wrote of "the supreme moral validity" of the deed. "These events cannot be approached, Mr. President, from an exclusively formal point of view." There were "overriding motives."

There always are. Just as total war involves total propaganda, so power in these circumstances recognizes no distinction between right and wrong, truth and falsehood, but only between victors and vanquished.

This may be an uncomfortable truth for liberal minded people to live with, but it is best to face it squarely. Blake's words are again to the point:

The Strongest Poison ever known
Came from Caesar's Laurel Crown.

But it is possible to wear this crown, as de Gaulle did, with honor and integrity. No one can say of de Gaulle that he was a fraud, a liar or a cheat. Or a creation of the media. And if he rendered unique services to France, there is no need to decry his greatness.

But neither should we rail against a Hitler or a Stalin as though they were different in kind from Bismarck and Frederick the Great, Napoleon and Richelieu, the czars and the Holy Roman Emperors, Cromwell and George Washington, and all the other rulers we read about in history books. Different times and circumstances produce different responses to power, but it remains, as Pascal defined it, power of a kind that requires uniforms and gold braid, orbs and scepters and maces and salutes to make it an object of appeal to the eye.

In this respect this book is true to its subject. It consists of portraits, not academic biographies. The authors are all correspondents of *The New York Times*, America's outstanding daily newspaper. They do not claim to say all that there is to be said about their subjects, nor do they necessarily agree with each other. Each writer brings his own insight into the workings of power based on his personal experience as a journalist in the field. Inevitably there will be conflicting

estimates of men and events depending on the point of view of the observer, which is indeed how power operates.

The resulting collection of words and pictures is a many faceted portrait of power in general which is more than the sum of its parts. Taken together these essays, photographs and personal contributions cover the history of our times — a period of more than 50 years which future historians will look back on as giving the 20th century its essential character. The years before 1914 belong to the old order of power, to the world of the 19th century when European civilization spread itself throughout the globe; the years after America's withdrawal from Vietnam belong to a new order whose form we are as yet unable to make out. Between lie the years which belong to the individuals portrayed in these pages.

But to find an appropriate arrangement for their portraits is like trying to fit a jigsaw puzzle together without knowing what the overall design is. The scheme that has been followed here is to place the portraits in an order which brings out as far as possible the dramatic interaction of men and events upon each other. Like actors in a play, each one has his role, his moment of destiny as it were, which determines the timing of his appearance.

On this basis the pieces of the jigsaw come together to reveal certain themes and sub-plots within the larger chronological design. One of the most notable of these themes which weaves its way through much of the book is the disappearance of the British Empire.

When Winston Churchill became Britain's wartime prime minister in 1940, he brought to the office a lifetime's experience of a power system which encircled the globe, a power system which was the linchpin of the old order and even in 1940 seemed outwardly more impressive than that of Soviet Russia or Republican America. It was certainly assumed to be more powerful than Hirohito's Japan. Five years later when Churchill met Stalin and Truman at Potsdam shortly after the defeat of Germany, Britain's power was gone. The war had exhausted her and the belief that she ruled the waves had been shattered with the sinking of the *Repulse* and the *Prince of Wales* and the fall of Singapore. After the war's end with almost indecent speed she had to leave India. She could no longer afford to prop up Greece and Turkey against the advance of Russia toward the Mediterranean, which had been her traditional policy since the 19th century when the Slav and not the Hun was the principal threat to her imperial interests. She quickly abandoned Palestine and Egypt. She had no power to prevent her interests being taken over in Iran. Decolonization followed rapidly in Southeast Asia and Africa. By the time Churchill became prime minister for a second term in 1951 Britain could scarcely be described as a world power. By the time he died in 1965 the British Empire was a thing of the past.

Here, then, was a situation in which new contenders for power quickly appeared. The removal of ancient landmarks in the form of British bases and British power cleared the stage for Gandhi and his associates in India, for Ben-Gurion in Palestine, Nasser in Egypt and the Shah of Iran in his own country. It was a factor in Mao Tse-tung's success in China and it was the context in which Stalin and Truman both operated in the early years of the cold war.

With the decline of British power came the rise of America to world dominance which her monopoly of the atomic bomb gave her in 1945. But the paradox of American history in the 20th century is that it places this enormous power in the hands of a single man, the president, who finds himself virtually incapable of using it abroad because of a constitution designed to safeguard her citizens against such power being used at home. American liberalism can only survive in the world if American power is actually deployed on equal terms with those who do not have such a constitution. In peacetime this rarely seems to happen, with the result that in peacetime American presidents are always building castles on sand which is being steadily undermined by more determined users of power. As early as the first months of 1946 Secretary Byrnes put the position succinctly when he complained that Soviet policy meant "a unilateral gnawing away at the status quo." But whose status quo? If it was to be a *Pax Americana*, then it would have to be with the 20th century's equivalent of gunboat diplomacy.

It is therefore an illusion of liberalism to suppose that mankind will ever become wise or good enough for the use of force to be unnecessary, or that an international order can ever exist in which everyone respects his neighbor's territory, rights and goods, or that it is power, of all things, which will wither away. The history of the years covered by these portraits should be enough to dispose of this illusion.

The four American presidents featured here, who between them span a 30-year period of history, illustrate this theme. Only, it seems, when America is fully committed to a world war and is certain of the rightness of the cause can her power be fully utilized. Because of its limited nature, the Korean War ended in military stalemate and stirred deep political animosities. Today, in the bitter aftermath of Vietnam, we have to acknowledge that the Truman Doctrine is dead and all we are left with is the empty rhetoric of Kennedy's Inaugural address. To reverse Dean Acheson's quip about Britain: America has lost a role and not found an empire.

The readiness of others to exploit the liberal illusion is another theme to emerge from these portraits. Those who wield power without the restraint of a Congress or a Parliament turn out to be the prime movers in events. They are free always to take the initiative. Indeed, this is the nature of their power: to maintain themselves against rivals they must be constantly seeking more of it. Hitler, Stalin and Khrushchev are the leading examples portrayed here, while more obscurely we feel it to be so with Mao Tse-tung and his successors.

In the light of these themes, the first portrait to appear has to be Hitler's. It was Hitler who dissected the way power works most clearly, grasped it most boldly and dispensed with all humbug in pursuing it. His appointment as Chancellor of Germany in January 1933 set in motion those forces which changed the face of the world. Without Hitler Churchill would not have enjoyed supreme power in Britain, and without Churchill Hitler might well have succeeded in

making himself master of the world. In their ability to capture the hearts and minds of the people they led, in their grasp of the broad implications of power, in their ruthlessness, the two men had much in common. Their two portraits therefore stand together, just as during the Battle of Britain they can be pictured facing each other in a duel of wills across the English Channel.

Following this arrangement, Stalin, another prime mover, is flanked by Roosevelt and Truman, Khrushchev is followed by Kennedy, while at the end of the book rises the ominous figure of Mao Tse-tung whose role in the future of the world, like that of China, remains unclear. The other portraits find their place between these prime movers and their counterparts.

In the case of de Gaulle it is hard to say which was his finest moment — his call to honor in 1940, or his actions on returning to France in 1944, or his return to power in 1958. But in comparing de Gaulle with his contemporaries, it seems right that his portrait should form the centerpiece of the gallery. Controversial though many of his actions were, his stature provides a standard against which others can be measured. Although Eisenhower commanded more material power and Kennedy displayed more worldwide popular appeal, for the 10 years during which de Gaulle represented France he was, in Kennedy's phrase, "the great captain of the western world."

A final point about this arrangement is to note that the portrait of the man also tells us something about his circumstances. With Adenauer, it is the rebirth of Germany; with Ben-Gurion, it is the creation of the State of Israel; with the Shah, it is the politics of oil. The portrait of Tito tells us about Stalin the bully and the relationship between small and big powers. The portrait of Hirohito tells us about the varying fortunes of Japan. And so with each one: it is a portrait of the life and of the times.

The inclusion of Mahatma Gandhi needs explaining. Many people revere Gandhi for his wisdom and his saintliness, but it is not for these qualities that he appears here. Nor is it likely that his name will go down in history because of them. Rather, as a practitioner of power politics who did more than anyone to call the bluff of the British in ruling so vast an empire with such an exclusive racial caste and on so flimsy an ideological pretext. Once India became free the old colonialism was finished everywhere.

Gandhi's portrait follows Churchill's because of the dramatic contrast in their two approaches to power. For Churchill, power lay in the pomp of a Durbar and the dash of a cavalry charge and the idea of Westminster as the mother of parliaments. But for Gandhi, who had seen in the massacre at Amritsar what all that could lead to and had personally suffered racial humiliation in South Africa, power lay in India's peasant millions who needed to do nothing more than patiently sit it out until the Raj would give up of its own accord.

The clash between Churchill and Gandhi was, in its way, as full of personal drama as the duel between Churchill and Hitler. The stakes were as high and the issue as far-reaching. In Britain, Gandhi is popularly remembered because of Churchill's description of him as a "seditious fakir ... striding half naked up the steps of the Viceroy's palace." But Gandhi was Churchill's equal in the art of political propaganda. Where other men of power dress up to enhance their image, Gandhi's characteristic lack of clothing made him the best known Asian leader in the world. Churchill was able to have Gandhi locked up at a critical moment in the war; but Gandhi was still around when Churchill was voted out of office and the new Viceroy was quick to make friends with him. Old India hands of Churchill's generation shuddered when they saw photographs of Gandhi's arm resting on Lady Mountbatten's shoulder, as did old Africa hands a decade and a half later when they saw Jomo Kenyatta dancing with the Colonial Secretary's daughter.

So Gandhi takes his place alongside the other members of this portrait gallery because his campaign of nonviolence, like the civil rights movement in the United States which it inspired, was concerned with power and was politically motivated. Faced in the one case with a paternalistic British Raj and in the other with a complex democratic system, both movements proved the most effective weapons available in the existing power struggle. But in both cases, when their political objectives were realized, they ceased to have further relevance. As weapons in the continuing power struggle they were immediately discarded.

The price that India paid for her independence was a million or so deaths in savage communal violence, together with the partition of the continent which later produced the further dismemberment of Pakistan. It may be that at the end of his life Gandhi regretted ever having associated himself with a political movement which had such tragic results. They were, after all, a negation of everything he stood for. The other Asian leader portrayed here, who also mobilized peasants in their millions, took a different line from the start. Mao Tse-tung grasped power through violence, an example which has found more imitators than Gandhi's, especially in Africa.

Nevertheless lip service to Gandhi's ideals continued to be paid long after his death. The site where his body was cremated became a national shrine, like the Cenotaph in London's Whitehall or Kennedy's grave in Washington's Arlington Cemetery, where visiting statesmen felt obliged to pay their respects. Khrushchev, for one, never failed to lay a wreath there, both before and after suppressing the Hungarian bid for freedom.

It is worth noting that in terms of this kind of power, a movement like Gandhi's would have stood no chance of success in Hitler's Germany or Stalin's Russia. And indeed none appeared in either country. Instead resistance to tyrannies so absolute as these has to be on a different level altogether, witness Helmuth von Moltke and his friends in the Kreisau Circle in Germany and Russian dissidents like Alexander Solzhenitsyn.

Attention must be drawn to one other common factor in all these portraits of power, and this is the power of the media. The 20th century has seen this new form of power grow to such proportions that, with television, it has come to dominate all others.

15

Take the case of British monarchy. It is arguable that without the power of the media the monarchy in Britain would have disappeared long ago. But when King George V broadcast for the first time on Christmas Day 1932 the effect took everyone by surprise. Harold Nicholson described it: "His was a wonderful voice — strong, emphatic, vibrant, with undertones of sentiment, devoid of all condescension, artifice or pose. The effect was wide and deep." "Surely there was magic in all this," he added. Though Queen Elizabeth's Christmas broadcasts have proved less successful, the effect of television coverage of royal events has been to popularize the monarchy as never before. The "magic in all this" has been a source of power to British politicians who now welcome the legal fiction of a constitutional monarchy as an alibi for their own weaknesses.

But if the Queen has taken a passive role in utilizing the media, the same can certainly not be said of the other practitioners of power in the 20th century. With Hitler, Churchill, Stalin and Roosevelt, use of the media was a cornerstone of their power. Each, it seems, was quick to grasp the lesson of the others' success and in a curious way they all borrowed from each other. In this respect Goebbels' diaries make instructive reading. In *Mein Kampf* Hitler had shown his deep understanding of mass psychology; working together, he and Goebbels built up the Nazi propaganda machine to the point where, in the closing stages of the war, it was the most powerful weapon the Germans possessed. In recognition of this, Allied propaganda went far to outbid it.

Goebbels wrote admiringly of Churchill's speeches during the Battle of Britain and of Stalin's slogan, "Better to die standing than live kneeling." But it seems that Goebbels was the one who first coined the phrase "iron curtain" about Soviet tactics in eastern Europe. Churchill in turn must have borrowed it from him. That Churchill understood the power of the media was obvious from his resort to broadcasting from the moment he took over as Prime Minister. In opposition it remained his most important weapon. Truman knew this and traded on it to bolster his own cold war policies. In messages to the new President shortly after Roosevelt's death Churchill had made use of the phrase "iron curtain" in an attempt to forestall the withdrawal of American power from eastern Europe. Some weeks before delivering the speech at Fulton, Missouri, which is now famous for the phrase, Churchill wrote to Truman saying: "I have a Message to deliver to your country and to the world and I think it very likely that we shall be in full agreement about it. Under your auspices anything I say will command some attention and there is an opportunity for doing some good to this bewildered, baffled and breathless world." Truman knew well what to expect.

The Fulton speech is well known. Less well known is Churchill's speech delivered to the Massachusetts Institute of Technology. The somber note of his words may seem melodramatic, but we shall probably never know whether there were hawks and doves in the Kremlin, the former arguing for the speedy conquest of all Europe — an easy task for the Red Army once Truman had called American forces home — and the latter fearful of the American bomb.

Whatever lay behind Stalin's moves, it is unlikely that Soviet archives will ever become available to scholars, even supposing such archives exist. A Ministry of Truth has no need of records like these.

Stalin's use of the media lies at the very center of his power. Being a small and unprepossessing man with no speaking style and none of the qualities of charisma attributed to other leaders, Stalin manufactured his own charisma. He proved that you could do what you liked with the media, whether it was your own or other people's.

Using different methods, Roosevelt and his successors came to the same conclusion. The fireside chat, the press conference, the controlled leak — an immobile President developed these aids to power to an extraordinary degree. In contrast, after 12 years of a President in a wheelchair, Truman's very mobility made news. While with Kennedy, the media achieved its greatest triumph — the packaging of a President in his every word and gesture, in his very looks, above all in the *réclame* of his death which has ensured his immortality in celluloid, print and videotape.

Today all exponents of power know that information has to be processed according to the needs of the moment. Manipulating the media has become as integral a part of the apparatus of power as the gun or the ballot box. In this respect Goebbels was once again right when he wrote: "History will acquit us if we win the war." After comparing a great number of newsreels put out by the various participants in the Second World War, one is driven to conclude that there is no real difference between them either in technique or in propaganda content. The self-deceptions of power afflict winners and losers alike; and if Goebbels and Hitler were living on fantasies as the Allies closed in on Berlin, so were Roosevelt and Churchill as they met with Stalin to sign the Yalta agreements.

The role of the communications media raises questions about the nature of historical reality which cannot be answered here. Suffice it to say that to draw attention to the power of the media is another way of saying that power itself acts as a magnet to the media, this book and its companion film series being themselves evidence of this. Power is mankind's opiate. In today's terms it is good for network ratings. Films about Hitler will always attract large audiences. Photographs of Queen Elizabeth and her family help boost the circulation of popular magazines. There will never be a shortage of villains to provide material for peak hour viewing. The President of the United States will always be accompanied by a television film crew, as indispensable a part of his entourage as security men and speech writers.

For an essential element of power is the creation of an image before which men can prostrate themselves. In Nebuchadnezzar's day it was a colossal image of gold set up in the plains of Babylon. Today, it is a televised image of man himself — man on the moon, man in a test-tube, man who, according to President Kennedy's speech writers, "can be as big as he wants." Thus it is appropriate that at the end of this book our last sight of power is a picture of the corpse of Mao Tse-tung preserved in crystal. Dead or alive, the image is the power.

HITLER

He knew his audience. He knew exactly what chords to play to get the maximum response. He began in a very moderate tone and then, when he got on his main theme, gradually worked them up to a pitch. It was almost like a rocket going up — very slowly at first and then, at the end, it bursts!
Drew Middleton

The Road to Ruin

by Drew Middleton

Hitler first appears in history as a thin-faced, rather grubby but venomous agitator on the extreme right of German politics in the turbulent years after World War I. In less than 20 years he is the supreme ruler of Germany, then the greatest military power in the world, the most powerful man in an age of giants.

Dictionaries define power as the ability to do or act; the capability of doing or accomplishing something. They do not distinguish between good and evil.

By that definition, Adolf Hitler was one of the preeminent practitioners of power in this century. He did, he acted, he

An anti-Nazi election poster at the end of the Weimar Republic.

accomplished; if the end results were the ruin of his dreams and of his Third Reich, a death toll in the tens of millions and drastic changes in the world balance of power, he was a moving force. In the end, Hitler's exercise of power produced the very results he sought most to avoid: the emergence of the Soviet Union as a great military force, the subjection of eastern Europe to communism, and the rise of the United States to world leadership.

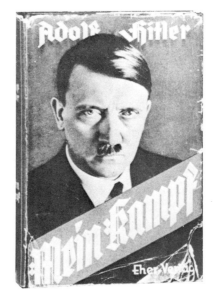

Like many of his fellow countrymen, Hitler thought that German might made German right. He made no secret of his will to power; it was what won him the adulation of so many of his fellow countrymen. He would give them everything they wanted. He would give them glory and honor. He would make them racially pure. He would make their children masters of the world. Anyone standing in the way would be ruthlessly cut down. And yet he seemed a kindly enough man; one you could even enjoy a joke with, if you knew him well enough.

Hitler served in the Kaiser's army as a company runner in World War I. His courage in the trenches won him the Iron Cross.

On the battlefield it could be proved that might makes right. True, Germany lost the war, but that was because of the republicans, the socialists, the Jews and the war profiteers who had combined to stab the army in the back, according to the legend which Hitler was to foster. These poisonous elements must be purged from German society and the peace treaty they accepted, the Treaty of Versailles, must be avenged.

In the aftermath of war, riots and street brawls were commonplace in Germany. Out of work officers and soldiers back from the front were accustomed to violence and welcomed a chance to fight it out with supporters of the recent Bolshevik revolution in Moscow. In their hatred for the new Republic of Weimar, which replaced the Kaiser's Germany, there was nothing to choose between Hitler's National Socialists and the Communists.

In the early 1920's, Hitler and his fellow malcontents gathered in Munich, a stronghold of reaction. Here Hitler's first attempt at a coup d'état collapsed at the opening burst of rifle fire. In prison, he brooded on the lessons of failure. Power, he realized, must be won by legal means if he was to rule Germany as he wanted. So, while there, he wrote a book, *Mein Kampf*, My Struggle, a blueprint for the Nazi march to power.

Few people at the time bothered to read Hitler's book, and those who did hardly took it seriously. At this stage, Hitler's posturing and the marches of the early National Socialists seemed ridiculous. They were a handful of crackpots, no more. Yet Hitler gave clear expression to the ideas which would later guide his actions and those of his followers. Germany must have *Lebensraum,* living space, he wrote, and that living space could be found only in the east. The people must have a leader, and that leader must have the will to use power ruthlessly to purify the race and recover Germany's greatness. One people, one Reich, one leader.

In *Mein Kampf*, Hitler also displayed his understanding of mass psychology — an understanding which amounted to

The fervor of National Socialist youth is displayed in Berlin in 1933.

genius. The propaganda techniques by which he turned his crackpot movement into the most powerful party in Germany are all laid down in *Mein Kampf.*

Hitler hated Jews. His anti-semitism was nurtured in the back streets of Vienna where such views were widely held. At that time, Jewish communities existed in most of the big cities of central Europe. To men and women who had lost their savings in the postwar inflation, or found themselves out of work in the depression at the end of the 1920's, these Jewish communities became a target for every kind of discontent. Hitler made the Jews a scapegoat for all Germany's misfortunes.

As the power of civil law inside Germany declined, so Nazi Jew-baiting grew in violence. Jews were publicly humiliated and beaten in the streets. Jewish shops were smashed, Jewish property and synagogues set on fire. The Jews were easy victims of Hitler's brown-shirted thugs. But Hitler knew that he could only win his way to power through the democratic system of Weimar Germany. The state, after all, still possessed greater actual powers than he and his party did, and he had to obtain those powers legally.

When Germany's economy suddenly collapsed in the wake of the world slump, Hitler saw his opportunity. In a series of elections following close upon each other, he courted every kind of vote. To the employers, he promised security against Bolshevism. To the conservatives, he promised order. To the radicals, he promised social revolution . . . His tireless campaigning paid off. Overnight, it seemed, the number of his supporters leaped into millions. No longer a party of crackpots, National Socialism was a mass movement equal in strength to the other powerful parties in the state.

In January 1933 Hitler was appointed Chancellor. His will to power had carried him to the top. Outwardly, legality was preserved, but it was the deathknell of the democratic Republic of Weimar. A huge torchlight parade by Hitler's supporters signaled his victory. No one really knew what his arrival in power would mean. His followers, of course, all looked for a share in the rewards of victory, but it would not be long before Hitler would throw his private army of brown-shirts, the S.A., to the wolves in order to win the confidence of the regular army.

With the powers of the state now in his hands, Hitler was able to exercise his skills as a propagandist on a vast scale. His intuition of what the German people liked to see and hear gave him a popular appeal among widely different groups of people. Giant spectacles revived memories of the glories of the past. Massive rallies excited the emotions of old and young alike. Through pageantry, through the rhetoric of National Socialism, through his deep understanding of mass psychology, backed where necessary by fists and jackboots, Hitler forged a power base which made him the sole undisputed leader.

Industry needed him for the freedom he gave them from union trouble; workers needed him to support their rising wages and hopes of a better future. Above all, the army needed him for the men and weapons denied them under the hated Treaty of Versailles. Under the terms of the peace treaty which ended World War I, Germany was restricted as to the armaments she could manufacture and troops she could maintain. Hitler ignored the treaty. He restored conscription.

Nazi rally in Nuremberg in 1935.

Hitler enters Vienna after the Nazi takeover of Austria.

Shock waves ran through the capitals of Europe. Some of Hitler's generals warned him against rearming, fearing retaliation from France and Britain, but the leaders of the western democracies were unwilling to risk another war. Hitler knew their fears and played upon them. Each success gave him renewed strength. Might *was* proving right.

In 1936, he took a further step toward destroying the Treaty of Versailles. He ordered 25,000 German troops to reoccupy the Rhineland in defiance of the peace terms. It was another gamble which some of his generals feared to take, but Hitler obeyed his own instincts. He knew France and Britain would do nothing but make noises. Once again, his will proved stronger than their irresolution.

Hitler replaced the generals who opposed him. To maintain the momentum of power, he had to have men who would obey his every order. One moment of faltering and all would be lost.

After the Rhineland came Austria, the leader's birthplace. All German-speaking people were to form part of Hitler's greater Germany. And after Austria, Hitler set his sights on Czechoslovakia, a nation created by the Treaty of Versailles whose borders included large numbers of German-speaking people. Hitler claimed them for his Reich. Although he was momentarily checked by the diplomatic intervention of France and Britain at Munich, his drive to power soon showed that these paper agreements were worthless. While he was content for the British and French to believe that "peace for our time" was at hand, he was disappointed that many Germans shared this view. His appetite for conquest was fed by the appeasement of the democracies.

Not just the Sudeten Germans but all of Czechoslovakia was next to be incorporated into Hitler's Germany; he claimed that it was his last territorial demand. But the living space which Germany needed according to the blueprint laid down in Hitler's *Mein Kampf* still lay untouched in the east.

In 1939, Hitler attacked Poland. Britain and France had at last committed themselves to war should he do so, but they were too late to deter him. He said: "We are faced with the alternative to strike or to be destroyed with certainty, sooner or later. No one knows how long I shall live — therefore anything is better now."

The young at that time vaguely recognized that back there in the past there had been something much more glorious, something much more appealing than this bourgeois Republic of Weimar. And I think there was a conscious looking back for something that was better than the present.

I don't think we ought to get the idea that all the Nazis were guttersnipes either, or street brawlers. There were some very substantial people who became Nazis.
Drew Middleton

Hitler and Ribbentrop.

On September 3, 1939, the Second World War began. War was the ultimate test of power. Hitler's judgment, his leadership, his physical stamina were subjected to almost unbearable strains. All moral questions aside, the manner in which he met the test stamps him as one of the most extraordinary men of all time. He had the best army in the world when the war began. His air force cowed all but the British. His navy, although small, was efficient. But it is doubtful that these military resources plus German industry would have won so many successes without Hitler.

Nothing, it seemed, could stop the German armies. Before the speed and ferocity of attack, known as the Blitzkrieg, one by one all the nations of Europe went under: Poland, Norway, Holland, Belgium, Luxembourg, Denmark.

Then it was France's turn. And France, one of the principal architects of the Treaty of Versailles, collapsed with a suddenness that shook the world. The British army was forced to evacuate in disarray at Dunkirk as the German Reich forged its way to the English Channel. Europe was at

his feet. Hitler enjoyed his triumph to the full. Turning France's humiliation into a piece of theater, he forced her leaders to sign their country's surrender in the very railroad car in which the Germans had signed *their* surrender in 1918.

The fall of France in June 1940 signaled Hitler's supreme victory. In six weeks the German armies had destroyed France as a military power. Even those generals who doubted Hitler's direction of the war were silenced by the astonishing success of his moves. The war had not lasted a year, but on the continent of Europe German power was paramount. The German flag flew in Paris in revenge for Germany's defeat in 1918. Nothing, it seemed, could halt Hitler's dream of conquest.

Although Paris was in German hands, Hitler could not afford to rest. The momentum of his drive for world power required further victories. His real prize lay in the east, but meanwhile the British must be made to sue for peace. He was prepared to make generous terms. "I can see no reason why this war should continue," he declared in the Reichstag.

At the same time, Hitler threatened the British with annihilation if they did not bend to his will. While he waited for peace moves which never came, his strategists prepared Operation Sea-Lion, the invasion of England. First, British air-power had to be eliminated. Hermann Goering's much vaunted Luftwaffe was given the task of bringing England to her knees.

For two months during the late summer of 1940, the fate

As Hitler re-armed, he brought back the Wehrmacht with its bands, its tanks, its aircraft. To an intensely militarist people, this had a great appeal. Even though, at this time, the German army was comparatively weak, it didn't look that weak to somebody who is seeing a parade of a division for the first time in his life. This looks like all the strength in the world and Germany is back on its feet again.

of the free world hung in the balance. What came to be known as the Battle of Britain ended in the middle of September when Hitler was forced to postpone his invasion plans and, with them, his timetable for the attack on Russia.

Hitler never understood the British nor the character of their new leader, Winston Churchill. His failure to subdue Britain in September 1940 was the turning point in his fortunes, though he did not realize it at the time.

The Luftwaffe was never able to replace the losses in trained pilots and aircraft it sustained in the Battle of Britain. But Hitler was still a conquering hero to most of his fellow countrymen. As yet the German people had suffered

hardly any ill effects of the war. They still followed their leader blindly and he was blind to what had really happened in the skies above the small island across the English Channel.

Hitler ruled continental Europe, west of Russia. Where would he attack next? His agents were in all corners of the globe disseminating Nazi propaganda and extending the influence of Germany. In France, the aged Marshal Pétain headed a puppet government.

In Spain, General Franco, himself a dictator and ostensibly a supporter of Germany, proved less amenable to Hitler's will. Hitler wanted a free run to Gibraltar, but Franco played for time. He was more realistic in his appraisal of Germany's position.

Late in 1940, Molotov, Russia's Foreign Minister, arrived in Berlin to confirm the year-old Nazi-Soviet pact. Signed in August 1939, it was Hitler's master diplomatic stroke, giving him a free hand to move against the west. Outwardly, Nazis and Soviets were in peaceful accord with each other, but secretly Hitler was already preparing to strike east.

Molotov left Berlin with Hitler's promise that Germany would never attack Russia. Meanwhile, plans for Germany's invasion of Russia went steadily ahead.

In the early morning of June 22, 1941, the assault began.

The attack on Russia was given the code name Operation Barbarossa. It was the logical culmination of Hitler's rise to power. Germany must have living space, he had written, and living space could only be found in the east. Take what you want by force. Might makes right. And the Slavs, after all, were unworthy to stand in the way of the master race.

To direct the campaign, Hitler moved his headquarters to a secret bunker in east Prussia, called Wolf's Lair. He had secured his southern flank by adding Greece and Yugoslavia

The Nazi-Soviet pact, signed in 1939, made allies of the two most powerful dictators in the world, who theoretically were the deadliest of enemies. Stalin got a free hand in the Baltic; Hitler was free to move west. They divided Poland between them.

Eisenhower used to say that any damn fool can be a strategist, but it takes someone who knows armies to get the food, the ammunition and the fuel there on time, so that the attack goes through. And I believe Hitler didn't know that and his generals knew he didn't know that.
Drew Middleton

Hitler isolated himself at Wolf's Lair for three and a half years. Surrounded by maps and generals he could dream of conquests greater than Napoleon's or Alexander's.

to his conquests; the states of eastern Europe were already subservient to him. From Wolf's Lair he could concentrate all Germany's resources on smashing the Soviet Union and wiping out Bolshevism forever.

For the first four months all went well. Then the velocity of the invasion slowed. Hitler intervened. He halted the direct attack on Moscow. Units were sent from that front to increase the pressure on Leningrad and to bolster the drive into the Ukraine in the south. The Führer's commands were obeyed but his generals were concerned with what they regarded as his interference in strategy.

Their protests were wasted. Hitler had proven himself right before — in Poland, in Scandinavia, in France and the Low Countries. He was buoyant, he said in September, because he had not hesitated. "When an inner conviction commands you to attack . . . I had to throw all my authority into the scales to force it [the attack] through. I note in passing that a great part of our successes have originated in 'mistakes' we've had the audacity to commit."

Victory seemed very near. Hitler, confident, was closer to complete triumph in the Eurasian land mass than any conqueror in history. Nor had he abandoned his hopes that military success would be accompanied by the elimination of the Jews and Slavs. In this period, the autumn of 1941, he was determined to solve forever the Jewish problem — by extermination.

Then in December came the Japanese attack on America at Pearl Harbor. Hitler at once declared war on America, thereby committing Germany to what was now truly a world war.

On the Russian front the war dragged on. The German armies were halted outside Moscow and Leningrad and could go no further. Hitler's top commanders advised withdrawal toward the German frontier, but he refused to consider any suggestion of retreat. The enormous casualties suffered by his forces left him unmoved, while the fate of the conquered races was of no importance to him. His own will, he believed, was enough to win the ultimate victory — a victory which would justify everything.

Hitler continued to make strategic decisions against the professional advice of his generals. The turning point came at Stalingrad, where he allowed an entire German army to be surrounded. Defying Hitler's orders, Field Marshal von Paulus, the German commander, surrendered. In a rage, Hitler began to suspect all his generals of treachery. He was determined to humiliate the once-proud officer corps of the German army. On July 20, 1944, a group of these officers attempted to assassinate Hitler by placing a bomb in his bunker. He survived, badly shaken. He ordered a terrible vengeance. To the very end of the war he hunted down his enemies in the officer class with the same venomous intensity he did the Jews.

The sun was setting on the Third Reich. Hitler still possessed enormous power. But, whereas he had used it adroitly in the first years of the war, he now used it foolishly. Great efforts were devoted to the extermination of the Jews. Millions of Russian civilians were shot or beaten to death. The Führer refused to listen to proposals for strategic withdrawals in the east even though he knew that the Americans and British were preparing to invade France. He never

I don't think that he was a personally brutal man. But I think he had that sort of icy coldness that could order the deportation of the Jews to concentration camps without giving it a second thought. And I think that, incidentally, is a characteristic of a lot of great people in power.
Drew Middleton

Supremely confident in his superior military power, Hitler anticipated a short campaign in the east. The majority of his troops were not even issued winter clothing.

seems to have understood the impact that continuous heavy losses had on the Wehrmacht. And fantasy reigned.

Germany would defeat the invaders in the west. Reserves would be free for employment in Russia and Italy. "I can hold the Russians as long as I like" he said, even as Soviet spearheads pushed deeper into Poland. The Normandy invasion struck Hitler not as a danger but as an opportunity. Even when the British and Americans began to move out of the beaches, Hitler predicted that his miracle weapons, the V-1 and the V-2 rockets, would bring the British to their knees.

As the last months of the war approached, Hitler retreated further and further into fantasy. Closeted with his staff, he talked of secret weapons and brilliant strokes which would give him final victory over his many enemies. But in the east, the Russians were already on German soil.

By March of 1945 the Third Reich which had stretched from the Atlantic to the Volga was compressed within the Oder and Rhine rivers. Day by day the Russians on the east and the Allies on the west tore holes in the German lines. The Russians moved to the encirclement of Berlin.

Hitler was fighting the war now with words only. "A talk by the Führer over the radio would be as good as a victorious battle today," wrote Goebbels in March 1945.

In the west the British and Americans had broken through Germany's defenses and were making for the heart of Hitler's Reich. Hitler himself was now in Berlin living with his mistress, Eva Braun, in a bunker below the Chancellery. Old men and children were being pressed into military service to fill up the gaps in his army. Puffy-faced from the drugs which kept him going, and visibly deteriorating from the strain, Hitler still possessed a demonic energy which excited a devotion from those around him.

As the Allies closed in on Berlin, he clung to the only power he was left with, the power to bring all of Germany down with him into death and destruction.

By day and by night, city after city in Germany felt the terrible effects of Allied mass bombing raids. The road to revenge, once garlanded with roses, now led to utter ruin, the result of the total war which Hitler himself had ordered. Even when the Russians entered Berlin, Hitler continued to believe a miracle would save him. Goebbels encouraged him by reminding him of episodes in the life of Frederick the Great. Other Nazi leaders kept their spirits up with predictions from astrology.

By April 29, the Russians were driving towards Hitler's bunker. On April 30 they were on the next street.

At last Hitler faced the reality of his own death. He had always lived with the knowledge that he had the power to take his own life, persuading himself that by doing so he could maintain a hold over Germany's destiny. "It is all finished," he said at the end. "National Socialism is dead and will never rise again. Germany is lost. It actually was not quite ready, not quite strong enough, for the mission I set out for the nation."

The final act took place in the bunker underneath the Chancellery. Hitler said goodbye to his staff. Eva Braun, whom he had recently made his wife, took poison. Hitler shot himself. Their bodies and those of Goebbels and his family were burned.

Hitler's pursuit of power was undisguised and brutal. World power, or going under had been his only alternatives. Though he went under, can posterity ever forget the ten years when his voice made the world tremble?

The last known photograph of Hitler.

CHURCHILL

*Nothing is more certain than that every trace of
Hitler's footsteps, every stain of his infected
and corroding fingers will be sponged,
and purged, and, if need be, blasted from
the surface of the earth.*
Winston Churchill

Voice of a Lion

by Drew Middleton

Power was Winston Churchill's natural environment. The power of a famous name, of influential connections, of an education which gave Englishmen the confidence and arrogance to rule the greatest empire the world has known. By the end of the 19th century, he had had his share of adventure in this empire and he even contrived to take part in the war in South Africa which opened the 20th century. The Boers took him prisoner in that war and when he escaped, put a price on his head. Churchill survived and the power of survival turned out to be one of his most notable characteristics.

Entering Parliament at the age of 25, he was to spend more than 50 years at the center of political power. As the 20th century advanced, so Churchill's experience of office grew.

He was First Lord of the Admiralty when the First World War broke out, which gave him civilian charge over the most powerful navy in the world. Later, as Secretary for War and Air, he directed the sending of British troops to support the White Russians in their civil war against the Bolsheviks. Knowing the truth of the Latin saying: "If you want peace, prepare for war," he warned his fellow countrymen against

Winston Churchill was born in Blenheim Palace, the seat of the Duke of Marlborough, and a citadel of power in Victorian England. But supreme power eluded him for more than 60 years. When, in 1940, he achieved it, he wielded it with imaginative boldness through five of the most critical years in the long history of Britain.

the rising power of the European dictators in the 1930's. His warnings were ignored, but in these years he established a new power base — the common people of Britain who were thrilled at the sound of his voice.

On May 10, 1940, Neville Chamberlain, leader of the policy of appeasement, resigned. Churchill took over as Prime Minister. He wrote later of this moment: "At last I had the opportunity to give directions over the whole scene. I felt as if I were walking with Destiny, and that all my past life had been but a preparation for this hour and this trial."

The prospects for Churchill could hardly have been worse. Within two weeks of his becoming Britain's war leader, the German armies were at the English Channel and Britain's Expeditionary Force had to be evacuated from Dunkirk. A month later, France gave in and Britain stood alone.

Hitler deluded himself that Churchill would sue for peace. Boasting in his strength, the Nazi Goliath planted his feet over Europe and taunted his enemy across the English Channel. As the crisis of the war arrived, the lion roared. In the late summer of 1940, the Battle of Britain decided the fate of the free world. And it was won, as Churchill said, by the few — Britain's fighter pilots.

During his long experience in government, Churchill had fought innumerable battles with the Civil Service. These conflicts left scars. But they also left him with a tremendous knowledge of how the system worked. When he became Prime Minister, Churchill knew exactly where to administer

Churchill as First Lord of the Admiralty at the outbreak of World War I.

British prime minister Neville Chamberlain reaches agreement with Hitler in Munich in 1938.

a rebuff, exactly how and who to cajole or order, exactly how the civil service mandarins could delay the orders of the political leaders.

The Prime Minister's memoranda, sometimes brutal, sometimes beguiling but always to the point streamed out of Downing Street. Supremely conscious of the importance of conciseness and brevity he warred on excessive wordage. "Pray give me your answer on one sheet of paper," was a customary ending. Seeing a civil service letter that called the water of the Thames "unpotable" he protested, "This means undrinkable. Why not say so?"

This application of his own powerful mind, backed by years of experience, upon the civil service has been largely overlooked by his biographers. Yet it should be seen as an exercise in power quite as important to the war effort as more publicized decisions and actions.

Lord Normanbrooke, then in the Cabinet Office, described the process:

> This stream of messages, covering so wide a range of subjects, was like the beam of a searchlight ceaselessly swinging round and penetrating into the remote recesses of the administration so that everyone, however humble his range or function, felt that one day the beam might rest on him and light up what he was doing. In Whitehall the effect of this influence was immediate and dramatic. The machine responded at once to his leadership. It quickened the pace and improved the tone of administration. A new sense of purpose and urgency was created as it came to be realized that a firm hand, guided by a strong will, was on the wheel.

Any study of Churchill's use of power is most profitable when it focuses on the period between May 1940 and January 1942. By the latter date, the United States had entered the war and the Prime Minister had to share his power as strategist and warlord with Franklin D. Roosevelt. Churchill naturally remained the supreme power in British political and military affairs but to understand him at the apex of his power as the leader of the West one must analyze his first 19 months as Prime Minister.

His exercise of power was not always spectacular but it can be argued that some of his less known decisions, taken by him alone, had as great an influence on the future course of the war as some of the sweeping military moves.

For example, in 1940 by Churchill's personal intervention, a permanent inter-service committee was formed to develop counter-measures to jam German electronic radio-navigational systems. "Being master, and not having to argue too much once I was convinced about the principles of this queer and deadly game I gave all the necessary orders . . ." he wrote later. "Being master" is the key phrase. He did not revel in power. But he understood it.

There was another exercise in power in this period that demonstrates both Churchill's daring and his moral courage. Italy had entered the war in June. A large and well-equipped Italian army was expected to attack the smaller British forces in Egypt from Libya. The British needed almost every modern weapon to halt the expected attack; most vital

Hitler knows that he will have to break us in this island or lose the war. If we can stand up to him, all Europe may be free, and the life of the world may move forward into broad sunlit uplands. But if we fail, then the whole world will sink into the abyss of a new dark age. Let us therefore brace ourselves to our duty, so bear ourselves that if the British Empire and its Commonwealth last for a thousand years men will still say, "This was their finest hour."
Winston Churchill

were tanks. In August 1940, Sir John Dill, then Chief of the Imperial General Staff, informed the Prime Minister that he wished to send to Egypt 154 tanks plus large stocks of field anti-tank artillery ammunition. The German invasion barges were being concentrated across the Channel. The balance in the Battle of Britain oscillated from day to day. In an invasion the tanks and ammunition would be desperately needed. There was only one man who had the power to take the risk and issue the order — Churchill. He took it. The Italian army was first halted and then destroyed.

The British intervention in Greece in the spring of 1941 provides another example of the use of power to attain political ends but at great risk. When the Nazis turned southeastward toward Greece, destroying the old royal army of Yugoslavia en route, the British, already overextended in Egypt, Libya and Ethiopia, were confronted with one of the toughest decisions of the year in which they

In order to win the war, Hitler must destroy Great Britain.

With every month that passes, the many proud and once happy countries he is now holding down by brute force and vile intrigue are all learning how to hate the Prussian yoke and the Nazi name, as nothing has ever been hated so fiercely and so widely among men before. And all the time, masters of the sea and air the British Empire — nay, in a certain sense, the whole English-speaking world — will be on his track bearing with them the swords of justice.

We shall not fail or falter. We shall not weaken or tire. Neither the sudden shock of battle nor the long-drawn trials of vigilance and interception will wear us down.

Give us the tools and we will finish the job.

Winston Churchill

Power in a national crisis, when a man believes he knows what orders should be given, is a blessing ... The loyalties which center upon number one are enormous. If he trips, he must be sustained. If he makes mistakes, they must be covered. If he sleeps, he must not wantonly be disturbed. If he is no good, he must be poleaxed.

Winston Churchill

fought alone. Should they, the self-proclaimed supporters of every nation that fought Hitler, enter Greece in an attempt to save that country? On purely military grounds the operation was unpromising. On political grounds it was necessary. If the British did not attempt to save Greece, then what store could other invaded countries place in their promises?

Churchill recognized this better than his military commanders or most of his cabinet colleagues. He decided. Britain went in. The Greek front collapsed. The British evacuated about 52,000 of the 60,000 men committed to Greece but lost large stocks of heavy equipment.

Had Churchill used his supreme power wisely? At the time, it seemed not. Another British Army had been defeated. The Germans were encouraged to reinforce their ultimately disastrous African adventure. But the political gain appears, in retrospect, to have outweighed the military setback. Britain had not abandoned an ally. Britain, speaking through her Prime Minister, had shown she meant to aid any

Never did so mocking a fantasy obsess the mind of mortal man. We cannot tell what the course of this fell war will be, as it spreads remorseless, to ever wider regions. We know it will be hard. We expect it will be long. We cannot predict or measure its episodes or its tribulations.

But one thing is certain, one thing is sure, one thing stands out stark and undeniable, massive and unassailable for all the world to see. It will not be by German hands that the structure of Europe will be rebuilt, or the union of the European family achieved.

Winston Churchill

country that opposed Hitler. Again, the message was read by the White House. Before long 74 American merchantmen started for the Middle East loaded with the tanks and ammunition that would replace those Britain had lost in Greece.

"They now say that I went into Greece for the wrong reasons," Churchill said in a conversation in 1948. "How do they know? The point is that it was worth it."

Winston Churchill enjoyed supreme power. But it cannot be said that, in any of these war crises, he hoarded it as did Hitler and Stalin. Although he remained as the director-general of the war effort until the end, he was wise enough to see that he, personally, could not exercise all the power that accumulated in Downing Street.

Once he had installed military commanders in whom he had faith, Alexander in the Middle East and Italy, Montgomery in northwest Europe, he gave them far more power than he had Wavell, Auchinleck and others in the

"Fraternal association" — Churchill's formula for the Anglo-American alliance.

opening years of the war. He was never hesitant to intervene on strategic matters. But, after 1942, there were more important matters with which he, and he alone, could deal.

He considered it his duty to do his utmost to use his power in the Western Alliance and his popularity in Britain and America to guide Allied policy toward the goals he conceived most rewarding for Britain and the West. In some of this he failed. And the reason for his failure is evident. After 1943 Britain's military, economic and financial resources began to wither. Britain's power, which was Churchill's base, slowly eroded. Only his matchless tongue, the vigor and incisiveness of his thought, the truculent tenor of his mind enabled him to exert in the closing years of the war an influence that was far greater than the power he commanded.

Roosevelt and Stalin, representing the new superpowers who were rising in influence, now placed Churchill in a relatively minor position. At Yalta, early in 1945, agreements were made which proved disastrous for the future of Europe. Soon after, Germany surrendered, and the war in Europe was over. But the Allies still had to deal with Japan. Many problems connected with the resettlement of Europe also had to be resolved. While the Allied leaders met at

A shadow has fallen upon the scenes so lately lighted by the Allied victory. Nobody knows what Soviet Russia and its communist international organization intends to do in the immediate future. From Stettin in the Baltic, to Trieste in the Adriatic an iron curtain has descended across the continent. I do not believe that Soviet Russia desires war. From what I have seen of our Russian friends and allies during the war, I am convinced that there is nothing they admire so much as strength. And there is nothing for which they have less respect than for weakness, especially military weakness.

Winston Churchill

Potsdam, Britain held a general election, the first since 1935.

Although the Conservatives had held large majorities in the House of Commons since 1931, Churchill's wartime government was a coalition of all parties. The leaders of the Labor Party held important posts in the Cabinet. Churchill's deputy prime minister was the Labor leader, Clement Attlee. Many voters thought that in supporting Churchill's wartime colleagues, they were voting for Churchill himself. But the polls gave Attlee a clear victory over the Conservatives. Churchill was defeated. It was a bitter moment. Perhaps the most bitter of his career.

"I awoke with a sudden sharp stab of almost physical pain," he wrote. "A hitherto unconscious conviction that we were beaten broke forth and dominated my mind. I should fall. The power to shape the future would be denied me."

Churchill was now Leader of the Opposition, but he could not be limited to this arena. He used his tremendous influence in the United States and in Europe for three purposes. The first was to alert the western world to the danger of Soviet ambitions. The second was to retain, at all costs, the Anglo-American solidarity he had built up during the war. And thirdly, to goad, cajole and push Europe into the unity

ABOVE RIGHT Churchill campaigning in 1945 when at the height of his popularity. RIGHT Despite his wartime record, he is defeated by Clement Attlee, leader of Britain's Labor Party. It was perhaps the most bitter moment of his career.

which he regarded as indispensable to her freedom. As Stalin and Truman faced up to each other in the cold war, Churchill joined in whenever he could with words which rang around the world.

Meanwhile, in the five years following the election of 1945, great changes took place in British society as a result of socialist policies. Among the most momentous was the decision to grant India independence. It marked the end of the British Empire. For Churchill, though out of office, this was a bitter blow and it was made more bitter by the triumph of a man whom Churchill had once called a "seditious fakir." In Mahatma Gandhi's long challenge to the British Raj another form of power was called into being to which Churchill had no answer.

"Set the people free!" Churchill's phrase became an election winner in Britain when in 1951 voters grasped the

Do not therefore believe these fantastic tales that the modern world, with all its science, is broken and ruined. Crazy doctrines! Clumsy fingers! Meddlesome maggies! Vicious and morbid trends of policy! These are what are manufacturing shortages and miseries by their vice and folly.

We propose, if and when we have the power, to set the people free as quickly as possible from the controls and restrictions that now beset their daily life.

Winston Churchill

Ten years after the war, we talked about the news conference at Casablanca in 1943 at which Roosevelt announced the doctrine of Unconditional Surrender.

The old man mused, "Did I look surprised? Well I certainly was. It was not the way I saw it being done. There were diplomatic courses open. But your armies were streaming across the Atlantic. I was Roosevelt's ardent lieutenant. The power was in his hands."
Drew Middleton

opportunity to escape from the drabness of postwar life. After six years of austerity they had had enough of socialist government. Attlee was out. The 77-year-old Winston Churchill brought the promise of better things and he was back, once more, at Number 10 Downing Street.

Churchill remained Prime Minister for four years. But the world had now shifted permanently into new power blocs and Churchill was too old to influence events outside Britain. When George VI died, he saw the Princess Elizabeth crowned Queen and accepted from her a knighthood in the Order of the Garter. Anthony Eden, his faithful lieutenant, succeeded him.

On his retirement, Churchill could have had any title he wanted, even a dukedom like his illustrious ancestor, the first Duke of Marlborough. But he chose to remain a commoner, living on quietly at Chartwell, his country home, until 1965 when he died soon after his ninetieth birthday.

In one way or another Churchill had served six monarchs, but he always recognized that in Britain power came from the people and rested in the House of Commons.

Well, this was the greatest man I've ever met. He was bold and brave in war, both as a soldier and a politician. He was magnanimous and far-sighted in peace. He saw the world in great historical perspectives. He was bull-headed certainly. He talked too much, often. He sometimes grasped at straws. He often was too conscious of the past and failed to come to grips with the present.

But he was also a great democrat — a "child of the House of Commons" as he described himself. Given great power he never sought to use it for base or ignoble ends.
    Drew Middleton

GANDHI

*I believe that Gandhi's views were the most
enlightened of all the political men in our time.
We should strive to do things in his spirit, not
to use violence in fighting for our cause, but by
non-participation in everything you believe is evil.*

Albert Einstein

Soul Force

by Paul Grimes

Round spectacles and false teeth. Worn sandals. A portable spinning wheel. A slim, well-thumbed copy of the *Bhagavad Gita*, a Hindu scripture. Two bowls. A pen and a letter opener. Three small make-believe monkeys: speak-no-evil, see-no-evil, hear-no-evil. A dollar watch. A spittoon.

These were almost all the worldly possessions of Mohandas Karamchand Gandhi, the Mahatma, or "great soul," when a Hindu fanatic assassinated him on January 30, 1948. But the possessions that he left behind are misleading. His real legacy was his experience: as he called it in the title of his autobiography, *My Experiments With Truth*. In his 78 years he had shown the world, through a persistent pursuit of truth and perfection, that nonviolence, love, renunciation and rigid adherence to principle could humble Britain, the

I feel in the innermost recesses of my heart, after a political experience extending for an unbroken period of close upon thirty years, that the world is sick unto death of blood-spilling, the world is seeking a way out, and I flatter myself with the belief that perhaps it will be the privilege of the ancient land of India to show that way out to the hungering world.

  Mahatma Gandhi

strongest empire on earth, and lead 400 million of its unwilling colonial subjects to self-respecting freedom. His uniquely powerful weapon, nonviolent civil disobedience, rendered military force almost ineffectual.

The goal of Gandhi and his disciples was independence only for India. But because of their success in the most populous colony in the world, other countries soon were able to win freedom, too. Gandhi taught that a united people could not be suppressed, so the granting of freedom to India in 1947 was followed over the next 15 years by independence for almost 100 possessions of Britain, France, the Netherlands and Belgium. Each freedom struggle was a little different, some were brutally bloody — but Mahatma Gandhi had led the way.

Today the legacy of Gandhi is dead. Some argue that there never really was one because once India became free, his highly principled strategy lost its validity. For example, how can a people combat poverty, India's biggest enemy, with *satyagraha*, a word created by Gandhi from two words to mean, literally, the "power of truth," or "soul force." To perform *satyagraha* meant to provoke change by refusing nonviolently to comply with what one believed to be wrong, by suffering whatever punishment this might involve and ultimately, by firm adherence to conviction, forcing the opponent to submit. *Satyagraha* could help gain independence, but it cannot feed, clothe, shelter and employ the needy. Industrialization and mechanized agriculture will do that, but Gandhi eschewed them. He would have based India's economic growth on development of a self-governing, self-sufficient village, "independent of its neighbors for its vital wants, and yet interdependent for many wants in which dependence is necessary."

He called for "constructive institutions" run by "constructive workers" to rebuild India from the village up, but most Indians did not listen. They craved not Gandhian ideals, but the material fruits of 20th century society, about which they learned as communication and transportation improved and the world diminished, showing them what they lacked.

India might have become free without Gandhi; in fact, the struggle toward independence began long before he was involved in it. There is no doubt, however, that he shortened it greatly. On a considerably smaller scale, he also showed a fruitful way to others, such as followers of Martin Luther King, who used a modification of *satyagraha* to help smash overt racial discrimination in the United States.

Gandhi's early boyhood seems to have been like many others in Kathiawad, then an amalgamation of princely states in a peninsula of Gujarat, western India. Gandhi's father, though of sparse education, was a "prime minister" to middle level maharajahs, a job that probably could have been inherited by Mohandas, had the boy wanted it.

Young Gandhi was short, thin, shy, awkward at sports and of halting speech — hardly the ingredients to build power and greatness. But even in his teens there were hints of extraordinary character.

An older friend convinced him to try eating meat, which observant Hindus abjure, under the belief that it would make him strong like the British, but in about a year he

Seventeen-year-old Gandhi prior to his departure for England to study law.

In 1915 Gandhi returns home from South Africa where, over a period of 21 years, he had worked out his concept of "soul force."

To Gandhi, fasting was a demonstration of renunciation, a means of self-purification and, politically, a means of communication when words failed. When he fasted for Hindu-Moslem amity, he said he did so because "nothing evidently which I can say or write can bring the two communities together."

abandoned it because he felt that to be weak was worse than to deceive one's parents. He was married at 13 to illiterate Kasturbai, the same age, and he soon became a demanding, lustful husband. When he was 15 he administered lovingly to his ailing father, but at the moment when the elder Gandhi died, the son was, by his own admission, indulging in "carnal desire" with his wife, "a blot," he said later, "I have never been able to efface or forget."

In September 1888, a month before he turned 19, he sailed for England to study law. He left his wife and infant son behind. But because of family apprehension and the strong opposition to the trip from his Modh Bania subcaste, which ousted him, he first took a solemn oath to avoid wine, women and meat. In England, where he remained nearly four years, he quickly acquired a British wardrobe, took lessons in ballroom dancing and elocution, and bought a violin. He believed that aping a British gentleman would raise his status. But even then he rigidly adhered to his vow, although most of his Hindu friends, like him vegetarians at home, avidly ate meat in England on the grounds that the religious inhibitions of India did not apply abroad. Gandhi, however, became an ardent advocate of vegetarianism and began the novel dietary experiments that continued throughout his life.

He developed a strong interest in different religions, and was especially captivated by the Sermon on the Mount of Christianity's New Testament and by the *Bhagavad Gita* of Hinduism. Over the years his reverence grew for the *Gita*, a poem of 700 stanzas that uses a battlefield conversation between a warrior chief and a Hindu god to extol renunciation of desire, rejection of worldly things and performance of acts of service without reward. Through his belief in the *Gita*, Gandhi gained a mastery over himself that gave him a mastery over others, even though few subscribed completely to his views.

In June 1891, two days after he was admitted to the Bar in London, Gandhi sailed for India and entered law practice in Bombay. He was eminently unsuccessful, proving unable to speak out in court. He soon returned to his native Kathiawad and got some cases through his family, but was grossly underemployed and unhappy. Had he not unexpectedly been offered a job in South Africa helping an Indian merchant press a business claim for £40,000, he might well have never found a purpose for his life and an outlet for the moral fortitude imprisoned within him.

Probably the most decisive event in Gandhi's life occurred at Pietermaritzburg, the capital of the province of Natal, about a week after he arrived in South Africa in the spring of 1893. Gandhi was on a train from Durban to Johannesburg, traveling first class. At Pietermaritzburg at about 9 P.M., a boarding white passenger found him in the first-class compartment and had a railway official order him to travel in the baggage car on the grounds that "coolies," as Indians were commonly called in South Africa, were not allowed in first class. Gandhi showed his first-class ticket and refused to leave unless removed by force. So a policeman threw him off the train and locked away his luggage and overcoat. Gandhi spent the night shivering and meditating in a bitterly cold waiting room.

Because of the importance of his legal assignment, he decided to continue the journey the next night as best he could, and he suffered further humiliation before reaching Pretoria, his ultimate destination. Meanwhile, as he waited at Pietermaritzburg, conversations with Indian merchants confirmed that such discrimination was common and hardly the worst of an Indian's fate in South Africa. He heard similar stories from Indians in Johannesburg, where he was refused a room in a first-class hotel.

Unlike most Indians in South Africa, Gandhi was unwilling to accept discrimination stoically, in order to earn a living. The longer he remained in the country, the more he was repelled by the way Indians were consistently and deliberately humiliated by whites. He learned of a vast array of jobs from which Indians were barred, of a poll tax, of restrictions on their ownership of land, of curfews against them and of regulations forcing them to walk in the street instead of on the sidewalk. He became determined to fight — not violently, but through moral force. He called a meeting of Indians in Pretoria, encouraged them to join forces to seek redress and offered to serve them without charge.

In South Africa, Gandhi gradually developed the philosophy and strong moral code that formed the base of his power. To the great initial distress of his wife, he renounced personal property (even hers), declaring that whatever he acquired was on trust alone and should be used for the good of the community. He believed that no domestic chore was beneath his dignity, even emptying chamber pots, normally the work of "untouchables" in Hindu households. He studied and experimented in nursing, hygiene, sanitation and diet, and on several occasions seemed almost miraculously to cure people so ill that medical science had forsaken them. From time to time he fasted to prove that he could abstain from the pleasures of food.

The revolutionary concept of *satyagraha,* or "soul force," evolved as Gandhi changed. This was to be the backbone of his belief in the strength of struggle without violence. Gandhi called *satyagraha* "the vindication of truth not by infliction of suffering on the opponent but upon one's self." He believed that patience and sympathy could wean the opponent from error. Thus, he sought not to humiliate his foes, but to persuade them to accept his position. He rejected the doctrine of "an eye for an eye" and abjured insults and vilification. He believed that to be successful, the practitioners of *satyagraha* should be "stronger and more spirited" at the end of a campaign than at the beginning.

The source of the *satyagraha* movement was Gandhi's farm at Phoenix, in Natal. His collaborators were always willing to go to jail if necessary to press their principles. In 1913, to protest a requirement that Indians have permits to cross the provincial border between Natal and the Transvaal 11 women *satyagrahis* from Phoenix crossed into the Transvaal without permits. The police ignored them, and they proceeded to Newcastle to exhort Indian coal miners to strike against a £3 poll tax. (Sixteen other Indian women, including Mrs. Gandhi, also crossed into the Transvaal but were arrested and sentenced to three months imprisonment.)

Many of Gandhi's closest followers — even Nehru, his political heir — did not completely repudiate violence as a means to an end, but they were willing during the freedom struggle to follow Gandhi's nonviolent path because they knew that even though there might be other ways, his was a winner.

Then the Newcastle workers went on strike and the *satyagrahis* who had inspired them were arrested, too. This inspired the miners even more, and they nonviolently submitted to floggings and other abuses inflicted on them by mine officials. When Gandhi arrived to take charge of the movement, he found himself with an army of perhaps 5,000 eager *satyagrahis* but without the wherewithal to feed or house them. So he decided to march them all across the Transvaal border, two days away, and thereby put 5,000 Indians in police hands, under the assumption that they would be arrested. Before the march began, he wrote to the government and detailed his plans, offering to let the police arrest his followers immediately rather than wait until they crossed the border. The police responded initially by arresting only Gandhi but then released him on bail because time was needed to prepare a case against him. Eventually large-scale arrests began, but more and more Indians joined the *satyagraha* volunteers. Meanwhile, news of the movement spread throughout the world, and the South African government was deluged with criticism of its actions. Ultimately the government yielded and the *satyagraha* campaign, having attained its goal, was called off.

Gandhi at his spinning wheel, "the machine gun of nonviolence."

After his *satyagraha* victory in South Africa, Gandhi sailed for England in 1914 to meet with Gopal Krishna Gokhale, at the time one of India's most prominent national leaders. They were caught in England by the outbreak of World War I, in which Gandhi supported the British, as he had in the Boer War in South Africa from 1899 to 1902. Toward the end of that year he had an attack of pleurisy, and despite the war, sailed for home. To his amazement a huge throng turned out at the Bombay harbor and in the streets of the city to welcome him. They sought *darshan*, an inner glow that many Hindus feel upon the sight of a venerated person or deity.

Although most Indians seemed to know of him, his face was not immediately recognized by the masses. So for his first few years at home he could travel about relatively anonymously, with the mass surge for *darshan* reserved for his public appearances. But by 1917 he was instantly recognizable in even remote villages, and his freedom of movement became severely circumscribed.

The compulsive quest for the Mahatma's *darshan* was, in a sense, to plague him for the remainder of his life as dense crowds flocked to his every public appearance — not really to hear his message, but simply to be in his presence. He spoke of the title Mahatma as an "affliction" that he renounced. Twice when he attempted to visit a famous Hindu temple in Benares, so many people sought his *darshan* that he could not have the *darshan* of the temple. "The woes of Mahatmas," he once said, "are known to Mahatmas only." He disliked protective security; his insistence that it be minimal ultimately contributed to his death.

Beginning in 1920, Gandhi fervently devoted himself to nonviolent noncooperation with the British authorities. He developed a three-stage program emphasizing first, the weaving of *khadi*, the Hindu word for hand-woven cloth, the making of which he thought would solve India's poverty; second, the larger objective of *swadeshi*, or economic self-sufficiency, which he felt would inevitably produce, third, *swaraj*, or self-government. He inspired tens of millions to work for that third objective, but he was never able to convince many outside his ashrams that *khadi* and *swadeshi* had to precede it. Nonetheless, Gandhi got the Congress movement, the political organization of the independence campaign, to formally urge the introduction of *khadi* as a substitute for foreign cloth.

Gandhi used *satyagraha* as a means of opposing British domination, but an early campaign turned violent and he fasted for five days in penitence, halting the *satyagraha* meanwhile. Nevertheless, the government decided to put him on trial in 1922 for "exciting disaffection" toward established law. Gandhi refused to defend himself, but in a speech before the court he said:

> I wanted to avoid violence, but I had to make my choice. I had either to submit to a system which I considered had done an irreparable harm to my country or incur the risk of the mad fury of my people bursting forth when they understood the truth from my lips. I know that my people have sometimes gone mad. I am deeply sorry for it, and I am, therefore, here to submit not to a

In May 1915, a few months after he returned to India, Gandhi established what he called an ashram, or retreat, at Kocharab, a small village near Ahmedabab, the main city of his native province of Gujarat. Two years later, when plague struck Kocharab, the ashram was moved several miles northward to the banks of the Sabarmati River. Here Gandhi gathered around him a coterie of devoted disciples who lived frugally, communally and self-sufficiently in a relentless pursuit of truth.

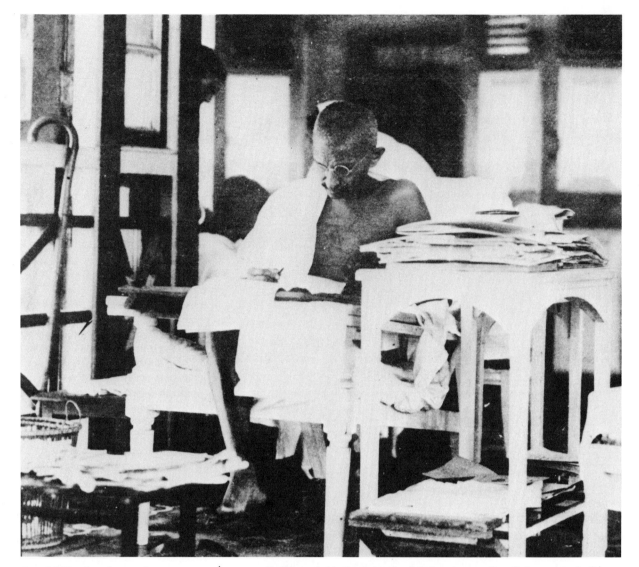

Q: *If England grants your demands, Mr. Gandhi, do you intend to have complete prohibition in the new Indian state?*
A: *Oh yes.*
Q: *Absolute prohibition?*
A: *Absolute.*
Q: *And do you intend also if India wins its independence to abolish child marriages?*
A: *I should very much like to.*
Q: *Are you prepared to return to jail again?*
A: *I am always prepared to return to jail.*

light penalty but to the highest penalty. I do not ask for mercy or plead any extenuating act.

I am here, therefore, to invite and cheerfully submit to the highest penalty that can be inflicted upon me for what in law is a deliberate crime, and what appears to me the highest duty of a citizen.

The British judge, C.N. Broomsfield, replied that "it will be impossible to ignore the fact that you are in a different category from any person I have ever tried or am likely to have to try." He sentenced Gandhi to six years "simple imprisonment." Then he said: "If the course of events in India should make it possible for the government to reduce the period and release you, no one will be better pleased than I."

In March 1930 Gandhi left forever the ashram or retreat on the Sabarmati River which he had established in 1917. He led a 24-day, 241-mile march to Dandi on the Arabian Sea to make salt in peaceful defiance of a British monopoly on its manufacture. He said he would not return to Sabarmati until India attained independence. Less than six months after freedom arrived, he was dead.

The "salt march" made Gandhi's name known throughout the world. It taught Indians that they need not be crushed

Following the salt march, Gandhi is once more imprisoned. By the end of his life he had spent a total of 2,338 days in British jails.

"Freedom," Gandhi once wrote, "is often to be found inside a prison's walls, even on a gallows; never in council chambers, courts and classrooms." His real work lay outside the 1931 London round table conference.

beneath British might. They allowed themselves to be physically beaten, but they did not cringe, thus proving their invincibility.

After nearly a month of making salt, Gandhi was arrested but was freed in January 1931 to attend a round-table conference in London on India's future. Before leaving for England he had a long interview in New Delhi with the Viceroy, Lord Irwin (who later was elevated to the title of Lord Halifax). It was an interview that provoked Winston Churchill to remark caustically about "the nauseating and humiliating spectacle of this one-time Inner Temple lawyer,

now seditious fakir, striding half-naked up the steps of the Viceroy's palace, there to negotiate and parley on equal terms with the representative of the King-Emperor."

The round table conference failed to reconcile the differences between Indians who craved to be free and Britons who insisted on continuing to rule. Within a week after Gandhi's return to India, he was again in jail. The British sought a formula to give Indians a right to vote, but when they proposed a separate electorate for the untouchables so that that group would not be completely disadvantaged, Gandhi balked at what he considered a move toward dis-

unity, and he announced a "fast unto death." He fasted six days before a compromise was agreed upon.

Gandhi supported the British against Germany and Japan in World War II, but in 1942, at Britain's weakest hour, he also initiated a "Quit India" campaign of civil disobedience against their rule. He and his principal colleagues were promptly arrested, provoking substantial anti-British violence across India. His wife, Kasturbai, died in prison in February 1944; Gandhi was released two and a half months later on medical grounds.

Probably the greatest challenge of his lifetime began just after World War II, when the Labor government of Prime Minister Clement Attlee took power in London and moved toward setting India free. Gandhi, whose powerful leadership had led the way toward what was to have been the fruition of his life's dream, was determined that a free India be a united one. In this quest he failed miserably.

The crowd at the funeral rites was so vast that the army had to be called in to organize the event.

"All the News That's Fit to Print"

The New York Times.

LATE CITY EDITION
Increasing cloudiness, cold today. Snow, not so cold tomorrow.
Temperature Range Today—Max., 18; Min., 6
Temperatures Yesterday—Max., 24; Min., 5.5
Full U. S. Weather Bureau Report, Page 31

VOL. XCVII No. 32,879.

Entered as Second-Class Matter, Postoffice, New York, N. Y.

NEW YORK, SATURDAY, JANUARY 31, 1948.

Copyright, 1948, by The New York Times Company.

THREE CENTS NEW YORK CITY

GANDHI IS KILLED BY A HINDU; INDIA SHAKEN, WORLD MOURNS; 15 DIE IN RIOTING IN BOMBAY

All Britain Honors Gandhi; Truman Deplores Tragedy

MOHANDAS K. GANDHI

The New York Times

THREE SHOTS FIRED

Slayer Is Seized, Beaten After Felling Victim on Way to Prayer

DOMINION IS BEWILDERED

Nehru Appeals to the Nation to Keep Peace—U. S. Consul Assisted in Capture

By ROBERT TRUMBULL
Special to THE NEW YORK TIMES.

NEW DELHI, India, Jan. 30— Mohandas K. Gandhi was killed by an assassin's bullet today. The assassin was a Hindu who fired three shots from a pistol at a range of three feet.

The 78-year-old Gandhi, who was the one person who held discordant elements together and kept some sort of unity in this turbulent land, was shot down at 5:15 P. M. as he was proceeding through the Birla House gardens to the pergola from which he was to deliver his daily prayer meeting.

Churchill fought the India Bill tooth and nail in '47, largely because of his own experience as a young man in India. Until the end of his life he looked on India as the India of the 1890's. He never understood the changes there and couldn't understand how a man like Gandhi, or Nehru — even though he had gone to his old school, Harrow, — could be responsible for India.

The Hindu majority wanted a united India. The Moslem League, representing a substantial religious minority, adamantly argued for a separate nation called Pakistan ("land of the pure") to be carved out of India in the east and west. In 1947, with independence only a few months away, Gandhi had to give in, but when the two free nations were created that August, he refused to attend the celebrations. Instead, he was in Bengal trying to end bitter clashes between Moslems and Hindus.

Gandhi had been working fervently for Hindu-Moslem harmony for nearly a year. At times he seemed to succeed in one area, but then violence would erupt in another. He lived to see what must have been his saddest chapter: the internecine slaughter of nearly one million Hindus and Moslems as each side struggled bitterly to salvage what it could and to flee to safety during the partition of the nation. Many Indians hailed Gandhi's efforts for peace, but many of his fellow Hindus disdained them on the grounds that they were unjustified because of alleged Moslem misbehavior and intransigence. It was this adverse reaction that ultimately led to the assassination of Gandhi by a young Hindu fanatic, Nathuram Godse, as the Mahatma walked to a prayer meeting in a New Delhi garden on January 30, 1948.

"He Ram" (Oh God), the Mahatma muttered after three bullets had been pumped into his spare body. Then he was dead.

It is ironic that with all Gandhi's emphasis on nonviolence, India remained essentially a country like every other, where violence often prevails. Gandhi's creed was dominant while it had a goal to attain — a goal that, he showed, could be gained no other way. Once the goal was reached, Gandhi's

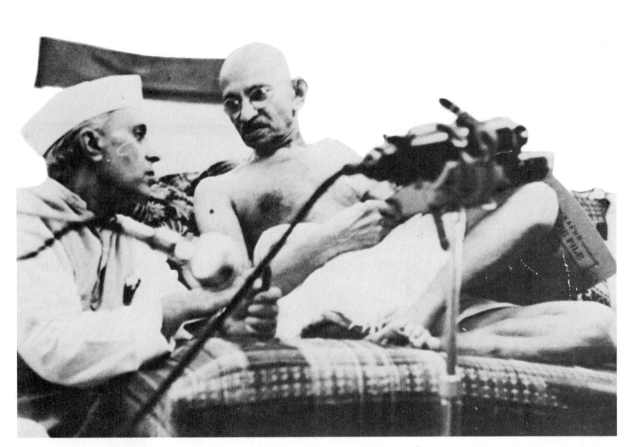

power was gone. For the sake of his memory, it is probably best that he died when he did — a martyr.

Friends and comrades, the light has gone out of our lives and there is darkness everywhere. And I do not quite know what to tell you and how to say it. Our beloved leader, Bapu as we called him, the father of the nation, is no more.
  Pandit Nehru

ROOSEVELT

I am prepared under my constitutional duty to recommend measures that a stricken nation in the midst of a stricken world may require . . . But in the event that the national emergency is still critical, I shall not evade the clear course of duty that will then confront me. I shall ask Congress for the one remaining instrument to meet the crisis — broad executive power, to wage a war against the emergency as great as the power that would be given to me if we were in fact invaded by a foreign foe.
Franklin D. Roosevelt

Manipulator-in-Chief

by Turner Catledge

Had Franklin Delano Roosevelt wanted to be a dictator, as his critics often charged, he missed his greatest opportunity on that misty noon of Saturday, March 4, 1933, when he was first sworn in as President of the United States. That day the nation practically demanded that he take full personal control of its affairs, and loudest in the chorus were some of those very conservative leaders who later denounced him for alleged dictatorship tendencies.

The country was in a state of economic collapse. Public morale was at zero point. National income had dropped more than 50 percent in 4 years. One fourth of the labor force was unemployed, with men and women of all skills frantically looking for jobs. Breadlines stretched block after block in every major city, and the means to care for the destitute were running out. Farmers were offering corn at 10 cents a bushel in the fields of the Midwest and some were even

From the beginning of his presidency, Roosevelt dominated the press with action. Television was not then a factor, although radio was in wide use and he took full advantage of it in his occasional fireside chats. The White House press conference was his principal contact with the public. During his twelve years and three months in the White House, he held 998 press conferences.
PREVIOUS PAGE The face of the Depression.

The depression in America forces some smaller banks to close.

burning it for fuel. On that very day, only hours before the inaugural ceremony, every bank in the country had locked its doors with no assurance of ever reopening or paying off depositors. The vaunted American private enterprise system was in disarray and leaderless, unable to respond to the call for "action, and action now" that Roosevelt could hear in the national mood.

Then came an astounding change. Within a matter of a few hours there was a gushing of hope. The country sensed that a leader had stepped forward who had the will to use governmental power and the determination to gather unto himself whatever authority he needed. Applause from the thousands congregated before the Capitol interrupted Roosevelt's inaugural address more than 30 times.

Looking back over the record of his twelve years and three months in the White House, one wonders whether Roosevelt ever would have tried to use the kind of power that his listeners thought him to mean. It was not his style. He was not essentially a commander or an administrator, but a manipulator. With him the use of authority was a kind of game. Even when he assumed the role of Commander-in-Chief in the war he always wanted a willing Congress at his side, or just behind him, and he contrived to have it so. On those occasions when he chose to use muscle instead of persuasion, he was less successful.

Roosevelt came from a family well acquainted with power. His wife, Eleanor, was a distant cousin, the niece of the Republican President, Theodore Roosevelt. FDR entered

67

the New York State Senate as a Democrat in 1910 and in his thirties he served for seven years as Assistant Secretary of the Navy in Woodrow Wilson's cabinet. In 1921, while holidaying in New Brunswick, he caught polio. At the age of 39 he was paralyzed in the legs, a cruel blow to an active and ambitious man. But it taught Roosevelt patience and self-control. It gave him, too, a sympathy for the underdog and deepened his interest in social problems. Slowly he learned to do without his crutches in public. In 1928 he was elected Governor of New York and was within reach of supreme power.

Roosevelt's first task on entering the White House in 1933 was to get the banking system going again. He immediately called a special session of Congress to meet the following Thursday, March 9. Meanwhile, he proclaimed a banking "holiday," a Presidential order to keep the banks closed. The authority he used was a clause he found in the yellowing "Trading with the Enemy Act," enacted during the First World War to give the President authority to prohibit exportation of gold. When Congress convened, he submitted a bill providing a licensing system for reopening the banks. His purpose was to save the banking system rather than to change it. This policy was a disappointment to some of the eager New Dealers then moving into Washington. They wanted him to go all the way and nationalize the banks. Congress responded promptly, passing the bill in the House after less than an hour's debate. The chamber echoed with shouts, "Vote, vote, vote." The banking act was signed into law within eight hours of its submission to Congress. The Capitol and the country could feel, almost physically, the presence of authority and powerful leadership. Half a million people wrote letters to Roosevelt, some likening him to God.

The new President had intended in the beginning to have Congress pass the banking act and then go home. But seeing himself so completely in control, he quickly submitted bills to carry out two campaign promises. One was a so-called "Economy Act," a move toward balancing the budget by heavy cuts in government expenditure, including veterans' pensions. The other was a bill to legalize beer. Congress passed both within a week, and in doing so gave him victories over two of the most powerful pressure groups ever to appear on Capitol Hill — war veterans and prohibitionists.

Roosevelt's skill at generating and using power was working miracles and the country was in a joyful mood for the first time since the stock market crash in 1929. Keeping up the momentum during the first three months of his presidency, Roosevelt deluged Congress with a flood of ideas and programs unlike anything known in American history. They represented an entirely new approach to the use of federal powers. This was the "New Deal."

Few presidents loved the exercise of power more than Roosevelt, but he was shaken when the Supreme Court ruled unconstitutional several of his favorite measures. Roosevelt's determination to bend the court to his will led to a titanic struggle between the Chief Executive and Congress. It was a bitter episode, but it taught Roosevelt that he could use his power more effectively through charm and

The Axis powers will never achieve their objective of world domination unless they first obtain control of the sea. That is their supreme purpose today and to achieve it they must capture Great Britain. We shall give every possible assistance to Britain and to all who along with Britain are resisting Hitlerism or its equivalent with the force of arms. Our patrols are helping now to insure delivery of the needed supplies to Britain; all additional measures necessary to deliver the goods will be taken. Therefore with profound consciousness of my responsibilities to my countrymen, and to my country of course, I have tonight issued a proclamation that an unlimited national emergency exists and requires the strengthening of our defense to the extreme limit of our national power and authority.

Franklin D. Roosevelt

persuasion than through sheer muscle. To be a manipulator and not a bully.

Roosevelt came to power in America a few weeks after Hitler was made Chancellor of Germany. The President's second term in the White House coincided with the Nazi director's drive for world power. But the looming threat of war in Europe hardly troubled the minds of most Americans. Nor was the rising power of Japan seen as a real danger, even though Japanese military strength posed a more direct challenge to American interests.

Protected by the Pacific Ocean on one side and by the Atlantic Ocean on the other, Americans felt confident of the security of their continent. Roosevelt was only too conscious of the danger. But the peace lobby represented a powerful force in American politics. Aware that Roosevelt had more power than any other president had been granted in peacetime, Congress attempted to shackle his conduct of

The success of the New Deal gave Roosevelt a landslide victory in 1936. He carried every state except Vermont and Maine.

The Atlantic Charter. Roosevelt and Churchill meet on board the Prince of Wales.

foreign affairs. Here Roosevelt found an unexpected ally. The Supreme Court now declared that Congress was itself acting unconstitutionally since the President had sole authority in foreign affairs, except for the Senate's duty to pass on treaties.

With hindsight, Roosevelt can be portrayed as a president given to bold actions, who delighted in the exercise of power, especially in foreign affairs. But he was also a cautious man who was deeply sensitive to the ebb and flow of public opinion. It was impossible to tell whether his caution and regard for public opinion were evidence of his commitment to the democratic process or more a matter of political calculation. At a time when the future of the free world hung in the balance, Roosevelt resorted to the shifting tactics and manipulation of the American system which were characteristic of the man.

He became bolder after his reelection for a third term in 1940. He moved more openly in extending aid to the British. He found less need to resort to subterfuge. He submitted a

daring proposal to Congress, namely the Lend-Lease bill, by which he intended to increase the flow of material to the British who had practically exhausted their ability to purchase.

As the British situation worsened, Roosevelt looked for other ways to help this stricken friend. He reasoned that if Congress authorized the lending and leasing of war goods, this implied an effort to make sure the goods arrived at their destination. At that time German submarines were sinking increasing numbers of British cargo ships. In April 1941 he negotiated another "executive agreement," this one with the Danish minister to send American troops to Greenland. He maintained that Greenland was part of the western hemisphere and therefore covered by the Monroe Doctrine.

At the end of May he issued a presidential proclamation declaring a state of "unlimited national emergency," deepening the state of "limited emergency" he had declared when war broke out in Europe in 1939. He felt no need to go to Congress for approval of either of these proclamations.

I believed that once Congress passed the Lend-Lease Act, we were in the war.
Turner Catledge

This nation will remain a neutral nation. But I cannot ask that every American remain neutral in thought as well. Even a neutral has a right to take account of facts. Even a neutral cannot be asked to close his mind or to close his conscience. I have said not once, but many times, that I have seen war and that I hate war. I say that again and again. I hope the United States will keep out of this war. I believe that it will, and I give you assurance and reassurance that every effort of your government will be directed toward that end. As long as it remains within my power to prevent there will be no blackout of peace in the United States.

Franklin D. Roosevelt

72

Congress had already granted the powers over a period of many years and he had them in his power bank. The proclamation of "unlimited emergency" stated the purpose of the President: to repel any acts or threats of aggression directed against any part of the western hemisphere. He proceeded to move American power into the North Atlantic. By another "executive agreement" with the government of Iceland, he sent American troops to a territory that was not a part of the western hemisphere. He feared that if the Germans got to Iceland first, it would be a serious threat to the movement of munitions to Britain, and thus would thwart the intent of Congress.

Then in rapid order he proceeded to institute a convoy system to step up deliveries to England. He ordered the Navy to protect the convoys, even to the extent of shooting to kill. He was not merely nudging the country toward involvement. He was actually shoving it.

In those pre-Pearl Harbor years, Roosevelt seldom claimed authority independent of Congressional acts. Occasionally, when it seemed he did, as when he sent troops to Iceland, he was able to cite an obscure clause in an act passed by Congress years before, although in an entirely different context. He was said to have compiled a catalogue of more than 60 such clauses, should he need them. When he found it necessary to use these tactics, he would usually ask Congress to confirm his action. It invariably did.

As tragic as it was, Pearl Harbor was actually a victory for Roosevelt. It solved his constitutional dilemma. He was deeply grieved that the Navy, which he loved so much, was caught by surprise. After Congress' declaration of a state of war with Japan on December 8, 1941, and Germany's declaration of war with the United States three days later, he eagerly seized the role of Commander-in-Chief. He loved the title; but most of all he enjoyed the realities of readily usable powers which were now at his command.

The actuality of war speeded a change in Roosevelt's approach to presidential power. He had fashioned the New Deal out of authority granted by Congress, act by act. Now, after Congress' declaration of war, he preferred to rely on less specific Congressional authority. He submitted a Second War Powers Act, in which the grant of powers was more generalized. On the authority he thus gained from Congress, and together with powers he now asserted as Commander-in-Chief, he gathered into an all-purpose agency all the administrative organizations he needed to prosecute the war.

In 1944, Roosevelt won power for a fourth term. The return to active political warfare stimulated him. But his health was weakening. When he reported to Congress on his return from the Yalta conference, he was a dying man.

Franklin Delano Roosevelt had no equal among American presidents in the acquisition, use and enjoyment of political

Roosevelt is "one of the men who will take the greatest part in shaping the immediate future of our civilization."
Winston Churchill

At Tehran in 1943, Churchill and Roosevelt met with Stalin. Three grand masters of power, with the world as their chess-board.

"All the News That's Fit to Print"

The New York Times.

LATE CITY EDITION
POSTSCRIPT
Considerable cloudiness and milder today; moderate winds.
Temperature Yesterday—Max., 51; Min., 38
Sunrise, 7:33 A. M.; Sunset, 5:43 P. M.

Copyright, 1944, by The New York Times Company.

VOL. XCIV No. 31,700.   Entered as Second-Class Matter. Postoffice, New York, N. Y.   NEW YORK, WEDNESDAY, NOVEMBER 8, 1944.   THREE CENTS NEW YORK CITY

ROOSEVELT WINS FOURTH TERM; RECORD POPULAR VOTE IS CLOSE; DEMOCRATS GAIN IN THE HOUSE

I come from the Crimea conference with the firm belief that we have made a good start on the road to a world at peace. Never before have the major allies been more closely united, not only in their war aims, but also in their peace aims. And they're determined to continue to be united, to be united with each other and with all peace-loving nations so that the ideal of lasting peace will become a reality . . . We haven't won the wars yet — with an 's' on wars. It's a long, tough road to Tokyo. It's as long to go to Tokyo as it is to Berlin, in every sense of the word. The defeat of Germany will not mean the end of the war against Japan. On the contrary, we must be prepared for a long and costly struggle in the Pacific. But the unconditional surrender of Japan is as essential as the defeat of Germany.

Franklin D. Roosevelt

power. His basic purposes were always noble, although his means were occasionally less so. By applying his particular skills in a thoroughly pragmatic approach to the awesome problems of his presidency, he brought capitalism in the United States back from the brink and then led his country into a crusade that saved democracy for another chance in the world.

But because of his habit of making decisions seem deliberately vague and of keeping policy fluid, Roosevelt's death on April 12, 1945, left many crucial matters up in the air. Perhaps the most serious of these was the lack of any clearly stated formulation of how America intended to face up to the postwar consequences of insisting on the unconditional surrender of Germany and Japan. In his last speech to Congress Roosevelt stressed the unity of the Grand Alliance with an optimism all the more poignant for the evidence already accumulating on his desk of Soviet duplicity. Whether Roosevelt ever fully appreciated the crude manner in which Stalin used power, which contrasted so markedly with his own technique of political manipulation, he died before he had to answer the challenges of the postwar world. But Stalin had the Yalta agreements in his pocket and no home electorate to concern himself with. With Roosevelt dead and Churchill ousted by voters in Britain, the Soviet dictator could be excused for thinking that history, with or without the help of Karl Marx, had, after all, placed the future in his hands.

Americans were stunned
when they learned that the
president they had known for
more than 12 years was dead.

STALIN

Wherever you turned in Stalin's Russia, Big Brother looked down on you. By the end of the 1930's there was no escaping him. His eyes were everywhere and a word whispered to a partner in the dark would somehow reach his ears. His power was the power of fear. Everywhere, with everyone, from the highest to the lowest, there was fear.

BRANDELL

PREVIOUS PAGES Stalin, according to czarist police files. BELOW Stalin, according to his own propaganda.

The Power of Fear

by Harrison E. Salisbury

The portrait of Big Brother drawn by the English writer George Orwell in his novel *1984* has a permanent place in the literature of the western world. Big Brother — alias Josif Vissarionovich Djugashvili — alias Josef Stalin. The word Stalin derives from the Russian word for steel, a name chosen to enhance its holder's image in the days before he had risen to power. By 1939 Stalin had become Big Brother. A man of steel in the Kremlin to forge the workers' Brave New World.

Whenever we look at Stalin we have to ask ourselves what purpose this public image was intended to serve. A man to love or a man to fear? An outstanding leader, or just one of the people? Stalin used the media to paint whatever portrait of himself suited his purpose at the time. But who was it that lived behind the image?

He was actually a small man — not more than five feet six in height. But to disguise his short stature, he surrounded himself with men as small as himself. A taller man would not survive long in his presence. Nor was he physically imposing, his left hand being slightly crippled from a boyhood injury. His piercing eyes were most disconcerting. Not to return Stalin's gaze steadily could be a man's undoing.

Stalin grew up in the Russia of the czars, a Russia which was one of the great imperial powers of Europe. Though she possessed enormous natural resources, she was not an industrial nation. Her power was symbolized by the reverence and glittering ceremony which surrounded her ruler and the dignitaries of a Church whose traditions went back to the creation of the Slavic state.

Stalin himself came from Georgia. His parents were peasants who had earlier been liberated from the condition of agricultural slavery known as serfdom. By 1917, when the old order inside Russia gave way under the terrible blows suffered in the war with Germany, Stalin had already been in trouble with the authorities and spent time in Siberia. He had learned his lessons in secrecy, deceit and double-dealing and ostensibly he was a rebel against the powers-that-be.

One man, at least, was determined to profit by the chaos of 1917. No one was more surprised than Lenin when trouble broke out in Russia. Hurrying back from Switzerland under German protection, Lenin engineered the October coup d'état and seized power in Moscow with his small group of followers, known as Bolsheviks. Stalin belonged to this group, although with his rough provincial manner he had little in common with the intellectuals of the movement who had enjoyed exile in the capitals of Europe. Recognizing that the center of power lay in Lenin's person, Stalin stuck closely to Lenin, at least as the official record shows.

Lenin died in 1924, after a series of strokes which incapacitated him during the critical period when Russia was in chaos and the Bolsheviks were maneuvering among themselves for the succession. At Lenin's funeral, Stalin was one of the pall bearers and delivered a eulogy over the body. Toward the end of his life, Lenin had dictated his last testament to his party in which he recommended that Stalin should be moved from his office of General Secretary. It was

This was the world that Stalin knew — a Russia of dynastic power upheld by secret police and a state religion; with imperialistic ambitions beyond her frontiers and anti-semitic outbursts within them. Stalin, the Georgian, would become more Russian than the Russians, more autocratic than the Czar.

Stalin's birthplace is transformed into a shrine.

Stalin used brute force to build what he called "Socialism in one country." Rudeness, intimidation, intolerance, cunning, deceit — these were the methods by which he had achieved power and his henchmen used the same methods.

Stalin is photographed apparently as Lenin's right hand man.

While Stalin worked his way up through the party office, a more spectacular contender for power was Trotsky, organizer of the Red Army. Trotsky acted his part on the open stage — a lover of the limelight, who welcomed outsiders with their newsreel cameras since he sought an international role for himself. For Trotsky, backward Russia was only a launching pad for world power.

not that Stalin had too much power, but that he might not use this power with sufficient caution. Stalin's main fault, in Lenin's eyes, lay in his rudeness. It was a fault Lenin considered fully tolerable among party members, but not in the General Secretary's office. Stalin, however, succeeded in keeping knowledge of Lenin's criticism from all but the inner core of party members.

New myths are born of the old. To preserve Lenin's place in history, Stalin himself would one day have to be de-Stalinized. But in those critical months following Lenin's death, the party could not afford to lose its General Secretary. Stalin bided his time.

Stalin resented the internationalist views of other Soviet leaders. He was especially suspicious of Trotsky, a latecomer to the Bolshevik cause and a Jew. Trotsky's brilliant organization of the Red Army gave him a power base outside the party organization. Playing upon his colleagues' jealousies of Trotsky, Stalin succeeded in driving him into exile.

Stalin's position as General Secretary of the party enabled him to build up a network of supporters personally loyal to himself and to undermine anyone who sought to create a rival power base.

Russia in the 1920's was in a desperate plight. The war and its aftermath had devastated the country and undone the slow but steady advance of the national economy which had been evident at the beginning of the century. She needed time to repair the damage. But Stalin could not afford to wait; his first priority was to oust the remaining leaders of the old Bolshevik group. To this end, he advocated the enforced collectivization of agriculture followed by a massive program of rapid industrialization, policies which outmaneuvered first one set of rivals, then another.

The results caused the most appalling suffering throughout Russia. Stalin cared nothing for the cost in human terms, while the damage he inflicted to Russian agriculture has never been fully made good. Outsiders may have been taken in by the showplaces they were allowed to visit, but the true picture of conditions inside Russia surpassed in horror anything Europe has known in the 20th century.

The system of secret police and labor camps, which Lenin initiated, was swollen to grotesque proportions to deal with the millions of men and women from all parts of the Soviet Union who at one time or another were declared to be enemies of the state. It is possible that as many as two million lives were lost each year in Stalin's slave labor brigades. The modern Soviet state is built on their graves.

Stalin's justification for his actions was that Russia's backwardness had left her a hundred years behind the other powers in the world. A 10-year effort, he argued, would enable Russia to catch up and take her rightful place among them. Without such an effort, she would forever be at their mercy.

Stalin's principal concern was for himself only. Displaying a paranoid suspicion of all around him, he embarked on a series of show trials in which one group of potential opponents after another was forced to confess to crimes against the party. Purges continued throughout the 1930's. Thousands upon thousands from all walks of life were sent to their deaths, including the entire staff of the Red Army and all the old Bolshevik leaders. The object was to glorify Stalin himself as the sole repository of party orthodoxy. Stalin in effect became Lenin, or, as he liked it to be put, Stalin is Lenin in our day.

Stalin's Russia did not exist in a vacuum. The advent of Adolf Hitler to power in Germany affected all Europe and signs of a second world war were everywhere at hand. Hitler publicly proclaimed his hatred for communism and Germany's need for *Lebensraum* in the east.

Stalin now carried out what he conceived as a master stroke. He had been negotiating in lackadaisical fashion for a defense pact with Britain and France. Simultaneously, he opened secret negotiations with Hitler at the end of August 1939 and struck a deal which enabled Hitler to launch World War II.

The two dictators agreed on a pact of neutrality, on a division of Poland, on spheres of influence in the Balkans and eastern Europe and on a trade pact which guaranteed Germany needed food and oil.

Stalin insisted that all foreign communist parties carry out a 180-degree switch — from violent opposition to the Nazis to full support. He was helped by the convenient fact that he had killed off most of the foreign communist leaders on whom he could lay his hands.

Stalin thought he had out-tricked Hitler. He would sit on the sidelines while Hitler fought France and England. At an opportune moment when the Wehrmacht had been weakened Stalin would stab his erstwhile comrade in the back.

Stalin made a fatal miscalculation. Hitler swept through France and western Europe and after smashing away at England with his bombers decided to turn east and finish off his enemy-ally. Stalin had the world's greatest espionage system. Intelligence agents' reports of Hitler's intentions flooded in. Reliable commanders on Russia's western front

Stalin's role in the Bolshevik power seizure was minimal. He was described as "a gray shadow." He was there but he was not seen. His activities were carried on in the corridors, not on the center stage. He made no speeches which are remembered. He took no stands which aroused controversy.

83

The German army is welcomed as liberator of the Ukraine.

reported the steadily increasing Nazi concentrations. Churchill and Roosevelt warned Stalin. But he was oblivious to all. A week before the Nazi attack Stalin took a few guarded precautions. He tried to get Hitler to reveal his plans. He fawningly pointed out how loyal he had been, how faithfully Russia had delivered the wheat and oil. On the evening of June 21, 1941, eight hours before the Nazi blitz, Stalin still insisted that the signs added up to nothing — at best a provocation by Nazi generals. Late in the evening he permitted alerts to go to his armed forces but prohibited any movement across the frontiers. Vainly Molotov and the Foreign Office called in the German ambassador and tried to contact some responsible official in Berlin.

Even after the attack at 4 A.M., June 22, Stalin refused to be convinced. Only after 8 A.M. — four hours after Hitler's planes and tanks swirled across the frontier — did he permit orders for a full scale resistance. No notice was given the population until noon — and then it was Molotov, not Stalin who spoke on the radio.

Stalin? He had collapsed. He retreated to his villa outside Moscow and barricaded himself in. He would see no one. Not even his generals and Politburo colleagues. "All that Lenin bequeathed us has been lost," he wailed, according to Khrushchev. He remained in this state for "a long time," in Khrushchev's words. Finally, he managed to pull himself together. He made a pathetic speech to his countrymen on July 3, marked by long pauses and punctuated by the sounds of water being gulped down. He called his fellow Russians "sisters and brothers." He had never done this before.

The losses in the German attack were unbelievable. By October the Germans had put Leningrad under siege. They were at the gates of Moscow. At least one light tank had even penetrated the city. All of the Ukraine was gone; Nazi tanks rolled toward the Caucasus. Kiev had been lost and a million Soviet troops with it.

The countryside was devastated. The toll in lives was astronomical. Moscow was under a state of siege and thousands of citizens fled in panic. Smoke poured from the chimneys of the secret police headquarters in the Lubiyanka as documents burned. Did Stalin join the exodus? His associates and historians say he did not. But there is a period of a week or more that looks suspiciously blank in the reconstructed record.

By that time the generals, Marshal Zhukov at their head and many like Rokossovsky who had been released from Stalin's prisons and sent directly to the battlefield, had brought the Nazi offensive to at least a temporary halt, aided by cruel winter weather.

Everything was now subordinated to the task of freeing Russia from the invader. Military traditions of czarist Russia, banned by the first Soviets, were revived. Stalin brought back ranks and salutes and epaulets and medals. He invented a title for himself, Generalissimo, one that had never been used before in Russia. He gave back to the people the heroes of the past. Russians, he reminded them, were the successors of Alexander Nevsky, who led the fight against the Teutonic Knights, and of Kutuzov, the general who defeated Napoleon, names which, to have uttered in the 1930's, would have cost a man his life.

Finally, the war in Europe was won. Stalin's victorious legions paraded past him in Red Square. They hurled captured Nazi standards and ancient German military emblems in a heap at the bottom of Lenin's tomb while Stalin, now Generalissimo Stalin, took the salute. At a Kremlin reception for his marshals and generals Stalin toasted the "Russian people" whom, he said, had remained loyal and true and fought the Germans to victory, whereas another people might well have despaired and turned against its leadership. It was a toast well earned. No people deserved them more. But it was all Stalin gave them.

There was one more act in World War II to be played out.

To win the war against Germany, and to save his own skin, Stalin unashamedly appealed to the spirit of pre-revolutionary Russia.

German soldiers are taken prisoner by the Russians during the defense of Stalingrad.

Twice Stalin had met with his World War fellow leaders, Winston Churchill and Franklin D. Roosevelt, once at Tehran, once at Yalta in the Crimea. He had, he thought, played his cards well, particularly at Yalta where he believed he had obtained a division of spheres of influence — at least with Churchill, if not with Roosevelt.

But he was taking no chances, especially in eastern Europe. As the Red Army moved forward he took care that regimes subservient to Moscow were quickly installed, particularly in Poland. He hoped to get a six billion dollar reconstruction loan from the United States, but with Roosevelt's death in April 1945 this prospect faded.

There was one last meeting of the wartime leaders — this time at Potsdam. In place of Roosevelt there was President Truman and after the British election Clement Attlee replaced Winston Churchill. It was a congress of victors but also a congress of deceivers. Truman informed Stalin about the American A-bomb, soon to be used at Hiroshima. But he was careful not to give Stalin too precise a notion of the terrible new weapon. Stalin had a secret too. The Japanese had been moving heaven and earth trying to get him to act as intermediary for their peace bids to the West. But Stalin kept his secret as Truman kept his. The atom bomb was dropped. Quickly Stalin reacted to Hiroshima. He declared war on Japan and managed to fight a 10-day battle which gave him what he wanted — the restoration of most of what Russia lost to Japan in the war of 1904-5. The deceit of Potsdam was a sinister portent of the era to follow.

Stalin turned back to the crushing labor of rebuilding the country. He uprooted more hundreds of thousands of his subjects, those whom he adjudged disloyal or untrustworthy — the Crimean Tartars, small tribes in the Caucasus, the peoples of the Baltic states. He sent them to the fearsome concentration camps in the east. There they were joined by millions of Soviet soldiers — those who had fallen prisoner to the Nazis and survived the terrible Nazi camps; ordinary citizens who had been left behind under Nazi occupation; hundreds of thousands of men and women culled from the refugee camps of western and central Europe. All fodder for the camp system.

There was no relaxation. Quickly Stalin turned again against his own with one wave of purges after another. New "plots," new "conspiracies." The Leningrad leadership of the party was wiped out in a paranoid "affair" in which they were alleged to have plotted to move the Soviet capital back from Moscow to Leningrad. The Jewish cultural leadership which had been the nucleus of Soviet propaganda work in World War II was wiped out at a single blow. A raging anti-semitic campaign was launched against Jews in cultural and artistic institutions. Jews were driven from posts in industry and banned from the high command of the army, the Foreign Office and the party leadership.

Stalin's circle grew more and more narrow. His paranoia was fanned by the crises of the cold war. And even more so

This was Yalta. A picture that speaks of treachery, of sickness and miscalculation, of decisions affecting the lives of millions.

After Potsdam Stalin found himself Big Brother of virtually all continental Europe. The temptation to grab more power was irresistible. Satellite governments were quickly installed in eastern Europe and the cold war spread to northern Iran, Greece and Turkey.

In 1948, Stalin attempted to throttle Berlin, which had been jointly allocated to the four powers occupying Germany.

by his failure to terrorize fellow communists. The defiance of Tito in Yugoslavia and the success of Mao Tse-tung in China threatened his sense of power. Their hidden supporters inside the Soviet Union must all be relentlessly rooted out.

Stalin's last years were fear-ridden, joyless, bleak — for himself and his country. Alone in the Kremlin he dreamed of immortality. Two doctors who devised "cures" for old age were awarded medals and titles. The press was filled with articles about Georgian mountaineers who lived to the age of 130 or 140. Stalin seemed to grow more suspicious of normal medical remedies. He took to treating himself.

Finally, in his last year of life, he began to concoct the greatest "purge" he had ever dreamed of. This time the victims were to be the older members of the Politburo, all of those who had survived the earlier waves of killing: Voroshilov (whom he now thought was a British spy); Molotov, his tough Foreign Minister (whose wife was already in prison but who went on serving his master faithfully); Mikoyan, his oldest surviving associate from the Caucasus; Beria, his police chief (due to vanish like all his predecessors); Bulganin, the heavy-drinking political marshal; Malenkov, who believed himself the chosen successor; Khrushchev whom he used to tease by making him dance the Ukrainian peasant *gopak* — all were to go.

But not this distinguished group alone. Together with the

men he called his "closest comrades-at-arms" Stalin proposed a "final solution" of Russia's "Jewish problem." He would deport all Soviet Jews, three or four million persons, to Siberia. He even contemplated sending along with them the entire Ukrainian population, more than twenty million people.

Then on the night of March 2, 1953, something happened to Stalin. Perhaps it was an old man's stroke that felled him in his villa just outside Moscow. Perhaps, and there have been many intimations of this, he was fatefully confronted by his impending victims — Beria, Malenkov, Khrushchev, Voroshilov, Kaganovich, and others. One version suggests they refused to accept his proposed "plot" and that, in a rage, Stalin fell into a coma. Other reports say that he suffered a stroke as he lay in bed and remained unattended for 12 or 18 hours because none of his guards or associates dared to open the bedroom door.

Whatever the cause, one thing is beyond doubt. At about 9:15 P.M. on March 5, surrounded by top party officials and attended by his daughter Svetlana and his son Vasily, Stalin died in his villa bedroom. His successors could hardly wait for the body to cool before they opened their struggle for the succession.

What, in the end, had Stalin's great power achieved? Russia had survived him. Despite the fearful toll of lives of his own countrymen, possibly 40 to 50 million in wars, starvation, executions and unnecessary deaths due to disease and cold, Russia had emerged as the number two power in the world. It had an industry second to that of the United States, (but soon that of Japan would exceed it). Its agriculture was still crippled by his savage self-inflicted blows. Russia was surrounded by sullen satellites which in the ensuing years would try their best to escape from her orbit. To the east lay the uneasy ally, China, soon to turn with ferocious force against its erstwhile communist ally. To the west the United States and Europe simmered in the hatred and security fears of the cold war, as alien an atmosphere as Russia had ever created in its long history.

At home the dictator's own paranoia had infected the total population. Abroad the paranoia was tangible as well. The Georgian shoemaker's son had garnered more power than any single man in the world and with it had made a world almost untenable for the existence of any man, including himself.

Stalin was buried beside Lenin in the great mausoleum in Red Square where his body remained for nearly 10 years. Then one night on Khrushchev's orders the tomb was stealthily opened, Stalin's embalmed remains removed, the tomb sealed again, Stalin's name chiseled off the red porphyry and his corpse buried in the little Kremlin park nearby under a simple stone that carried only the single word: Stalin.

His imprint on the history of our time cannot be so easily effaced. When Khrushchev in turn fell from power in 1964 his successors found they had a gap of 40 years of Soviet history on their hands — ever since Lenin's death, in fact. Half of this period belongs to the postwar world — the years covered by the presidencies of Truman, Eisenhower and Kennedy. For Eisenhower and Kennedy, confrontation with

We're now confronted with something quite as wicked, but in some ways more formidable, than Hitler.

Because Hitler had only the Herrenvolk *pride and anti-semitic hatred to exploit. He had no fundamental theme.*

But these 13 men in the Kremlin have their hierarchy, and a church of communist adepts whose missionaries are in every country as a fifth column. Obscure people awaiting the day when they hope to be the absolute masters of their fellow countrymen and pay off old scores.

They have their anti-God religion, and their communist doctrine of the entire subjugation of the individual to the State. Behind this stands the largest army in the world, in the hands of a government pursuing imperialistic expansion as no Czar or Kaiser has ever done.

I must not conceal from you tonight the truth as I see it. It is certain that Europe would have been communized, like Czechoslovakia, and London under bombardment some time ago, but for the deterrent of the atomic bomb in the hands of the United States.

Winston Churchill

*Double and treble the sentries
    guarding this slab
And stop Stalin from ever
    rising again
And with Stalin the past
By the past I mean neglect of
    the people's good
The false charges and the
    jailing of innocent men
Stalin has not given up
He thinks he can outsmart
    death
We took him out of the
    mausoleum
But how to remove Stalin's
    heirs
Some of them tend roses
    thinking, secretly
That their enforced leisure
    will not last
Others even heap public abuse
    on Stalin
But at night they yearn for the
    good old days
Why care some say
But I can't remain silent
Not while Stalin's heirs walk
    this earth
Stalin still lurks beside the
    mausoleum.*
    Yergeny Yevtuschenko

Soviet power, represented by Khrushchev himself, was the basic condition of life, being Stalin's legacy to them all. But Truman entered the White House trusting in the spirit of Yalta which had been Roosevelt's dying message to the American people. Stalin then had eight more years to live. He was at the height of his power, with his victorious Red Army dominating the continental land mass of Europe and Asia. Thus it fell to Truman in the seven and three quarter years of his presidency to have to meet every move Stalin made. They turned out to be the most decisive years of modern times. The spirit of Yalta soon disappeared to be replaced by a duel of will between the two most powerful men in the world — the Soviet dictator, growing more and more paranoic as his end neared, and the American president who never expected to hold such power in the first place, but who quickly learned how to use it in the cause of freedom.

He constantly thought of things that would further secure him in his one-man rule and he eventually began to dream of founding a dynasty. He would be Josef the First. The only problem was, who would be Josef the Second? He could not bear to think that there would be a successor to him.

TRUMAN

Let us not fail to grasp this supreme chance to establish a world wide rule of reason, to create an enduring peace under the guidance of God.
Harry Truman

Years of Decision

by Turner Catledge

I'd hate to break it down as to what his charm was. When he walked down a street of Independence, Missouri, or Kansas City, he stood out because he was dressed so well. He was a haberdasher and he continued to be in his dress. He had some kind of magnetism that I found very hard to understand. To me he was an uncommon common man.

Turner Catledge

President Truman's last known word on the atomic bomb took the form of a note written at the Potsdam conference and directed to Secretary of War, Henry Stimson.

Harry Truman faced a major crisis every day of the seven and three quarter years of his presidency. He was called to office by tragedy, the death of President Roosevelt, on April 12, 1945. From then on he was to live with, and greatly influence momentous events, national and global, until he turned the office over to Dwight D. Eisenhower on January 20, 1953.

Truman's years in the White House were lived under the shadow of the mushroom cloud. The jaunty little man from Missouri, who never expected to be President, suddenly found himself the most powerful man in the world by virtue of America's monopoly of the atomic bomb. Face to face with those giants of international power politics, Churchill and Stalin, Truman had to take decisions which would shape the postwar world for generations, perhaps centuries, to come.

Truman had not had a single day's experience or instruction in the country's foreign policy. He had been abroad only once, as a soldier on a troop ship to France in World War I. Throughout his brief tenure as Vice President, Roosevelt had deliberately excluded him from any discussion of the

Sec War

Reply to your 41011 suggestions approved Release when ready but not sooner than August 2

HST

atom bomb and all other matters of foreign affairs within the executive branch, except those that came up during cabinet meetings. At the time of the greatest diplomatic crisis in American history, the person standing next in line to a dying man for the presidency knew only of the tasks at hand from what he read in the newspapers and heard on Capitol Hill.

Once during his chairmanship of the committee investigating defense production, Truman's curiosity had been aroused by an unusually large project in the state of Washington. Finding it a highly hush-hush matter, Truman sought some information from Secretary of War Stimson. Stimson, who hardly admired Truman's type, or the prying of a Senate committee, shunted him aside with a sort of W.C. Fields' "get away boy, you bother me." Truman did not take the rebuff lightly. According to Stimson, Truman threatened him with "dire consequences." He noted in his diary, "Truman is a nuisance and a pretty untrustworthy man."

After Truman's first cabinet meeting, held within two hours of entering the White House, Stimson lingered behind. Very secretively he informed Truman that the project he had inquired about previously involved development of a new explosive of incredible power; he wanted to discuss it with the President at his very earliest convenience. The Secretary was so brief and circumspect that Truman was left puzzled. Stimson wrote in his diary: "The new President on the whole made a pleasant impression but it was very clear that he knew little of the task into which he was stepping."

Truman's first serious consideration of the atom bomb came two weeks later. Stimson paid a visit, this time bringing with him General Leslie R. Groves, commanding general of the Manhattan Engineering District, the official name of the secret bomb project. Stimson and Groves reviewed with him in detail the history of the bomb, describing it as the

It was hardly ever considered by anyone that Harry Truman would become President of the United States, even by those who had known for more than a year that Roosevelt was dying. This went for Truman himself. His nomination for Vice President was an inside job of Democratic Party bosses, who were determined to prevent the renomination of Vice President Henry W. Wallace.

"All the News
That's Fit to Print"

The New York Times.

Copyright, 1945, by The New York Times Company.

LATE CITY EDITION
Partly cloudy, less humid today.
Cloudy and warm tomorrow.
Temperature Yesterday—Max., 72; Min., 66
Sunrise today, 5:17 A. M.; Sunset, 8:06 P. M.

VOL. XCIV..No. 31,972.   Entered as Second-Class Matter, Postoffice, New York, N. Y.   NEW YORK, TUESDAY, AUGUST 7, 1945.   THREE CENTS NEW YORK CITY

FIRST ATOMIC BOMB DROPPED ON JAPAN; MISSILE IS EQUAL TO 20,000 TONS OF TNT; TRUMAN WARNS FOE OF A 'RAIN OF RUIN'

It is an atomic bomb . . . it is a harnessing of the basic power of the universe. The force from which the sun draws its power has been loosed against those who brought war to the Far East.

Harry Truman

most terrible weapon in human history. They predicted it would be ready for use by August.

Stimson later described Truman as being impressed but not overwhelmed. Stimson spoke of the bomb only as a war weapon, without voicing any opinion about its possible continuing impact on international politics. Truman also seemed concerned with it only as a war weapon, and a tactical weapon at that. Stimson emphasized that the policy had already been settled that the bomb would be used when ready. He proposed that the President set up an interim committee, with Byrnes as chairman, to keep him advised on future nuclear policy. It is not known how much Stimson told the President of misgivings within the military establishment. General Eisenhower recoiled at the thought that the United States should be the first to use this horrible machine. General Marshall hoped that some way might be found to warn the Japanese. At least they would have the alternative of surrendering and avoiding its devastating

96

consequences. These qualms were pushed aside for practical as well as policy reasons.

Truman raised no questions or doubts. He fully agreed that it was necessary to proceed. Up to and including using the weapon. He then let the matter rest for the time being. A moment after the meeting he remarked very pensively to an aide that soon he would have to make the most terrifying decision any head of state ever had to make. At no time did he consider halting the program.

Truman's induction into "Summit" diplomacy came at the Potsdam conference in July 1945. Germany had surrendered unconditionally on May 7, 1945, the day before Truman's 61st birthday. In June, to preserve the spirit of Yalta, and despite Churchill's plea to delay, Truman ordered all American forces to begin withdrawing to their zones of occupation. The war in the Pacific was still on and the United States and Britain were still trying to persuade the Soviet Union to join them in it. The atom bomb had not yet been dropped.

Little of great significance is remembered from the Potsdam conference yet it was noteworthy for two important reasons: It gave the other Allied leaders, Churchill and Stalin, an opportunity to observe the new President; secondly, it marked the occasion when Truman found himself without question the world's most powerful leader. For it was at this time that Truman received from Stimson full details of the successful test of the bomb in New Mexico. And it was from this meeting that he sent back the fateful message: "Release when ready, but not sooner than August 2." He expected to be on his way home by that date.

The first bomb was dropped on Hiroshima August 6. Two days later the Soviets declared war on Japan. A second bomb exploded over Nagasaki August 9. The Japanese surrendered August 14.

The end of the war came with a suddenness for which neither the government nor the country was prepared. Crises broke around Truman's head with the violence of the tornadoes which during his childhood used to send him and his family running for cover. Labor, long restrained from seeking large wage increases, came roaring out of the wings with demands that would compensate for their "sacrifices." Private business and housewives alike clamored for release from price controls and rationing. Industrialists thought their performance in production of war materials entitled them to resume dominance over the economy. Political liberals sought to resume the Roosevelt crusade to put private industry in its place. Strikes, boycotts, government seizures of mines, steel mills and railroads followed one after the other, as the little man from Independence, Missouri, sought to steer the country's reconversion to peaceful life. His reward? Congress turned a deaf ear to his schemes. In his first congressional election after taking office, Truman's party lost control of both houses. Not only did the majority shift, but Capitol Hill, under control of the Republicans with many Democrats following, practically declared war on the White House. Ignoring the President's requests for remedial measures Congress on its own initiative passed one bill after another; then they merrily repassed them over Truman's vetoes.

Once over bourbon in my office in New York, I asked Truman whether he ever had been tempted to call off the bomb. "Hell no," he replied. "What a damn fool I would have been — even what a traitor — to have allowed tens of thousands of American boys to be killed and wounded in an invasion of Japan while the atom bomb, capable of ending the war, lay idle on some factory floor."
Turner Catledge

97

Signed at TOKYO BAY, JAPAN at ____
on the ___ SECOND ___ day of ___ SEPTEMBER ___, 1945.

重光葵

By Command and in behalf of the Emperor of Japan and the Japanese Government.

梅津美治郎

By Command and in behalf of the Japanese Imperial General Headquarters.

Accepted at TOKYO BAY, JAPAN at 0908 I
on the ___ SECOND ___ day of ___ SEPTEMBER ___, 1945,
for the United States, Republic of China, United Kingdom and the Union of Soviet Socialist Republics, and in the interests of the other United Nations at war with Japan.

Douglas MacArthur
Supreme Commander for the Allied Powers.

United States Representative

Republic of China Representative

United Kingdom Representative

Union of Soviet Socialist Republics Representative

Commonwealth of Australia Representative

Dominion of Canada Representative

Provisional Government of the French Republic Representative

Kingdom of the Netherlands Representative

Dominion of New Zealand Representative

Truman didn't stop to lick his wounds. He had too much to do. The peace of Europe was in serious jeopardy due to the aggressive and deceitful action of the Soviet Union who proceeded to grab Poland and stepped up the pressure to extend communist control over other central European nations in defiance of the Yalta agreements. Truman found clear evidence of Soviet intentions in papers Roosevelt left on the Oval Room desk. Later he was to get a personal preview in a meeting with Molotov when the Soviet Foreign Minister stopped by Washington on his way home from the United Nations organizing conference in San Francisco. In a meeting at Blair House Molotov indicated clearly to Truman Soviet intentions regarding Poland. The President became so incensed he gave Molotov, or the Soviet Union, a tongue lashing and then ushered him to the door. Later he told Joseph E. Davies, former American ambassador to Moscow, and advocate of a softer approach to the Russians: "I gave him the one-two straight to the jaw."

Within a year after the 1946 election debacle, the Truman Administration promulgated the most massive international peacetime aid program ever conceived in the world's history

and a few months later won approval in Congress by over-whelming majorities. It was a two-pronged program known as the "Truman Doctrine" and the "Marshall Plan." The purpose of the Truman Doctrine was to block the possibility of a communist takeover of Greece and Turkey. Initially the United States would take over from Great Britain responsi-bility for the national security and economic rehabilitation of the two countries. The Marshall Plan was a wide-ranging scheme for the economic rescue of war-exhausted Europe, including Germany. To finance these commitments Con-gress appropriated nearly $25,000,000 during the next four years.

Promulgation of the Truman Doctrine and the Marshall Plan was conclusive evidence that the United States ac-cepted the existence of a "cold war" with the Soviet Union. Stalin acknowledged the same by forbidding any of the newly communized countries to accept aid from the Marshall Plan, although under the plan's terms they were eligible, as was Russia itself.

The early weeks of 1948 were a particularly somber time for Truman, the United States and the free world. Czecho-slovakia succumbed to brutal pressure from the outside and intrigue from the inside and fell into the communist bloc. All

The highest hope of the American people is that world cooperation for peace will soon reach such a state of perfection that atomic methods of destruction can be definitely and effectively outlawed for ever.
    Harry Truman

We have no hostile or aggressive designs against the Soviet Union or any other country. We are not waging a cold war. The crisis that exists is not between the Soviet Union and the United States. It is between the Soviet Union and the rest of the world.
    Harry Truman

We shall not realize our objectives unless we are willing to help free people to maintain their free institutions and their national integrity against aggressive movements that seek to impose upon them totalitarian regimes. This is no more than a frank recognition that totalitarian regimes imposed upon free peoples by direct or indirect aggression undermine the foundations of international peace and hence the security of the United States.

Harry Truman

of Scandinavia was threatened. The plan for four-power rule of Germany was being undermined by the Russians. The Yalta agreements were falling one by one. The United States sought to formulate a master military alliance among the western European non-communist nations (NATO). The communists, meanwhile, were closing in on Chiang Kai-shek in China. Entrapment of American forces in Korea loomed as a definite possibility. Fighting in Palestine was reaching serious proportions as Jews attempted to establish an independent state in the face of violent Arab opposition. Most potentially dangerous of all to the United States, Britain and France was an attempt by the Soviets to push them out of Berlin. This generated a fear of war that lasted for months, and brought forth a major effort from the two powers in the Berlin airlift. This airlift was a notable success for the Truman Administration.

In spite of all this activity, Truman was trying to mount a campaign for reelection, with signs pointing overwhelmingly to failure. He might have been disturbed or disheartened at times by the polls, as friends later said, but he left no record of ever believing anything but that he would win, which he did after a razzle-dazzle "whistle stop" campaign in which many times he appeared more aldermanic than presidential. He went after the 80th Congress with a vengeance and succeeded in transferring his wrath to millions of voters. His Republican opponent, following advice of party leaders, took the high-road, thinking it impossible to lose. The Republican feeling was expressed by Representative Claire Booth Luce of Connecticut in a speech to the faithful: "Let us waste no time in measuring the unfortunate man in the White House against our specifications. Mr. Truman's time is short, his situation is hopeless. Frankly, he is a gone goose." That remained the attitude of most Republicans, even when the tallying of the votes on election night indicated Truman's reelection.

Truman did not win a majority of the popular vote because of the diversion of Democratic votes to Henry Wallace, Progressive, and Strom Thurmond, Dixiecrat. He received 24,105,812 — 49.5 percent, to Dewey's 21,970,065 — 45.1 percent; this translated into 303 electoral votes to Dewey's 189. In the same election Democrats regained control of Congress with comfortable majorities in both houses.

Going into his second term, Truman's crisis list continued to expand. Mixed with the higher problems of state were scandals in his administrative bureaucracy involving officials and politicians close to him. He did not try to interfere with the processes of the law and two of his most trusted officials went to jail. Then came the Korean War and something Truman feared most of all — the return, by his order, of American troops to actual battle.

It started on the afternoon of Saturday, June 24, 1950, when the army of North Korea suddenly poured across the border into South Korea, then under the protection of the United States as a trustee for the United Nations. The U.N. responded hastily. On Sunday afternoon it convened the Security Council which quickly voted 9-0 — after the Russians had walked out — to label the North Korean action a breach of the peace and to call for an immediate cease-fire. That night Truman called his top military and diplomatic advisers to the White House. With their approval he ordered General Douglas MacArthur, then in Japan, to take charge and evacuate all Americans from Korea. Later that night he expanded MacArthur's orders to include giving direct support to the South Korean forces. The next day the United Nations Security Council called on all U.N. members to help South Korea repel the attack. Thus the Korean War became officially a United Nations action. Meanwhile, Truman met with Congress and his full cabinet. No one opposed what he had done.

"Everything I have done in the past five years has been to try to avoid making decisions such as I had to make today," he said.

In still further instructions to MacArthur, Truman authorized him to send American ground troops into Korea. The war was underway. Even though officially a United Nations action, the burden of the fighting was to be done by Americans who, before it was over, suffered more than 80,000 casualties.

One of the most interesting episodes of the Korean War was Truman's discharging of General MacArthur. MacArthur started the campaign with some brilliant military strokes. Then things went sour. He made some tragic misjudgments, one being that the Chinese would not enter the fight, which they did in great force and to the embarrassment of American, or United Nations, forces. He found it increasingly difficult to accept the guidelines and limitations set by the United Nations policies which were meant to

What would suit the ambitions of the Kremlin better than for our military forces to be committed to a full scale war with Red China? It may well be that in spite of our best efforts the communists may spread the war. But it would be wrong, tragically wrong, for us to take the initiative in extending the war. I have thought long and hard about this question of extending the war in Asia. I've discussed it many times with the ablest military advisers in the country. I believe with all my heart that the course which we are following is the best course. A number of events have made it evident that General MacArthur did not agree with that policy. I have therefore considered it essential to relieve General MacArthur so that there would be no doubt or confusion as to the real purpose and aim of our policy. It is with the deepest personal regret that I find myself compelled to take this action. General MacArthur is one of our greatest military commanders. But the cause of world peace is much more important than any individual.

Harry Truman

101

Victors and vanquished. The trial of leading Nazis as war criminals takes place at Nuremberg.

confine the action and avoid drawing other communist nations into the action. MacArthur became highly defiant of Washington. He went public with his gripes. When events moved to the point where peace was to be considered, he insisted on handling the peace negotiations "on the field of battle," like great warriors of old. Truman thought him disrespectful to him personally and insubordinate to the presidency. The first he might have overlooked; the second, never. So Truman fired him, setting the stage for MacArthur's last hour of glory in his address to a joint session of Congress.

Truman's presidency was truly a great and fascinating story in the history of American and world statesmanship. For him it was also a great personal drama. Suddenly, at a crucial point in history, the helm of the world's foremost power was handed by fate to this former Senator and small-town politician who was forced to enter upon the task totally unprepared for the job. He had one decided advantage. He was not overestimated by anyone, including himself. Although known previously for certain traits of narrowness, ineptness and impetuosity, he was able along the way to draw upon the resources of his own spirit, his own courage, hope and humor, and his own instincts and good intentions. He had an uncanny ability to listen and learn and a willingness — even eagerness — to face large challenges and make decisions without the slightest remorse.

It was these qualities that enabled Truman to bring to his office an open-mindedness rare among men of power. His long and bitter duel with Stalin, which lasted throughout his presidency, brought in its train an astonishing turnabout in America's attitude toward her former enemies, Germany and Japan. Because of the cold war, from being almost universally hated these defeated powers won the right to be considered new and respected partners in an alliance dedicated to freedom. Power legitimizes such unexpected twists of fortune. For Truman, who had ordered atomic destruction of Japanese cities, signing a peace treaty with Japan brought personal satisfaction. But no one can have felt the drama more keenly than Hirohito, the Emperor of Japan, who knew both the illusion and the reality of power and who succeeded in utilizing both to retain his Chrysanthemum Throne through 50 of the most tumultuous years of Japanese history.

HIROHITO

The ultimate result of the wartime destruction, in which the major cities were laid waste and more than 80 percent of the nation's manufacturing plant was destroyed under incessant bombing, was the complete replacement of the former outmoded equipment with the most up-to-date machinery in existence.

The Chrysanthemum Throne

by Robert Trumbull

When the slender, round-shouldered young man called Hirohito mounted the Chrysanthemum Throne as the 124th Emperor of Japan in 1926, court scholars were called upon by ancient tradition to give his reign a title that would also survive the Emperor long after his death. They selected for Hirohito the name Showa, which means "Enlightened Peace."

The choice seemed incongruous during the decades of aggressive Japanese militarism. In that period Hirohito was

Emperor Hirohito in a familiar pre-war pose.

often pictured in a resplendent uniform and seated upon a magnificent white horse, reviewing the troops that had been called to war in the Emperor's name by the officer clique who actually ruled Japan as the monarch's surrogates.

Years later, the selection of Showa to designate the Hirohito era appeared to have been uncannily prophetic. Now the former martial figurehead was usually seen in a rumpled business suit, waving a crushed fedora to the crowds. They had come to regard him as their leader in a march toward a peaceful and democratic Japan. The economic prowess of their nation would soon amaze the world.

The change in Japan's direction, and the imperial image, stemmed from a single courageous act by Hirohito himself. Defying imperial tradition as well as the powerful warmakers whose bellicose policies had smirched his name, the Emperor decreed his nation's surrender to the strength of the Allied powers, especially the United States, that a prostrate and devastated Japan faced at the end of World War II.

Under the tradition that the monarch's role is merely to lend the mystic power of his august name to decisions made by others, no Japanese emperor before Hirohito had exercised such a controlling voice in his country's destiny for centuries past, if ever.

For hundreds of years Japan had been governed, always in the Emperor's name, by military dictators called shoguns. This period ended in 1868 with the so-called Meiji Restoration, which theoretically returned power to the Emperor. The incumbent monarch was Hirohito's grandfather Mutsuhito, known since his death in 1912 as Meiji (Enlightened Rule). It was he who moved the imperial court from the shrine city of Kyoto, where the emperors had been virtual prisoners of the shoguns, to Tokyo.

Hirohito was born on April 29, 1901. Following ancient custom, the infant prince was removed from his parents' custody to be brought up in a separate household. His training as a future emperor was strict and formal. Hirohito was sickly and myopic as a child and had to wear thick glasses throughout his life. In later years he declared that the happiest time in his life was the visit he made in 1921 to London and other European capitals, something no imperial prince had done before him. In England the 20-year-old Crown Prince became a special friend of the Prince of Wales.

In accordance with Japanese custom, Hirohito became Emperor at the instant his father expired on Christmas Day 1926. But the formal coronation in ancient Shinto ceremonies at the ancestral palace in Kyoto was not held until November 10, 1928, nearly two years later.

By 1933, the year that Hitler became Chancellor of Germany and Roosevelt was inaugurated as President of the United States, the government that Hirohito formally headed had come under almost complete control of the militarist faction, who were able to bring down any cabinet by withholding the approval of the High Command for appointments to the key posts of Minister of War and Minister of the Navy. Hirohito was disturbed by the trend, according to a former adviser and confidant, Marquis Koichi Kido, but he was unable to halt it.

During this period of armed expansionism, the militarists

Crown Prince Hirohito's wife, the Crown Princess Nagako, with their first child, Princess Teru, in June 1926.

Hirohito, as Crown Prince, meets British leaders on a visit to England in 1931.

carried on an intensive campaign of propaganda supporting the theory of the Emperor's divinity. The public reacted with such fervor that the government was forced to go along. A law was proclaimed making it an offense to suggest that the Emperor was other than divine, or that he was a constitutional monarch subject to earthly laws. Anyone passing the palace was required to bow low in the direction of the Imperial presence, a ritual that began the day in every Japanese schoolroom. Police enforced a law that no one could look directly at the Emperor when he passed by on the street, and it was required that windows looking down on his route be shuttered till he had gone by. All this was done so that the militarist rulers, like the former shoguns who had kept the emperors virtually imprisoned in Kyoto, could claim the sanction of the gods for actions taken in the monarch's name.

Hirohito, according to accounts of contemporaries that surfaced later, was deeply annoyed by the unsought deification of his person. The Emperor was said to have rejected totally the divinity concept and, furthermore, to have thoroughly understood the purpose of the campaign. He was only too well aware of his own powerlessness to stop the militarists exploiting the false image of an infallible Imperial being to further their own design.

In December 1941 a militarist-dominated cabinet headed by General Hideki Tojo as prime minister decided, against the earnest advice of many others besides Hirohito, that Japan must attack the United States. This followed an American decision to prevent the Japanese from obtaining the oil and other materials vital to continued expansion into China and Southeast Asia, where the imperial forces had seized part of French Indochina. Tojo thereupon activated a plan to strike at the United States Pacific Fleet, based in Pearl Harbor, with carrier-based aircraft.

The decision to go to war was made at a conference attended by Hirohito and the cabinet. The Emperor was enthroned on a dais. With misgivings, but feeling powerless to do otherwise, Hirohito affixed the imperial seal to the documents. It was reported later by former aides that he had insisted that the United States be told beforehand of the impending attack on Pearl Harbor. In fact, a final message to Washington containing the warning was held up, by a delay in decoding, until after the bombs had fallen.

Although Hirohito's name was attached to numerous declarations exhorting his subjects to a supreme effort in the war, and assuring them that final victory was certain, the Emperor's role in the prosecution of hostilities was purely formal until the later stages. By then much of Japan lay in smoking ruins and it was clear that defeat was unavoidable.

In the same year he travels to Belgium where he is received by King Albert I.

A Tokyo crowd demonstrates
in support of the Axis powers
against Britain and
America.

At a cabinet conference in the palace on New Year's Eve of 1944, the Emperor declared that the country was indeed in a "desperate situation." Six months later Hirohito, deciding to take the initiative in bringing the disastrous conflict to an end, appealed personally to the Soviet Union to approach the United States for peace terms. Japan and the Soviet Union had signed a neutrality pact in 1941 which was still in operation, although Stalin had promised Roosevelt that Russia would attack Japan once Germany had been disposed of. In Moscow Hirohito's plea was ignored.

In the Potsdam Declaration, issued on July 25, 1945, by the United States, Britain and China (by radio), the Allied powers called for Japan's "unconditional surrender," a demand that Hirohito's cabinet summarily rejected. The first atomic bomb was dropped on Hiroshima on August 6, bringing a new dimension to warfare. Two days later the Soviet Union abruptly declared war, repudiating the pact with Japan. On August 9 the second atomic bomb fell on Nagasaki. On the following night the historic conference was held in the Emperor's air raid shelter at which Hirohito broke with imperial tradition to spare his country further suffering.

The scene was a narrow underground chamber about 30 feet long, whose concrete walls were covered with wood panelling. Access was by a stairway from the imperial library, where the Emperor and Empress had established their living quarters after the climactic firebombing of Tokyo on May 25. The imperial compound was out of bounds to the American bombardiers, but windblown debris had set the palace aflame, burning it to the ground. (For many years after the war, Hirohito insisted on remaining in the temporary headquarters because of the parlous housing situation of millions of his subjects. A new palace was not built until the 1960's, after Japan had long since regained prosperity.)

While Hirohito listened without expression, seated on his throne-like chair at the head of the long conference table, arguments were presented for accepting the Potsdam surrender terms. A strong militarist element in the cabinet still insisted upon continuing the fight, if only to obtain a softer settlement from the Allies. Finally the prime minister, Admiral Count Kantaro Suzuki, took the floor. Since it was obviously impossible for the cabinet to agree, he said, he had concluded that the decision must be made by the Emperor. There was an astonished gasp from the assembled dignitaries.

Hirohito, who knew what was to happen, rose from his chair with a sheaf of notes, written in Japanese characters, held in a hand that trembled slightly. He was perspiring heavily, as were all the men in the hot, airless room. His first words were high-pitched from nervousness. Collecting himself, the Emperor offered a few introductory remarks summarizing the hopelessness of the situation, with many pauses to swallow and to brush a hand across his damp face. To those who described the occasion later, it seemed that he was close to breaking down.

The Emperor "shook himself slightly," according to one account, then continued in an emotionless monotone:

> I cannot help feeling sad when I consider the people
> who have served me so loyally, the soldiers and sailors

In a decree notifying the Japanese nation that the hostilities had begun, one significant sentence was said to have been inserted in the text by Hirohito personally. "It has been truly unavoidable and far from our wishes that our Empire has now been brought to cross swords with America and Britain."

who have been killed or wounded in the battlefield overseas, the families who have lost their homes and so often their lives as well in the air raids here. I need not tell you how unbearable I find it to see the brave and loyal fighting men of Japan disarmed. It is equally unbearable that others who have given me devoted service should now be threatened with punishment as the instigators of war. Nevertheless, the time has come when we must bear the unbearable ... I swallow my tears and give my sanction to the proposal to accept the Allied proclamation on the basis outlined.

August 15, 1945: Despite the best that has been done by everyone, the gallant fighting of the military and naval forces, the diligence and assiduity of our servants of the state and the devoted service of our one hundred million people, the war situation has developed not necessarily to Japan's advantage, while the general trends of the world have all turned against her interest. Moreover, the enemy has begun to employ a new and most cruel bomb, the power of which to do damage is indeed incalculable, taking the toll of many innocent lives. Should we continue to fight, it would not only result in the ultimate collapse and obliteration of the Japanese nation, but it would also lead to the total extinction of human civilization.

Emperor Hirohito

Hirohito turned and left the air raid shelter as the others rose and bowed low in his direction. The war, in effect, was over.

Hostilities ended officially on August 15 when a stunned nation heard the Emperor's voice on the radio for the first time as he read the Imperial Rescript of surrender. The broadcast was made from a recording that die-hard militarists had attempted, unsuccessfully, to steal from the radio station. In exquisite Japanese circumlocution, using the archaic phrasing of the court language, the Emperor began the heart of his message by saying that "the war

Following Japan's acceptance of surrender terms, Hirohito promulgates a new constitution under American auspices.

In 1945 the Russians, British and Australians, among others, were demanding that Hirohito be put on trial as a war criminal. But MacArthur felt that the sovereign was needed to keep the bewildered and disorganized nation sufficiently disciplined and unified to implement the general's forthcoming decrees, which would revolutionize the life style of the country.

"All the News That's Fit to Print"

The New York Times.

LATE CITY EDITION

Clearing early today; cooler. Clear and cool tomorrow.
Temperatures Yesterday—Max., 88; Min., 72.
Sunrise today, 6:32 A. M.; Sunset, 7:36 P. M.

Section 1

NEWS INDEX, PAGE 33, THIS SECTION

Copyright, 1945, by The New York Times Company.

VOL. XCIV. No. 31,998.
Entered as Second-Class Matter, Postoffice, New York, N. Y.

NEW YORK, SUNDAY, SEPTEMBER 2, 1945.

Including Magazine and Book Review.

TEN CENTS
New York City and Suburban Area (5c Elsewhere)

JAPAN SURRENDERS TO ALLIES, SIGNS RIGID TERMS ON WARSHIP; TRUMAN SETS TODAY AS V-J DAY

The beginning of the postwar transformation of Japan is remembered by Japanese as Showa 20 — that is the 20th year of the reign of Hirohito, or 1945. It was in that year that the victorious American soldiers arrived, under General MacArthur, to begin the seven-year occupation and, with it, the complete revamping of Japanese society.

situation has developed not necessarily to Japan's advantage." Continuing, he called upon his 100 million subjects to join their sorrowing sovereign in "enduring the unendurable and suffering what is insufferable" to insure the peace.

As the Americans landed in Japan from ships and planes to begin the occupation, the power of the Emperor over his people was demonstrated at once in the peacefulness of their reception by the Japanese populace. It would not have been unreasonable to have expected them to react with surly hostility at the very least, possibly with sabotage and stealthy murder. Not a single instance of such a thing occurred during the whole of the occupation, which lasted nearly seven years.

After the surrender Hirohito met MacArthur wearing a formal morning coat with gray-striped trousers and a stiff, standup collar with black and white striped tie.

The Emperor and the general sat down alone with their two interpreters. MacArthur, in his memoirs, noted that the Emperor's hand shook as he accepted an American cigarette. Then the Emperor said quietly: "I come to you, General MacArthur, to offer myself in judgment of the powers you represent as the one to bear sole responsibility for every political and military decision made and taken by my people in the conduct of the war." The general felt a thrill of sympathy and admiration. "He was an emperor by inherent birth," MacArthur wrote later, "but in that instant I knew I faced the First Gentleman of Japan in his own right."

In that instant also, Hirohito became MacArthur's powerful ally in the democratization of Japan.

On January 1, 1946, at the request of occupation authorities, Hirohito made another historic broadcast to his people: he read out an Imperial Rescript denying his own divinity. "The ties between us and our people have always stood upon mutual trust and affection," said Hirohito. "They do not depend upon mere legends and myths. They are not predicated on the false conception that the Emperor is divine and that the Japanese people are superior to other races, and fated to rule the world."

It is related that when the broadcast was over, Hirohito turned to the Empress and said: "Do you see any difference? Do I look more human to you now?"

Without doubt, the Emperor swiftly became more human in the eyes of his people. The ensuing campaign was to popularize the monarch in a new posture as "the symbol of

the unity of the nation," in the words of the postwar constitution. With the encouragement of the American authorities, he visited many parts of the country with a minimum of protocol. Gone were the famous white horse, Shiroyuki (White Snow), and the resplendent uniforms. The Emperor now frequently moved among the people on foot, raising his plain gray fedora to acknowledge cheers.

The Emperor's subjects did not always find it easy to adjust to the strange new relationship. On one occasion, when Hirohito was visiting a factory, a worker shoved himself in front of the monarch with his right hand outstretched, in the familiar American manner. The Emperor, startled, hesitated a moment. "Let us do it the Japanese way," he said quietly, took one step backward, and bowed. The workman, abashed, returned the traditional greeting with a lower bow.

At first there was ridicule of "imperial parasites" and public demonstration against the continuance of the monarchy. But as more and more Japanese observed that the Emperor was a person like themselves, even to the incessant use of "Ah so," denigrating the throne ceased to be a popular pastime. In a few years, it could be said that the Emperor and his family were held in greater public affection than ever before.

Though no longer hailed as divine, and with his role in the political structure now reduced to purely ceremonial functions under the new constitution, Hirohito still embodied the

We are gathered here, representatives of the major warring powers, to conclude a solemn agreement whereby peace may be restored. It is my earnest hope and indeed the hope of all mankind that from this solemn occasion a better world shall emerge out of the blood and carnage of the past. A world founded upon faith and understanding. A world dedicated to the dignity of man and the fulfillment of his most cherished wish for freedom, tolerance and justice. I now invite the representatives of the Emperor of Japan and the Japanese government and the Japanese Imperial General Headquarters to sign the instrument of surrender at the places indicated.
General Douglas MacArthur

essence of Japanese civilization. In him, and only him, was vested the ultimate expression of *Yamato damashii*, the spirit of Japan. And he remained, as a constitutional monarch, the vehicle through which the government retained continuity through the vicissitudes of changing political tides.

Thus the dimensions of power resting with Hirohito were rooted in mystic concepts of the Emperor as the repository of the national identity. As in the two and a half millennia of imperial history that went before, the influence of the throne rests in its existence as a symbol upon which a nation can focus its collective affection and respect, above shifting temporal authority.

Hirohito's success in personifying a national will for survival places him alongside another man of power who rendered a similar service to his country. Like Hirohito, Franco, the Caudillo of Spain, was for many years a target for worldwide vilification; but just as the ideal of "enlightened peace" which Hirohito's person symbolized enabled Japan to rise above the catastrophe of 1945, so the symbolic nature of Franco's hold on power enabled his fellow countrymen to rise above the passions of Spain's terrible civil war. In each case, durability in power played a large part in making it possible for their two countries to put on new faces to meet a new world.

Displaying new-found affection for their Emperor and an ancient and inherent love of poetry, the people eagerly awaited the annual publication of Hirohito's personal composition, which he presented every year at a poetry-writing contest.

Sublime is the moment
When the world is at peace
And the limitless deep
Lies bathed in the morning
sun.

FRANCO

"*Franco is like St. Thomas Aquinas's definition of God,*" one official told me, and he was not being admiring. "*He is the Unmoved Mover.*"
Richard Eder

Caudillo of Spain

by Richard Eder

For almost 40 years, from 1936 to his death in 1975, Franco dominated one of the major countries of Europe.

Caution, coldness and a total attention to the realities of power made him the only dictator linked with the Axis — he never fully joined — to survive; and the only one to go on to shape the destiny of his country in the postwar era. He grasped power as a miser grasps money: single-mindedly; not in order to enjoy it nor even in order to use it, but steadily to preserve it.

Every phase in his life coined power. There was the vigor and gallantry of his youth, when his exploits in Morocco made him a general at 33. There was the calculation of middle age, maneuvering him into total command of the

Nationals after joining them with a prudent tardiness; winning the war; executing with utter coldness tens of thousands of beaten Republicans; and seizing the opportunity provided by the cold war to obtain United States backing. There was the controlled passivity of later years, allowing younger men to build the country into a considerable economic prosperity but never allowing them political control. Finally, even extreme old age was turned into a kind of power: Spain had clearly outgrown him in his last decade but by that time he was too old to overthrow.

Like many strong men, Franco dominated his followers not by his resemblance to them but by his differences. He was most untypical of what Spaniards considered themselves to be like and, especially when he was old and relatively inactive, his hold stemmed partly from the puzzlement he afforded his countrymen. He was aloof, uncommunicative, and nothing seemed to compel him: not love, not emotion, not religion nor ideology, and least of all the expectations he raised by any previous action or statement. He was as unfathomable to his subjects as a chicken farmer is to

Franco let each faction on the Nationalist side see in him what it hoped to see; and disappointed each one successively.

The most conspicuous horror of the civil war was the punishment behind the shifting lines. It can be argued that the Republican authorities made a greater effort to control the killings than did the Nationalists, but they were notably unsuccessful. On the other hand, the massacres of Republicans at Badajoz and Malaga are conceded even by historians friendly to Franco.

his chickens; and if after passing through and exploiting all the right-wing creeds of his time his governance of Spain resembled anything, it was the careful calculations of an old-fashioned and dour property-owner — and one who was deliberately mute about the terms of his will.

No wonder there were continual rumors about his foreignness, the main one being that his forebears, the Bahamondes, were Jewish. He did, in any case, come from a relatively un-Spanish part of Spain: Galicia, in the northwest. He was the scion of several generations of a naval family, part of a community that kept itself aloof from normal civilian life. Unable to join the naval academy, which closed its enrollment temporarily just after the Spanish-American war, he entered the military academy in Toledo.

Short, sallow, with a receding chin and a squeaky voice and disproportionate self-assurance, Franco was not a naturally popular figure in military life. He was nicknamed "Franquito" and the term set him apart, at first in mockery but eventually in admiration.

Spain had a large and largely unemployed army in the early part of the century and the only chance for advancement was in the campaigns against the turbulent tribesmen in Spanish Morocco. Franco pushed his way into the African service and distinguished himself by energy, shrewdness and bravery. During two long tours in Morocco he was noted for placing himself at the head of his troops and disregarding danger. He was, in fact, gravely wounded. By the age of 23 he had gone from second lieutenant to major, arguing vehemently whenever he felt that promotion was being delayed.

Ten years later, at 33, he became the country's youngest general. This was in 1926; in the interim Franco had served as commander of the Spanish Foreign Legion, developed a reputation as an astute tactician as well as a determined fighter, served with a number of officers who would later lead the Nationalist forces in the Civil War — Mola, Sanjurjo and Millan Astray — and carried out several missions putting down rioters and insurrectionists in Spain itself.

Spain was in an unsettled state and had been, off and on, since the beginning of the 19th century. There had been dynastic wars, endless changes of government, assassinations, rioting and military *pronunciamentos.* By the beginning of the 20th century the remnants of the Spanish empire had been lost, the gulf between Spain's impoverishment and the economic progress of her neighbors had deepened, and there was a massive growth in the strength, often armed, of radical popular movements, especially the Socialists and the Anarcho-Syndicalists. The split between what has been called "the two Spains" — that which clung to a ferocious interpretation of the country's religious, national and military traditions, and that which agitated for social change, progress and the adoption of a local and often wildly distorted version of advanced European ideologies — was growing fast.

Through the Twenties and Thirties the dialogue between the two sides was conducted by their extremes, with violent actions and reactions. A military coup led by General Primo de Rivera and acquiesced in by King Alfonso XIII — Franco was close to both — led to a brief dictatorship. This was

The unsettled state of Spain on the eve of the civil war. Civilians were forced to walk with their hands in the air to demonstrate that they were not carrying guns.

followed by the deposing of Primo de Rivera and then of the King, and the establishment of a republic. The battle between the two Spains intensified, each side becoming determined not merely to defeat the other but to exterminate it. Moderate men at the head of the Republican government were undermined by radicals on both sides and by the thickening climate of violence. Churches were burned, priests murdered; workers, liberals, leftists were shot down. When a number of leading generals — Mola, Sanjurjo, Goded, Varela and others — began to set up machinery for insurrection, arguing that it was necessary to prevent chaos and a dictatorship of the left, Franco was noncommittal. He was army chief of staff and Spain's most prestigious military man, known to be of the right but hesitant about defying the legality of the Republic's government.

A move by the government to isolate the generals it most feared polarized matters. Franco was sent to the Canary Islands. By the time the uprising began in July 1936, Franco had joined the conspiracy. Its nominal leader was General Sanjurjo who was killed in an air crash while flying to join the rebellion. Later another possible rival, General Mola, also died in an air crash.

In its early days the military position of the National side seemed doubtful. Much of its advance was stopped by loyalist troops. The navy, which was to have joined in, was neutralized when crewmen mutinied and killed their Nationalist officers. It was Franco who made the most progress. Using planes provided by the Germans and Italians, he ferried troops across to Spain from Morocco, where he had taken command. Within two months these forces, which included Moorish levies, had secured much of the south and

The Spanish Civil War left half a million to a million people dead, and to many Spaniards its horrors remained fixed in the mind as a kind of punishment for what they would call their national ungovernability.

125

driven up through Extremadura to take Toledo and link up with Mola's forces in the north.

With the insurgents holding the south, the west and the north, and the loyalists the center and east, including Madrid, Barcelona and Valencia, the next three years saw a brutal war of attrition. The rebels received powerful help from the Axis in the form of men, aviation and material. The Germans and Italians were conducting military research on Spanish soil, including such notorious laboratory demonstrations as the aerial massacre of Guernica. As for the Republicans, they were virtually cut off from assistance, even to such necessities as oil, by the future Allies. Only the Russians provided substantial assistance — and commissars — although volunteers came from all over to fight in the International Brigades.

If Franco was only one of several leading generals at the start of the war, within three months he was named to supreme command. With Sanjurjo dead he was the most obvious man to take charge, but there was more to it than that. In the maneuvering that went on before the decisive meeting of the generals at Salamanca, Franco characteristically did not push himself forward; a number of generals close to him did it for him. What was to be most significant was that these men represented the various political groupings on the Nationalist side: Falangists, Monarchists, conservative Republicans. Without making explicit promises Franco managed to imply to each group that he was one of them. It was to be the pattern of his power. In any event, when the generals met at Salamanca Franco was not only named supreme military commander but head of the National government as well. And when that had been voted, reluctantly by some, the decree was quietly altered on its way to the printers to make him not only head of government but chief of state as well.

Some monarchists felt betrayed — they were working for the restoration of a king, after all. But it was not time to make an issue out of an arrangement they took to be temporary. Indeed it was temporary, but a longer "temporary" than they had bargained for. It was to be 39 years, in fact, before the Bourbons would return in the person of Juan Carlos, who finally became king after Franco's death.

Franco came out of the civil war ostensibly linked to the Axis. Many of his supporters were pro-Nazi, including his brother-in-law, Serrano Suner. Yet out of caution and a growing conviction that the Germans would not win, he hedged his bets. Apart from frustrating Hitler's desire for a full-scale alliance, he continued throughout the war to furnish Britain with strategic materials and provide other useful services to the Allies. After the war Churchill even voiced his appreciation. His wartime cabinets balanced pro-British monarchists with pro-German Falangists.

With the Allied victory certain, he got rid of the vociferous pro-Nazis — including the brother-in-law. He began to stress that his regime had not been so much pro-Axis as anti-Soviet. Nevertheless, the postwar Allied boycott was a serious threat. He made defiant speeches to crowds in Madrid. But many Spaniards believed it was his moment of greatest danger. And then, after several years of diplomatic

*Evita Peron of Argentina
visits Franco on behalf of her
dictator husband.*

isolation, relieved only by gifts of wheat and friendship from
Peron in Argentina, the cold war came to his rescue. In the
1950's the United States signed agreements providing economic and military assistance in exchange for bases.

In his last couple of decades Franco added to his uncom-
municativeness a policy of doing as little as possible. He
would let his ministers act, and over the years they did act to
modernize the economy and relax some of the regime's orig-
inal harshness. The face of Spain changed dramatically;
economically and socially it moved closer to the rest of
Europe, even if it remained politically apart. But Franco's
own concerns, though he obviously intended the country to
prosper, focused more and more on the maintenance of public order and the dismantling of any combinations that could
infringe on his power.

It is an old truism that over any long period of time, using
power uses up power. What made Franco so durable was
that he divided the use of power from the maintenance of
power. His ministers would use the power he loaned them,
suffer the discredit when things went wrong, and be
dropped. He himself made as few decisions as possible; only
when some real crisis was at hand would he take significant
action. And even then it was usually less than seemed called
for. "He was brilliant at mediocre solutions," one Spaniard
observed.

The civil war was an unspeakably savage climax to 120
years of a flickering fight for power in Spain. The depredations, the national paralysis and the impoverishment caused

by the violent snatching of the prize back and forth among the factions never had the effect, as it did in many countries, of stimulating a national awareness that the question of who has power is less important than devising a civil framework inside which it can be peacefully contended for.

If the civil war was terrible enough to finally convince most Spaniards that such a framework was necessary, Franco, who seized power so bloodily, remained to provide another lesson. Holding on to power for so long, and doing so little with it, he de-mystified it. He made it seem boring. He was like a plaster cast holding a shattered limb together, constricting it, repressing it, and as strength returned, becoming a focus for the entire body to rebel against.

Franco's extraordinary durability was consistently marked by his willingness to drop whatever and whoever was not useful to him, however useful it or they may have been previously. In the course of 40 years this included just about every group that felt it had a claim on him.

In his own way he did unite a whole new generation of Spaniards, if only in the pleasure, and perhaps the surprise, of finding that they could perfectly well do without him.

To most foreigners the Spanish Civil War remained a much simplified moral drama of right and wrong. Mentally they rated Franco as a war criminal and they never forgave him for getting away with it. In Italy, the end of the Second World War saw Mussolini strung up by his ankles in Milan; after Himmler had taken poison, his corpse was displayed to cameramen for all the world to see. Goering and his fellow Nazis were arraigned before special tribunals, as were Tojo

and other Japanese war chiefs, many of them being condemned to death. In France, the aged Marshal Pétain was tried for high treason and sentenced to death, though the sentence was commuted on account of his age and former service to France. Elsewhere in Europe Quislings and other collaborators were summarily executed. But nothing of the kind happened in Spain; Franco was able to creep steadily forward after his high-powered associates had come to grief.

Germany, by contrast, lay prostrate before the Allies. With Hitler's disappearance there was a power vacuum which for the time being was filled by the occupying armies. No Emperor Hirohito was available to provide a focus of national revival, nor was there any continuity of civil leadership, many of those who might have given it having been killed off by the Gestapo in the last months of the war. In such inauspicious circumstances how could Germany be reborn? The answer was provided by Konrad Adenauer, at first sight as unlikely a figure as any that could be found in Germany.

Neither the anti-Fascist slogan of the Loyalists (OPPOSITE) nor the threat of persecution as a war criminal were sufficient to deter Franco, who crept slowly forward, like Aesop's tortoise, to survive his less fortunate associates.

ADENAUER

"The West must face the question of which danger is the greater," Adenauer told me in an interview, "the danger threatening the West from Russia or the prospect of a German contingent in a European army for the defense, defense remember, of western Europe."
Drew Middleton

Germany Reborn

by Drew Middleton

Konrad Adenauer bore little resemblance to other men of power. He was 73 with no experience in international affairs when he became Chancellor of the newly formed German Federal Republic. He was a devout Catholic who believed that Christian political parties were an answer to communism. His speeches were logical, colorless and devoid of emotional appeal; his manner was stern, at times authoritarian, although he was a devoted father to his family. And he was the first German leader to proclaim himself as much a European as a German.

Measured against the times, his achievements are striking. Adenauer negotiated the establishment of the Federal Republic with the United States, Britain and France, the three occupying powers in West Germany. He organized and then led his political party, the Christian Democratic Union, to a decisive victory in the first free national election in Germany since 1933. As Chancellor he presided over the German economic miracle which transformed a devastated country into one of the strongest economic powers in the world. He was a leading spirit in the reconciliation of France and Germany which laid the foundations for the establishment of the European Economic Community or Common

"Today, I regard myself primarily as a European and only in the second place as a German," Adenauer told an international audience in Luxembourg.
PREVIOUS PAGES The devastation of Cologne after the Allied bombing. Only the cathedral remains a recognizable landmark.

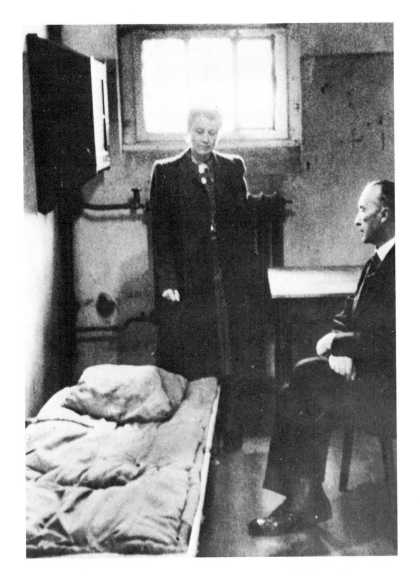

During the war Adenauer, although anti-Nazi, refused to have anything to do with politics and deliberately remained out of the various plots hatched against Hitler and his regime.

Adenauer and his wife visit Brauweiler prison where he was held in 1944.

Market. He negotiated the rearmament of West Germany and its entrance into the North Atlantic Treaty Organization.

When he left office, old and venerated, the Federal Republic was the strongest economic power in Europe, firmly democratic and a major contributor to the defense of the West. All this was accomplished by unremitting industry, by sound judgment of what would bring out the best in his countrymen and by a keen perception of the opportunities that the cold war offered him and his nation.

Before 1945 Adenauer's only taste of power had been as mayor of Cologne during the Weimar Republic of Germany. A devout Roman Catholic and incorruptible politician, he had opposed the Nazis and had been driven from office by them. In the convulsions which marked the end of Hitler's Third Reich, Adenauer was scheduled to be shot and for a time was detained by the Gestapo in miserable prison conditions.

Adenauer was finally released from the camp in November 1944. Emaciated and worn, he made his way to the village of Rhöndorf in the Rhineland and refuge with his family. There he stayed through the last winter of the war. Spring brought an American offensive, the fall of Cologne and the opening of Adenauer's second career.

135

Adenauer lived at Rhöndorf, condemned to political inactivity until his arrest in 1944.

The day after Cologne fell two American officers appeared at Rhöndorf to ask Adenauer to resume his old job as Chief Mayor of Cologne. He agreed to act as the chief adviser to the military, but secretly, because three of his sons were still serving in the German Army and the sons of a known collaborator faced instant death.

When the war ended, Adenauer resumed his old title of Chief Mayor and remained in the post until October 1945 when the British, who had by then taken over the Rhineland as part of their occupation zone, dismissed him. He was dismissed ostensibly because he had not implemented military government policy with sufficient energy. The true reason may have been Adenauer's outspokenness about Germany's future as part of Europe.

At 70 Adenauer could have retired to Rhöndorf, his family and his garden. But he was too active, too energetic and too ambitious a man to consider retirement. In addition the war and its aftermath had jolted him out of his parochialism. He was thinking now in terms of Germany and Europe and not simply of the Rhineland and Cologne. Before he could do anything he had to construct a political base. He found it in a new party, the Christian Democratic Union, generally known as the CDU.

In a Germany threatened by communism from the east and by a kind of political defeatism in the west, the reconstitution of parliamentary government was a daunting task. Adenauer, and indeed all German politicians, had to cope with Allied suspicion, strongest among the French, of any revival of German unity and political influence. The CDU in its efforts to win followers was opposed by a strong Socialist Party which had managed to survive the Hitler years and which was led by Kurt Schumacher, a tough veteran of Nazi concentration camps and a highly emotional and effective speaker. The Labor Government, then in power in London, openly favored Schumacher and the Social Democratic Party (SPD) over Adenauer and the CDU.

Events, however, eliminated some of the Allied suspicions of the Germans and promoted the revival of the economy and the growth of political life. By the summer of 1948 the Russians had ousted a pro-Western government in Czechoslovakia and blockaded western Berlin. The Soviet threat to western Europe was increasing.

Allied efforts to keep the western sectors of the former capital alive with the largest airlift ever organized were successful. German workmen helped unload the supplies. The people of West Berlin under a Socialist mayor, Ernst Reuter, stood firm despite Soviet pressure. The airlift, largely an American and British operation, broke the blockade. When the affair was over the Germans, particularly the Berliners, had improved their position. True, they remained a defeated, occupied nation. But they had supported the West in a time of trial and many allies now considered them as friends and helpers.

German youths hurl bricks and abuse at an intrusive East German tank.

The events of 1948 had a larger impact. It was clear to many allied statesmen and soldiers — Field Marshal Montgomery was the first to voice the view openly — that western europe could not be defended without a strong West German economy and, in time, the inclusion of German forces in the defense of the West. Currency reform was introduced in the western zones; the American and British zones were merged into an economic unit called Bizonia, and the economic "miracle" of German recovery began. The miracle, it should be remembered, required some priming. Between 1945 and 1955 the West German economy benefited from $3.5 billion in economic aid from the United States.

With great shrewdness Adenauer played his cards. One card was resistance to western zones. The second was resistance to the Soviet Union and its plans for a Germany united but theoretically neutral under communism. If the first card irritated the allied military governors, this irritation was more than balanced by the satisfaction they found in Adenauer's sturdy anti-communism.

Adenauer had three tasks in this formative period of the Federal Republic. He had to convince the three Western powers, including a hypersensitive France, that Germany was abiding by the rules laid down by the occupation powers. He had to convince the Bundestag that Germany, as far as it was able, was pursuing an independent course. And, finally, he had to awaken his countrymen to the need for a united Europe and, at the same time, convince Germany's future partners in such a Europe that the old enemy would be a good friend. In pursuing these tasks he displayed political wiliness and parliamentary acumen. And as a tactician he was head and shoulders above any other German politician. He may have had, as his enemies said, a vocabulary of only 300 words, but his sentences marched straight as soldiers to the point.

The Chancellor's greatest feat was to secure full sovereignty and equality of rights for the Federal Republic in return for its remilitarization within the North Atlantic Alliance. This occurred under the London and Paris protocols of 1954. Yet five years earlier the demilitarization of Germany had been the basic condition for the gradual relaxation and abolition of Western occupation!

In achieving full sovereignty, and militarization, Adenauer displayed to the full those qualities of statecraft that had grown since he first became Chancellor. He had one significant advantage. During his years in office he had stamped his personality upon the minds of his countrymen to such an extent that even members of opposition parties found it hard to conceive of a Germany that did not have *der Alte*, the Old Man, at its head. Toward this end he directed his political power and his popular prestige.

The most fundamental problem facing Adenauer in the debate within Germany over rearmament was the psychological state of the German people. Anti-militarism was not simply the result of the disasters of 1944 and 1945. It owed a great deal to the attraction of the new prosperity. Why, an intelligent German could ask himself, should we spend money to arm when the Americans, the British and the French are pledged to defend us? Adenauer's answer, endlessly repeated in private meetings, was that the Americans, in particular, would not send more troops to Germany unless the Germans were making an adequate contribution in men and money. His objective was two-fold. On the one hand he sought a treaty admitting Germany to full equality with other sovereign states in the world; and linked to this treaty he sought a second establishing a European Defense Community in which Germany would play a full part. All his shrewdness and tenacity were thrown into the pursuit of these objectives.

Finally on March 19, 1953, the two treaties were submitted to the Bundestag. The German Contract was approved with a majority of 62, the EDC treaty by one of 59. Was this a triumph? Superficially, yes. But two great trials lay before Adenauer, one known, the other unknown.

The known trial was the second general election in West

The attack by the North Koreans, armed and advised by the Soviet Union, in June 1950 supported those who in Washington and London favored some measure of German rearmament.

Germany's brief history. It was bitterly fought. The Socialists attacked on all fronts, even making the charge that in his heart Adenauer was opposed to reunification of all Germany. This was an adroit move. Adenauer had never entirely lost his early parochialism. He knew that in a Germany reunited in freedom, his CDU would have to fight a much larger Socialist party. The Socialists continued to portray him as a man who wished to keep Germany divided. To this charge they added that his Catholicism created an unbridgeable gap between the Chancellor and German Protestants.

But Adenauer weathered the storm with the help of an adroit move of his own. He disclosed that he had written to John Foster Dulles, U.S. Secretary of State, asking for a four power conference dealing with Germany's future to be held not later than the autumn. He also negotiated with the Soviet Union for the return of German prisoners of war who had been held all these years in Soviet camps.

By election day the tireless Adenauer had traveled throughout the country. He found it prosperous; industrial production was rising, unemployment falling. Although the Socialists continued to hammer away at his so-called provincialism and his resistance to German reunification, he did not consider them a real threat. He was right. The CDU received twelve and a half million votes compared to just under eight million for the SPD.

Der Alte's program, despite all he had done in the Federal Republic, was still far from completion. He had signed the German Contract, the treaty which was to give West Germany full sovereignty and equality of status, and the Bundestag had ratified the treaty establishing the European Defense Community. But other countries lagged behind, notably France, and the Federal Republic waited for sovereignty while the high commissioners for the three allies carried out their duties.

One of Adenauer's political virtues was patience. When his party stormed over French delays, he counseled patience. When the Cabinet suggested a stiff note to France, he reminded them that this would do more harm than good, that patience was the answer.

The Chancellor undoubtedly was right. France was going through a series of political convulsions in which power in the Elysée Palace was far more important than the future of Europe. Even the suggestion of interference from Bonn would have wrecked the fragile, half-constructed edifice of European unity.

As it was, the French National Assembly took a long step in that direction when on August 30, 1954, it voted by 319 to 264 to remove the EDC treaty from its agenda. It had not voted against it. It had not rejected it. It had decided not to debate it now or in the future. The European Defense Community was dead. And with it died Adenauer's hopes for early sovereignty for the Federal Republic.

For once the iron facade broke:

> Must we now assume that the French do not wish for an understanding between our two countries? The conception of Europe cannot be killed by a procedural discussion in the French National Assembly with the help of a hundred communists.

The Federal Republic must now obtain its full sovereignty. The Occupation Statute cannot be sustained nine years after the war. And implicit in sovereignty is the right of self-defense. We are not asking for the right of rearmament as unlimited and without shackles. We shall exercise the right to rearm in the light of European policy.

These were forceful words that were read with attention in London and Washington. The solution to the impasse was found by Anthony Eden, the gifted British Foreign Secretary. Like most solutions to complicated issues, it was simple.

Eden proposed to extend the Brussels Treaty, concluded in 1948 by Britain, France, Belgium, the Netherlands and Luxembourg to include West Germany and Italy and to adapt it to the new conditions. A month later, in September 1954, the British took another important step. To meet French fears, real or imaginary, of a rearmed Germany, Eden announced Britain's commitment to maintain four divisions and one tactical air force stationed in Europe. But, the Foreign Secretary added, Britain would enter this commitment only on condition that the nine powers assembled in London would reach agreement on all outstanding issues. One day later agreement was reached.

Nine foreign ministers signed a series of preliminary draft agreements to be embodied in a new treaty. These provided for the end of the occupation regime in Germany, the restoration of the Federal Republic's full sovereignty, the rearmament of that country within NATO and the inclusion of Germany and Italy in the mutual security assistance system of the Brussels pact.

Adenauer believed that "Power must never be allowed to concentrate in undue measure in any one place lest it imperil the freedom of the individual."

In May 1955 the Chancellor presides over the treaty signing ceremony in Bonn which officially ends the 10 year occupation of West Germany by the Western powers, Britain, France and the United States.

"You must not forget," the Chancellor told me, "that a new war would be fought in Germany. If Germany has no part in its own defense, how can I or any German be sure of the part Germans would play?"
  Drew Middleton

Adenauer finally had won. And France had lost. For her intransigence over EDC had produced exactly the result the French had striven to avert. Germany had started on the path that was to make her the primary industrial and military power in continental Europe.

No German statesman since Bismarck rivalled Adenauer in accomplishment. By patient negotiation, far-sighted planning and unrelenting work he won back West Germany's freedom and independence. What were the qualities that enabled him to exercise his power so adroitly?

First, and frequently forgotten, experience in government. He once told me, soon after taking power as Chancellor, that there was little difference between administering the West German state and the city of Cologne. The problems, he observed, were the same. It was only the scale that was larger now. Like Churchill, he knew how to make the civil service run, through long and sometimes bitter experience.

I have seen at Buchenwald how men were tortured, gassed, burned and slowly starved to death for their political and religious convictions. The responsibility for these terrible crimes, for the excruciating sufferings and agonized deaths of hundreds of thousands of men and women and children, too, in these camps, this responsibility falls squarely on the German people. They have long borne that responsibility in the eyes of God; they must be made now to bear it in the eyes of their fellow men.
Clare Booth Luce

An elderly couple are escorted back to East Berlin after attempting to cross the border and join the refugees flooding into the West.

A second quality was patience. He never appeared to hurry. He never allowed the impatient to push him into action he considered imprudent. When he took office he understood, far better than most of his colleagues, Germany's position. He knew that would change, as much as a result of the widening rift between East and West as by German actions. They must be patient, prepared to come forward at the right time with policies that would fit the general policy of the major Western powers.

A third quality was his impassiveness. It was a maxim of Adenauer's to "never show that you're hurt in debate." Socialists, communists, a few far rightists hammered away at this tall, calm figure. Some of the things they said hurt. Neither by word nor gesture did Adenauer ever show his wounds.

Finally, of course, he understood power. He had so little at the start but he husbanded it, using it adroitly with an excellent sense of political timing. When his second election victory consolidated his position and that of his party, he was neither elated nor overbearing. There was, he said, "so much that remains to be done."

Beneath this was his devout Catholicism. "Man's fortune and happiness will always be in the hands of God," he said. And he firmly believed that there are "greater chances of happiness" along "our road" than in the "world of communism."

Europe no less than Germany was fortunate that there was an Adenauer available at such a time to guide the destinies of a shattered nation back to freedom and prosperity. And Adenauer himself was fortunate that in neighboring France there was a man with whom he could share the experience of national humiliation along with the vision of a new Europe. In the towering personality of Charles de Gaulle, Adenauer found a friend and an ally, one who helped end the animosity between their two countries which had bedeviled the history of Europe for centuries and who showed that force of character alone can give a man power. In the darkest days of the war, when his material resources were negligible, de Gaulle stood out among all his contemporaries as a man of supreme integrity.

The friendship of de Gaulle and Adenauer sprang from the shattering experiences their two countries had suffered in war. De Gaulle helped end the feud which had so bedeviled European history for the past hundred years.

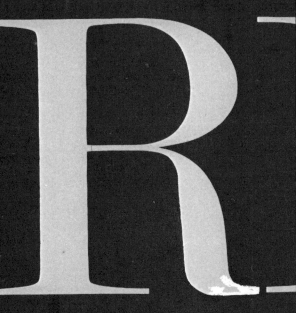

DE GAULLE

R

F

*On the first page of his memoirs
Charles de Gaulle wrote: "All my life I
have thought of France in a certain
way. To my mind, France cannot be
France without greatness."*

Republican Monarch

by Drew Middleton

The outbreak of war in September 1939 found Colonel
Charles de Gaulle commanding the tanks of the Fifth Armored Division in Alsace. He circulated a memorandum to 80
military and political leaders proposing that his tanks be
moved northward to close the gap that existed northwest of
Montmedy where the Maginot Line, theoretically the shield
of France, ended. No one paid much attention. The prevail-
ing wisdom was that the Germans by failing to attack at the
outset of the war had lost their chance. Nevertheless General Gamelin appointed de Gaulle commander of the Fourth
Armored Division then being formed. The newly made
Brigadier General asked for 200 tanks and received 120.

On May 10, 1940, after months of phony war, the German
armies attacked Holland and Belgium and fell upon France
with a massive concentration of armor and artillery, supported by dive bombers and parachutists. The Germans
called it the Blitzkrieg.

This new kind of mobile warfare was exactly what de
Gaulle had been advocating in the books he had written

De Gaulle as tank
commander and proponent
of mobile warfare.

before the war. But the French High Command was committed to the defensive strategy of the Maginot Line and were quite unprepared for the speed of the German onslaught.

De Gaulle, however, delivered one of the few successful counterattacks made by the French. On June 5 and 6 he threw two battalions of heavy tanks and one of light tanks against the Germans near Abbeville on the Somme River. The French did some damage, won time for the preparation of a futile defense in the north but lost heavily — about 200 men and many tanks. But the German bridgehead across the Somme held. De Gaulle fought on with his untrained, ill-armed division winning his fifth citation for valor.

Paul Reynaud, his old political patron, had become Premier. He gave de Gaulle the post of Under Secretary of War in a reconstituted cabinet. The new junior minister's first job was to visit London and plead with Churchill for the dispatch of more Royal Air Force fighters to France. The British prime minister refused. But he was impressed by de Gaulle's cool fortitude.

Marshal Pétain, now Vice-Premier in the government, criticized de Gaulle's arrogance and ingratitude. But such remarks were irrelevant in the time of a collapsing state. On June 10 Maxime Weygand, who had succeeded Gamelin, declared Paris an open city. The government fled first to Orleans and then to Bordeaux.

Sir Edward Spears, the chief British liaison officer, soon realized that of the French military attached to the government only de Gaulle was intent on continuing the war against the Germans. Reynaud resigned. Pétain, a hero of World War I and de Gaulle's former commanding officer, became the new head of state. Known as the Vichy government, this new regime was ready to make peace with the Germans and

Leaders of the Vichy government surrender to Germany in the very railroad car in which Germany had signed its own surrender in 1918.

LA RÉPUBLIQUE VOUS APPELLE!..

RASSEMBLEMENT DU PEUPLE FRANÇAIS

Following his "call to honor," de Gaulle in the immediate postwar years exhorted his fellow countrymen to rise above narrow party interests.

collaborate with Hitler's Third Reich. De Gaulle was offered the opportunity to escape by airplane to Britain and there carry on the war. He accepted Sir Edward's suggestion and on June 17 — the Germans and French were already negotiating an armistice — he left with Sir Edward in a tiny airplane. "He carried with him in that small airplane the honor of France," Churchill commented.

The next day this relatively obscure officer established his place in a world at war. Speaking over the BBC he called on all French soldiers, sailors and airmen, on all French workmen in Britain to get in touch with him. "Whatever happens," he said in his sonorous French, "the flame of French resistance must not and shall not die."

This was what he described as his "call to honor." It was the birth of Free France, or Fighting France as it came to be called, and announced de Gaulle's entry into the world arena. Oddly the date was the 125th anniversary of the Battle of Waterloo, an equally disastrous French defeat.

The period between that first broadcast and de Gaulle's final return to France was the formative period of his life as a political leader. With limited military resources, with, initially, little support in France he had, as Churchill pointed out, "no real foothold" but "never mind, he defied them all."

"Them" meant the Anglo-Saxons, first the British and

then the British and the Americans. De Gaulle's immediate objective was to make both governments realize that he was "responsible for the interests and destiny of France."

He had little to support his claim. In July 1940 the Free French forces consisted of about 7,000 soldiers plus a few warships that operated under British command. But to the British, continuing the war at great odds, even this was something and de Gaulle was recognized as chief of all the Free French. The long duel for power with Churchill and Franklin Roosevelt had begun.

In retrospect British and American irritation with the General is understandable. At that period with only Fighter Command of the R.A.F. between Britain and invasion, a tough but harried prime minister had more on his mind than the towering, demanding French general. Churchill admired de Gaulle's combativeness and intransigence. But he also found them trying. "Of all the crosses I have to bear," he told an aide, "the heaviest is the Cross of Lorraine" which de Gaulle had taken as a symbol of the Free French.

De Gaulle's assumption of French leadership that summer ostensibly reflected his devotion to France. "C'était à moi d'assumer la France" he said, meaning that he was prepared "to take France upon myself." But leadership also promoted his desire for power. He saw himself, quite rightly, as the indispensable Frenchman and he saw power as part of that role. "The deep root of action by the best and strongest of men," he wrote, "is the desire to acquire power."

And in his relations with the British and Americans he was learning how power was won.

"The statesman," he concluded, "must concentrate all his efforts on captivating men's minds. He must know when to dissemble and when to be frank. He must outbid his rivals in self-confidence and only after a thousand intrigues and solemn undertakings will he find himself entrusted with power."

The road to power was not an easy one. An early test came when the Royal Navy destroyed the French fleet at Mers el Kebir in Algeria. De Gaulle was torn between his resentment as a Frenchman and his recognition as a strategist that the British attack had been necessary to prevent the fleet from falling into German hands.

As the war wore on de Gaulle found his responsibilities widening and his trials increasing. French colonies in sub-Saharan Africa rallied to the Cross of Lorraine. In metropolitan France men realized that the war had not ended in June 1940, that the Luftwaffe had been whipped by the British, that Washington was supporting London. The resistance, partly Gaullist and partly communist, began to take shape although the communists remained aloof until Hitler attacked Russia in June of 1941.

De Gaulle soon learned that Franklin Roosevelt was a more formidable barrier to his ambitions for France and, of course, for himself, than was Churchill. The blow that might have felled a lesser man came in November 1942. The Americans and the British landed in North Africa and announced that General Giraud, a militarily gifted but politically inept French general, had been appointed French commander-in-chief. For the moment, as the Allied armies plunged west-

Inside occupied France, de Gaulle's name was synonymous with resistance. The BBC had made his voice familiar throughout his homeland.

151

The United States and Britain had made arrangements with certain French generals and officials in North Africa who appeared willing to desert the Germans and resume the war against the hereditary foe. Roosevelt had picked, for reasons still obscure, General Henri Giraud to lead the French forces in North Africa. There was an optimistic forecast that most of the French civil servants in the three states would rally to freedom's cause. Things went wrong almost from the start.

ward into the rain sodden hills of Tunisia, de Gaulle appeared side-tracked.

The battle in North Africa was being fought over territory which the French claimed as their own. With each military victory came fresh political complications. Whom should the Allies deal with? The French administration on the spot, appointed by the Vichy regime, or de Gaulle's nominees? Giraud was a good soldier, but no politician, while de Gaulle now had two years experience in the art of statesmanship.

In the struggle for power, de Gaulle drew on the loyalty of the team of men who gathered round him during his first days in London. Gaullism, as it began to be called, was by

At the Casablanca conference in January 1943, two rival contenders for power, Giraud (far left) and de Gaulle (on Churchill's right), were brought together in what was described as a "shotgun wedding."

now closely associated with the spirit of Free France and with the Cross of Lorraine. Giraud's position was steadily undermined by de Gaulle's men.

As Allied victories in the desert continued, Roosevelt tried to get Churchill to break with de Gaulle. But Churchill refused to dump the one Frenchman who had defied Hitler before the Americans had entered the war.

De Gaulle then learned that the Americans and the British were not intending to allow the Free French to take part in the liberation of Tunisia and Libya. De Gaulle bluntly informed Eisenhower that if this were the case, he would pull out his own Free French troops and send them to the Soviet Union to fight alongside the Red Army.

153

Paris liberated! De Gaulle sets out on his historic walk down the Champs Elysées.

At last the day came when de Gaulle headed back for France, following the Allied landings in Normandy. But when he first set foot again on his native soil, it was in the humiliating knowledge that his Free French forces had been left out of the invasion plans for security reasons. He himself was not even entrusted with detailed information about the landings. The wound went deep and lasted long. In later years, he cultivated the idea that France had freed herself, which was true only in the sense of his own moral victories. Though they distinguished themselves in the fighting, neither the French units in the field nor the partisans contributed as much to the Allied cause as the Gaullists liked to claim.

In the weeks after the invasion de Gaulle's identity with France fused with his own thirst for power. For he was convinced that he, and only he, could establish the France that he wanted. This would not be, he said, "a regime of parties disastrous for France."

In August 1944 de Gaulle entered Paris. His personal courage then probably did more to solidify his hold on the French than all his speeches and writings. On August 26 the tall, unbending leader of Free France marched from the Arc de Triomphe in company with resistance leaders, including a bevy of communists, to the Cathedral of Notre Dame. As they approached the great church, shots rang out. People flung themselves to the ground. De Gaulle, however, marched stolidly on, glancing neither to the right nor to the left. It was a display of raw, personal courage. And, perhaps,

De Gaulle was labelled a dictator by friends and enemies alike. During my years in Paris I believed this description was wrong. De Gaulle was a republican monarch, a Washington untrammeled by Congress. He was also a consummate performer with an unrivaled sense of timing, and a dominant and authoritative orator.

Drew Middleton

something else. A visible indication of de Gaulle's faith in his destiny, an expression of the man's sublime self-confidence. Because physical courage publicly displayed always excites admiration, that steady progress through the bullets kept de Gaulle on the path to supreme power in France.

In the autumn of 1944 the drive for power against the communists demonstrated de Gaulle's political sagacity. He proclaimed that there was only one power in France: the state, which he represented. That state, France, he said, had never ceased to exist. He meant that he, representing the state, had carried on the war after "the false state" headed by Pétain had surrendered. The position is a shaky one. The Chamber of Deputies, legally elected, had turned over full power to Pétain in 1940. Legally, de Gaulle, when he issued his "call to honor" in June 1940 was provoking a civil war. But in those days in 1944, in the heady atmosphere of victory, few thought in legalistic terms and those who did kept quiet.

On September 9, 1944, the General announced the establishment of a provisional French government. A month later that government was recognized by the United States and Britain. Yet de Gaulle remained unsatisfied. The Americans, British, Russians and Chinese had met at Dumbarton Oaks to draw up plans for a future United Nations. The French were excluded and, to de Gaulle, vilified by American comments that France's part in the war had been that of a small country. This was an insult.

De Gaulle countered by going to Moscow to seek an alliance with the Soviet Union. The treaty itself, while it solaced de Gaulle, was of little moment and was unilaterally abrogated by the Soviet Union 11 years later after France had entered the North Atlantic Treaty Organization.

More important to the development of de Gaulle as a man aspiring to power was the impression made upon him by Stalin. "Stalin was possessed of the will of power," the General wrote. "Trained by a lifetime of plotting to mask his features and his soul, to dispense with illusions, with pity, with sincerity, to see in each man an obstacle or a danger, everything in him was maneuver, mistrust and obstinacy."

The political storms that burst on France after Germany's surrender were too much for de Gaulle. The country was in torment. The men of the resistance paid off old scores

against collaborators. The strength of the communists, thriving on their false claim to be the only true resistance force, increased. The old parties, no whit discountenanced by the failures of 1940, reappeared. The political struggle was more important than economic recovery, or so it seemed. And the economy, after five and a half years of war, occupation and war, was a shambles.

Refusing to have any part of this system, de Gaulle retired from the scene in January 1946 to hold himself ready, he believed, for a return to power on his own terms. He had no wish, as he put it, to preside, powerless, over the powerlessness of the state, and however long it might take he had the force of character to retain his integrity while he waited for the call to act again to serve France.

In the meantime de Gaulle warned his fellow countrymen of the new dangers which beset them in a world dominated by the superpowers of Russia and America.

During the 12 years of his retirement, de Gaulle looked on as France's position in the world steadily declined. A long war in Indochina against the communist-inspired Vietminh drained her resources. French parachutists fought bravely, but the war ended disastrously for them.

French generals in Indochina felt badly let down by their allies and by their own governments in Paris. The war had cost the lives of 92,000 Frenchmen, all to no purpose. It was the parachutists in the French army who were especially embittered. They spearheaded the abortive Anglo-French attempt to seize the Suez Canal in 1956, and they had to bear the brunt of a long and savage fight against Algerian nationalists.

Any talk of making terms with the nationalists produced riots in Algiers. The settlers were citizens of France, fully represented in the National Assembly. There was no solution which would satisfy all parties. Rioting spread to Paris. The cry of "Algérie Française" was taken up on the streets and sounded out on car horns. No combination of parties survived long in government and no politician could feel certain of the loyalty of the army.

In the confusion, different groups for different reasons turned to the old warrior living in retirement at Colombey-les-Deux-Eglises.

For 12 years de Gaulle lived in retirement at Colombey-les-Deux-Eglises, a small country town some hundred miles from Paris, where he wrote his memoirs. Even as a child, visiting Paris, he had been moved, he wrote, by "the symbols of our glories; night falling over Notre Dame, the majesty of evening at Versailles, the Arc de Triomphe in the sun, conquered colors shuddering in the vault of Les Invalides."

By 1958, France seemed to be on the verge of civil war. The settlers of Algeria, fearing a sellout by the politicians in Paris, were preparing to take the law into their own hands. Enfeebled at home and ridiculed abroad, France looked for a savior.

At a famous press conference, de Gaulle declared that he was available to serve France once again. He belonged to no party, he said, and therefore he belonged to everybody. "Now," he concluded, "I shall return to my village and remain there at the disposal of my country."

De Gaulle insisted that he must be legally invested with special powers and given a definite term in which to work for order. He had no intention of seizing power; it must be entrusted to him with the full authority of the state. President Coty strongly supported him and de Gaulle had his way.

Men of the right saw de Gaulle as their champion. The army would certainly obey him. Men of the left feared a new kind of dictatorship. De Gaulle proposed a thoroughgoing reform of the constitution designed to give France a strong executive. Submitting his proposals to a national referendum, he campaigned vigorously to win the people's support. France gave him an overwhelming "Yes."

Well past the age when most men retire, Charles de Gaulle had now reached the summit of power. He was President of France, with a constitution tailored to his liking. He was supported by a slavish majority of Gaullist deputies in the National Assembly and served by an able civil service dependent on him for jobs.

De Gaulle also had style. His commanding figure could not fail to impress visitors. Conscious of the dignity of his office, de Gaulle welcomed them to France as though Paris were the center of the world. Critics said that he would be a better-informed President and France better governed if he had to stand before a Parliament or a Congress and answer questions twice a week. But none of his fellow statesmen could touch him for sheer presence — that force of character which had brought him through the dark days of the war.

The de Gaulle government settled and sobered France. But, although no one except a few unrepentant members of the opposition dared mention it, much of the progress was due to the Fourth Republic. The devaluation of the franc, the formation of a French nuclear force, the economic revival, all had their genesis in the now scorned "regime of partisan politics."

Power, among other things, provides those who wield it with the opportunity to repay old scores. De Gaulle had never forgotten or forgiven the slights, real or fancied, of Britain and the United States during the war. It is impossible to say how much these memories influenced him. They certainly played a major part in the decisions that led to two of his most important acts as President.

Twenty years later it is forgotten how strong the movement for European unity appeared. Hand in hand went the drive for a cooperative defense effort against the mounting power of the Soviet Union. Future historians will argue whether de Gaulle's actions were for good or ill. But no one can argue that he twice vetoed British admission to the European Economic Community and that he withdrew France from military integration in the North Atlantic Alliance.

With these two climactic acts de Gaulle was at the summit of his power. His peers in Europe, Adenauer in Germany,

Macmillan in Britain were restricted by parliaments. He alone was free to act, confident that a subservient and largely Gaullist Assembly would approve. There was something else within him: his innate sense of drama, a feeling that he, Charles de Gaulle, was moving and shaping the world of postwar Europe.

But there was another factor. Both the Common Market and NATO represented threats to the sovereignty and freedom of action of that France which de Gaulle had served since boyhood and with which he increasingly identified. "When he says 'de Gaulle,'" a fellow countryman said, "read 'France.'" What de Gaulle dismissed in his vetoes and in

France's withdrawal from NATO was the concept of a united Europe in which his beloved France would only be one member of a federation. This could not, would not be. His power was enough to prevent it. And prevent it he did.

De Gaulle's Fifth Republic transformed France. He gave her a political stability which she had not known for half a century. Under his rule, the currency was reformed, industry revived, the economy expanded. The settlement of Algeria relieved the country of a political abscess. Party strife was muted. All this confirmed de Gaulle's confident assertion of personal power in the crisis of 1958. He sought no monument for himself, but only for France.

As his power in France grew, and his ego with it, de Gaulle spread his wings abroad. He attempted, vainly, to revive France's position as a great international power. There were visits overseas. To Mexico where he promised credits that were beyond France's capacity. To Québec in Canada where he exacerbated an already difficult situation by shouting "Vive Québec libre." Such actions did him some good in France. But they failed to disturb the world balance between the Soviet and American empires. A gesture toward Communist China, a plea for disarmament, invocations of the grandeur and glory of France made headlines but failed to change the course of world events.

As President de Gaulle's power and ego grew, so did his belief in the solitude, majesty and aloofness of the true leader who, as he had written, was capable of "willfully misleading the very people one is thinking of using."

But 10 years of high-handed, one-man rule was proving irksome to many Frenchmen — especially the young. In 1968 student demonstrations against the Gaullist system coincided with a widespread workers' strike. Unrest spread throughout France and for a time de Gaulle seemed isolated.

At first he tried the techniques he had used before to secure acceptance of the constitution of the Fifth Republic. But these appeals failed to still the uproar. It was a year of student trouble in other countries too. The activists in this movement knew the power of television coverage upon a mass of uncritical viewers. Although de Gaulle's government controlled France's broadcasting networks, it could not suppress all news of what was happening in the streets of Paris and other major French cities.

De Gaulle met the crisis with characteristic defiance. "I shall not retire," he declared. "I have a mandate from the people; I shall fulfill it." Having assured himself that the army remained loyal, he dissolved the Assembly and campaigned with all his old vigor in the elections. The choice, he said, was between himself and the communists.

The result was an overwhelming victory for the Gaullists. Yet something had changed. Though de Gaulle's system might survive to keep the communists out of power in future elections, it was clear that de Gaulle's personal style of government could not continue much longer.

He resigned a year later and soon after, he died. To his country, he left his name to join those of other French immortals; to the world, he left his France, strong, self-confident and independent. Aloof in his integrity and untainted by the moral degradation that comes from holding

power, de Gaulle was a unique figure who made everyone else seem of lesser stature — even a high principled president of the United States under whom he had once served as an ally in war.

De Gaulle's coffin is carried by the young men from Colombey-les-Deux-Eglises. De Gaulle's widow, Yvonne, is in a black veil (center); in the uniform of a French naval officer (right) is the General's son Philippe.

EISENHOWER

We must be willing individually and as a nation to accept whatever sacrifices may be required of us. A people that values its privileges above its principles soon loses both. This is the work that awaits us all. To be done with bravery, with charity and with prayer to Almighty God.

Dwight D. Eisenhower

Years of Caution

by Drew Middleton

Dwight D. Eisenhower's life was full of contradictions. He became supremely powerful relatively early in his chosen profession and he exercised that power decisively behind a mask of bland affability. Just as in World War II he had seen the opportunity for high rank, so he saw in the decline of the Democratic Party's fortunes the opportunity for supreme civil power. Always reluctant on the surface, he maneuvered himself into the position where he was indispensable as far as the Republicans were concerned.

Once elected President he used his power to the full, although content to allow others to take some of the credit. Repeatedly in international affairs he used the military and economic power of the United States to further his policies. But although he spoke with alarming candor of the possibility of using atomic weapons or of intervention by the American forces, there was also an inbred caution.

In 1939 Eisenhower was one of many ambitious young American army officers with no combat service. He was marked as an exceptionally hard-working and capable staff officer who had the ability to see broad strategic plans in relation to their necessary logistical support. He was favored by the elimination through age or accident of more senior field commanders. But his own pleasing manner commended him to his allies and he showed a readiness to use able subordinates and if necessary to discard or discipline those who failed him. Chosen to command the Anglo-American expedition against French North Africa, Eisenhower picked his way through political and diplomatic minefields to win military victory in Tunisia and Sicily.

His big chance came in the autumn of 1943 when he was selected to direct the planning of the greatest Allied amphibious operation of the war — the invasion of Europe. From his headquarters in London Eisenhower exercised supreme command over an enormously complex military organization. Final responsibility for success or failure was his alone. By June 1944 the plans were ready.

No leader in war can avoid the hard decision, the one that involves great risk for his forces and, ultimately, for his career. Perhaps the most difficult decision Eisenhower made in the entire war was over the launching of the invasion.

On June 5, 1944, the meteorologic staff at headquarters reported that the weather conditions off the coast of France were so bad that if Eisenhower persisted in his plans, as he later said, "a major disaster would almost surely have resulted." The staff added that on the next morning a period of relatively good weather would follow, lasting perhaps 36 hours. It was up to Ike.

The general recalled later that he considered the decision for only a short time. It was a momentous one. Tens of thousands of troops, thousands of warships, landing craft and bombers and fighters were waiting. If the 36 hours of good weather did not materialize, landing craft might founder, and the supporting fighters and bombers would be unable to find and hit their targets. The first waves of troops might get ashore and be isolated by bad weather, an easy prey to German counterattacks.

Quickly he reviewed all the factors in his mind as he paced the floor of his office. Finally he decided that the consequences of delay justified a great risk. He ordered the attack to go ahead on June 6.

Eisenhower's generalship, that is, his use of the enormous power invested in him, was challenged seriously in the late summer of 1944. In the ensuing crisis in command, he displayed a steely conviction that his plans were right and those of his challenger wrong. The challenger was Montgomery.

The Field Marshal, then commander of the 21st Army group of British and Canadian troops, surprised Eisenhower with a plan to "end the war." If the Supreme Commander would support him with all the supplies, Montgomery would lead his army group to Berlin and end the war. The plan challenged both Eisenhower's authority and the mission laid down by the Combined Chiefs of Staff before the invasion. This stipulated pursuit of the retreating Germans on "a broad front with two army groups, emphasizing the left to gain necessary ports and reach the boundaries of Germany."

The youngish general who assumed command of American forces in Britain in 1942 impressed both Americans and British by his personality. To the Americans, diplomats, soldiers and civilians, his warm, breezy manner was a breath from across the Atlantic. To the British, now in their third year of a war that with one or two exceptions had been a losing one, Eisenhower's confidence, his enthusiasm, his affability was a tonic.

Eisenhower's arguments were that there was no way to maintain a force east of the Rhine in view of the lack of railroad bridges and stocks of food and fuel and that, while "at no point could a decisive success" be attained, the other Allied forces would have found themselves in "precarious positions."

The Supreme Commander's general strategy prevailed. Montgomery had to be content with the airborne assault on Arnheim which demonstrated that the Germans were still capable of vigorous defense and cast doubts on the Briton's concept of a dash to Berlin.

Eisenhower never doubted he was right in following the "broad front" strategy. And he was irritable then and later when his colleagues charged that he had overlooked the political importance of the capture of Berlin by the Anglo-American armies.

By early 1945 the Supreme Commander, if not drunk with power and success, was at least beginning to feel their effects. Convinced that "Berlin has lost much of its former military importance," he pointed the final Allied offensive at the Erfurt-Leipzig-Dresden area. He conveyed this plan in a personal message to Stalin, who naturally endorsed it because it enabled the Russian armies to drive straight on to Berlin without interference from their Western friends. The telegram, according to Churchill, was sent to Stalin without first being shown either to him or to the British Field Marshals Montgomery and Brooke. So, in one stroke, Eisenhower had helped the Russians to take Berlin unassisted and thus reap the political and propaganda dividends and, secondly, offended his allies, among them Churchill who had vigorously defended him in Parliament and the War Cabinet.

The incident discloses a rather startling defect in Eisenhower's political perception. Trained by an army that thought almost entirely in military terms, he was incapable of seeing the political advantages to the Soviet Union that would result from the Red Army's capture of the city and its subsequent occupation. This inability to see what hundreds of his subordinates saw was not confined to the Berlin affair. It also affected his perceptions as President of the United States.

Eisenhower was a much more complex and politically sophisticated man than he appeared to be. By the end of World War II he had dealt on equal terms with leaders such as Franklin Roosevelt, Winston Churchill and Charles de Gaulle. He had observed the workings of governments, his own and others, at first hand. No American politician of the immediate postwar years had greater experience in dealing with major international issues. He was also an ambitious man and a patriotic one. Moreover he had a strong sense of duty. These elements combined to prepare him, in his own mind, for the presidency.

At the same time he was fortunate, politically, in the posts he held between the end of the war and his campaign for the presidency in 1952: military governor of Germany, Chief of Staff, president of Columbia University, and Supreme Commander of the newly formed North Atlantic Treaty Organization. These, together with his war record, provided him with an almost Olympian status in the public eye.

Because the invasion would be launched from Britain and because the initial assault would be commanded by Montgomery, Eisenhower willingly gave the latter a great deal of freedom. Wisely, too. For, in his estimate given me after the war, he considered Monty "the only man who could fight and win the set piece battle that would establish us in France."
Drew Middleton

The war ended with General Eisenhower enjoying personal popularity and power such as few Americans have ever been granted.

Eisenhower on a whirlwind tour of Indiana in the 1952 campaign.

During his period of command as Supreme Commander Allied Powers Europe, his headquarters were besieged by a stream of visitors from the United States, most of them politicians, senators, governors, congressmen and local leaders. To most, when they raised the question of a run for the presidency, he said, "I'm not interested."

But he *was* interested. In conversations with his old friends he dwelt more and more upon American domestic problems. He was irritable when he discussed Senator Robert Taft and others whom he saw as standard bearers of a new and dangerous American isolationism. Any ambitious man, favorably placed for the presidency, when he discusses such problems may be assumed to be thinking of how he would handle them as president. The power of the presidency appeared more and more attractive to Eisenhower as he became convinced that he could use it for the good of his country.

A reasonable assumption is that from 1945 Eisenhower had his eye on the White House. His coldly logical mind, which was so much at odds with a generally ebullient, expansive nature, concluded that his best chance to be nominated and win the election lay in remaining outside the arena until the very last moment. So it was not until early in 1952, election year, that he confirmed that he was a Republican and that he "tentatively agreed" to return to the United States when his stint at NATO was over, "and, if nominated at the convention, would campaign for the presidency."

The outwardly reluctant candidate won the nomination easily and, after an arduous campaign, defeated Governor Adlai E. Stevenson for the presidency. He was the leader of the most powerful nation on earth; the West's standard bearer and spokesman in the duel with communism.

What did Eisenhower represent politically? My impression over the years was that he was a fundamentalist, even a primitive Republican who believed in what were, to him, peculiarly American virtues of hard work, thrift, obedience. He accepted the conventional wisdom of the lower middle class into which he had been born: that every American had a chance to do anything in life he wished; that in America class didn't matter; that "Duty, Honor, Country," the West Point motto, was the only creed that a man needed. It was difficult for the new President to understand that to some of his countrymen these concepts were so much hogwash. He sincerely believed that, as he often said, he and his brothers "had been poor as kids but we never knew it; we all worked hard and enjoyed it."

Oddly enough, even when Eisenhower had been nominated and elected, some of his new colleagues, politicians and officials, perhaps moved by wartime memories, still believed that he would act as chairman of the board and not as a powerful executive. His first opportunity to prove otherwise came during the campaign when he decided, against the best professional advice, to campaign in the largely Democratic South. He wanted to be, he said, "President of all the people." His own strategy, not that of the experts, paid off. The Republican national ticket swept five southern states.

Nor was he content to follow expert advice on what he should and should not say in his speeches. "I was determined to emphasize principle and to voice my own convictions," he wrote in his description of the campaign.

Powerful though he was, the new President labored under an important handicap in choosing his Cabinet and his associates. All through his military life when making an appointment, he had had before him the long, thorough record of an officer's qualifications and abilities. Politicians and officials are not subject to such thorough reporting. Eisenhower was ingenuous in some ways. He believed that the man who "had made his million" had made it through the application of those simple American virtues in which he believed. He was attracted by the young and plausible politicians of his party, men like former Senator Richard M. Nixon, now his vice president.

There is a distinct pattern in Eisenhower's use of power. He was readiest to use the presidential power in international and defense issues — and most successful in those fields.

As soon as he became President, Eisenhower, who had

Eisenhower possessed a consummate ability to mask his drive for power behind the front of the honest soldier seeking only to serve his country and, when it became fashionable, deliver Western civilization from assorted Nazi and communist hordes.

"All the News
That's Fit to Print"

The New York Times.

LATE CITY EDITION
Warm, humid, showers likely late
today. Fair, not so warm tomorrow.
Temperature Range Today—Max., 80 ; Min., 68
Temperature Yesterday—Max., 79 ; Min., 62
Full U. S. Weather Bureau Report, Page 35

Copyright, 1953, by The New York Times Company.

VOL. CII..No. 34,883.   Entered as Second-Class Matter,
Post Office, New York, N. Y.   NEW YORK, MONDAY, JULY 27, 1953.   Times Square, New York 36, N. Y.
Telephone: LAckawanna 4-1000   FIVE CENTS

TRUCE IS SIGNED, ENDING THE FIGHTING IN KOREA; P.O.W. EXCHANGE NEAR; RHEE GETS U. S. PLEDGE; EISENHOWER BIDS FREE WORLD STAY VIGILANT

*"Our job is to use our power,"
Eisenhower told me in 1953,
"to solve some of these
disputes around the world, to
protect our freedom and that
of our allies and to encourage
these new countries to follow
democracy. Sure, we're going
to have new problems;
progress won't be steady. But
that's the job we have to do."*

Drew Middleton

made a visit to Korea in the hiatus between the election and the inauguration, began to consider courses of action by the United States to bring the war to a close. One course was "a major offensive" that would involve expanding the war "outside of Korea" in which the United States "would have to use atomic weapons" to "keep the attack from becoming overly costly."

The President wrote later that he recognized British alarm over the use of atomic weapons, and the "possibility" that the Soviet Union, then firmly allied to the People's Republic of China and to North Korea, would retaliate with its own atomic weapons, with the unprotected cities of Japan as a likely target. In the event, this major, expanded offensive was never launched. But the planning for it by Eisenhower reveals his willingness to use his own and his country's power for what he considered to be justified national ends.

In the spring of 1953, perceiving the dangers of a communist invasion of French Indochina, he sent a message to Congress asking for greater economic and military aid for the French. In the light of subsequent events and as evidence of the change in the national temper, it is instructive to recall that this step was hailed as a decisive action to "save Indochina."

But, although he provided generous military and economic aid to the French throughout the war in Indochina and sent military advisers to the French forces, Eisenhower was wary about direct American military commitment in the form of ground or air forces.

He was always apprehensive about what he saw as clear threats to the security of the United States. He confirmed the death sentence on Julius and Ethel Rosenberg convinced that their treason involved "the deliberate betrayal of the entire nation."

But where the threat to the country was less clear, where it involved a more subtle challenge to the American system, Eisenhower often appeared confused and uncertain. His attitude toward Senator Joseph McCarthy during the latter's campaign against communists in government reflected a restraint not shown in the handling of foreign crises.

As he so often did, Eisenhower rationalized. He saw a long term value in restraint by a president, in reliance on due process of law and "the basic rights of free men." McCarthy eventually was brought down by the media, by his Senate colleagues and by the rising revulsion of a high proportion of his countrymen. But not by Eisenhower.

He came to office as a reluctant candidate. But

Eisenhower was not a reluctant President. And when, in September 1955, he suffered a heart attack, his first thoughts as he recovered were to get back to work. The illness naturally aroused questions about Eisenhower's ability to withstand the strains of another election campaign. But Eisenhower and his closest associates were convinced that he, and only he, could win the election for the Republicans. He also believed that his team of Cabinet members and high officials was the strongest possible and that he was in a better position than anyone else to prevent global war and advance a permanent peace.

These are cogent reasons embellished with high-sounding goals. Clearly Eisenhower had grown accustomed to and liked the power of the presidency. The decision to run for a second term, despite the heart attack, was not a difficult one.

My own impression was that Eisenhower by 1956 had lost some of his old alertness, his quickness to grasp a complicated situation. In September 1956, just as the British and French were preparing for the ill-fated Suez adventure, I visited the President in the White House. He made a surprising comment when we discussed Suez.

"Harold Macmillan was in yesterday," Eisenhower said, "and he told me that if the British had to go down, they'd go down with the flags flying, the bands playing and the guns

President Eisenhower discusses the world situation with Britain's Harold Macmillan. They had been colleagues in North Africa during the war.

firing. What do you think he meant by that?" Macmillan was then Chancellor of the Exchequer and, after Prime Minister Anthony Eden, the most powerful man in the British government.

I was taken aback. It was inconceivable that Eisenhower had not understood the message in Macmillan's words: that the British and French intended to move militarily against Nasser over Suez. I said as much wondering, as I did so, why the President of the United States with all the facilities of the Central Intelligence Agency at his command should ask me.

"Oh, I don't think so," the President said, "that sort of gunboat diplomacy is a thing of the past. Nothing's going to happen."

It happened. And, in the resulting crisis over the attack by the British and French, ostensibly launched to halt an Israeli attack, Eisenhower took the side of caution which, in this case, meant siding against America's allies. America's financial power was exerted to bring the adventure to a close. Eden, an old friend, left office ill and disheartened. Nasser and the spirit of Egyptian nationalism flourished in the Middle East.

Yet two years later Eisenhower sent the Marines into Lebanon at the same time that Macmillan, now prime minister, ordered British paratroops into Jordan.

Perhaps the last and most characteristic act of all in Eisenhower's years of power came in 1960 over the U-2 crisis. The U-2, an American spy plane, was shot down over the Soviet Union and its pilot, Gary Powers, captured. The accepted wisdom in the State Department and in the C.I.A. was to say nothing, the procedure usually followed when a spy is captured by a potential enemy. But deep in Eisenhower's character was the instinct to tell the truth. He told it. Powers was an American spy.

The truth infuriated Nikita Khrushchev, Russia's leader. It scuttled the 1960 summit conference in Paris. Yet, in a very real way, Eisenhower had been true to himself.

Eisenhower was a man who understood the use of power in its most dramatic and outwardly brutal form, as expressed in war. But he also understood what the unchecked employment of power could do to a country and to a people, with the result that when the successful professional soldier became a peacetime president he displayed a caution which could be construed as weakness, or at least as loss of opportunity. After the furious duel between Stalin and Truman, Eisenhower's time in the White House provided eight years of calm, punctuated by the climactic events of 1956 when the Soviet Union brutally suppressed Hungary's bid for freedom and Britain and France attempted unsuccessfully to retain power in the Middle East. Eisenhower's failure to see the historic significance of these events, caught up as he was in his campaign for reelection, resulted in a subtle shift in the power structure of the world.

Although successful in pulling off the stroke which restored the Shah of Iran to his throne, American power, however it might be deployed, proved unable to avert Fidel Castro's takeover of Cuba. In the Middle East, the Arab-Israeli feud was left unresolved with Nasser of Egypt and

Ben-Gurion of Israel confirmed as powerful figures in their own right, each championing a cause which would threaten the peace of the world long after Eisenhower ceased to be President. Hungary's agony made all the high-sounding phrases uttered by John Foster Dulles in the President's name ring hollow, and emboldened Nikita Khrushchev to pursue cold war policies which forced Eisenhower's successor to the brink of nuclear war.

Finally, a new kind of power came into being in the grouping together of states calling themselves the third world, some with newly won independence from the colonial empires, some confirmed in a determination to resist outside pressures from whichever direction they might be applied. Ultimately Mao Tse-tung's China would dwarf all others, but during Eisenhower's term the most striking figure representing this new kind of independent power was Tito of Yugoslavia. Tito's early life as an underground revolutionary and partisan leader was dramatic enough, but it was his epoch-making defiance of Stalin that gives him his importance in any study of power.

Ike and Tito relaxing during the Yugoslav president's visit to the United Nations in 1960.

TITO

Stalin once said: "What is Tito trying to be, the Stalin of the Balkans?" The Russians traditionally distinguished only between vassals and enemies, and since Tito was not a vassal, he became an enemy and Stalin saw his power being threatened by this upstart.

The Power of Resistance

by David Binder

"I will shake my little finger," Stalin had boasted to his Soviet party comrades, "and there will be no more Tito. He will fall."

It was 1948 at the beginning of the breach between Yugoslavia and the Soviet Union. Stalin was at the pinnacle of his power. He dominated eastern and central Europe to the banks of the Elbe, was influential in China where communist armies were nearing final victory and had an influence in western Europe where communist parties were large and active.

Нове мере против бандитизма

награда од 100.000 рајхсмарака у злату!

The Germans put a price on Tito's head of 100,000 gold marks — dead or alive!

But Stalin erred as seldom before or afterward, and his mistake opened a crack in the monolithic facade of the international communist movement that has steadily widened ever since. In the process, it has erased the vanguard role in that movement erected by the Soviet Union for itself in 1917 with the triumph of the Bolshevik Revolution. The success of Tito's break with Stalin paved the way not only for Yugoslavia's own "path to socialism," but also for China's split with the Soviet Union, for Rumania's independent foreign policy in 1964, and the varying degrees of independence achieved by other communist regimes.

This was the foremost historic accomplishment of Josip Broz Tito and the battle-hardened party comrades who rallied around him to keep Yugoslavia free and independent in a divided and uncertain world, only three years after leading their peoples to liberation from Nazi and Fascist occupation.

Tito, one of 15 children (all but six died young), had an urge to excel even as a boy. He was born May 25, 1892, in Kumrovec of a Croat father and a Slovene mother near the frontier between those two provinces of the Austro-Hungarian empire. He was good in school, but rebellious; growing up as a peasant he sought work in industry at age 16 and became an apprentice locksmith. Ambition and curiosity took him all over central Europe in the next five years and in 1913 he worked for a short period as a test-driver for the Daimler factory in Vienna. He had learned German and some Czech. Drafted into the Austro-Hungarian army he was selected for non-commissioned officer training and became a champion fencer. After the outbreak of war he served briefly on the Serbian front; in Galicia he was picked to lead long-range patrols behind Russian lines. His attraction to command showed up again after being wounded and taken prisoner; he was put in charge of his detachment of prisoners of war.

He had known poverty as a child and now he came to know the brutality of war, and the helplessness of prisoners. Once he was beaten by Cossacks for disobedience: "Thirty lashes I shall never forget." There was adventure, too, in watching the unfolding of the Bolshevik Revolution in 1917 for a few days in Petrograd, joining the International Red Guard in Omsk (he did not enter combat) during the civil war, spending months with a nomadic tribe in Siberia taming horses, marrying a Russian, repatriating only in 1920. Josip Broz was only sporadically active in the Socialist movement in Yugoslavia until 1925, but thereafter he was a dedicated party worker, as an organizer in Adriatic shipyards and, after 1927, as a full-time party official.

He was repeatedly jailed for communist agitation, his longest sentence being five years. In the 1930's Tito had firsthand experience of Stalin's great purges which carried off many of his Yugoslav comrades. But he was a loyal communist and in 1937 he took over the leadership of the Yugoslav party, reorganizing it to make the most tightly knit political force in Yugoslavia, though still illegal. It was personally loyal to him.

Josip Broz (left) and Moshe Pijade serving prison sentences in 1931. It was during this period that Broz began using the underground name Tito.

As Tito related to his biographer, Vladimir Dedijer, his reaction to Stalin's letter of March 27, 1948, containing extraordinary insults and demands was as follows: "Scanning the opening lines I felt as if a thunderbolt had struck me." A communist party member since 1920, a loyal functionary of the Comintern in the 1930's, a leader who started the Yugoslav Partisan uprising the moment Hitler attacked the Soviet Union in 1941, Tito was totally unprepared for the vilification that suddenly poured in on him from Moscow and the Soviet satellite capitals. He had spent most of his political lifetime honoring the Soviet Union as "the first land of Socialism" and obeying the orders of its leaders. Stalin was revered in his army's ranks and many a young partisan fell with Stalin's name on his lips. Pre-war slogans had called for creation of a "Soviet state" in Yugoslavia and Tito's close associate, Edvard Kardelj, had spoken in 1945 of the prospect of eventual incorporation of Yugoslavia into the Soviet Union as a constituent republic. Now the oaths and allegiances of three decades were suddenly going up in smoke. It was an awesome moment for, just as in 1941 and 1942, when Tito's partisans fought without a shred of outside support, Yugoslavia stood utterly alone.

The seeds of the split lay, however, not only in the uniqueness of Yugoslavia's war of national liberation, but also in the experience and character of Tito himself. While there had been courageous underground and guerrilla actions against the Fascist forces in Greece, Norway, Poland and France during World War II, none sufficed in numbers or cohesiveness to triumph over the invaders. True, his partisan units received substantial military supplies from the

Yugoslav partisans with British armored cars and American tanks supplied by the Allied wartime military missions.

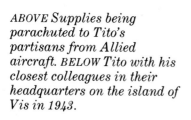
ABOVE *Supplies being parachuted to Tito's partisans from Allied aircraft. BELOW Tito with his closest colleagues in their headquarters on the island of Vis in 1943.*

western allies after 1943 and help on the ground from the Soviet army late in 1944. But it is also true that his victory was largely an exercise in self-help against overwhelming odds. For he fought not just against the German-Italian occupation armies, but also against the Serbian Chetniks of Draza Mihailovic, and against the Croatian separatist movement called Ustase in what was a bloody civil war within the war. From 1941 to 1945 a total of 1.7 million Yugoslavs had perished, more than one tenth of the pre-war population — a ratio exceeded only in Poland. Of these, 305,000 were partisan fighters. The war consumed the old Yugoslavia, a corrupt and fragile monarchy that barely disguised its fatal flaw of domination by Serbia of the other diverse parts of the country; in short it was a revolutionary war. Even in wartime there had been differences between Tito's command and the Soviet leadership. He was chided for introducing the red star on partisan caps and the formation of Proletarian Brigades as being too forward. The Yugoslavs, for their part, were disappointed first by the failure of the Russians to send them desperately needed munitions and then by continuing Soviet recognition accorded to the royal government-in-exile.

Tito had made it a cardinal point to spread his party "throughout Yugoslavia," having found when he took over that there were "whole regions with no party organization." At the outbreak of war the Yugoslav Communist Party was

I think it is fair to say of Tito and the Yugoslavs that they liberated themselves. There has been a repeated Soviet historical line from the outset that the Red Army played the principal role in liberating Yugoslavia, but there's no question that the bulk of the fighting and the bulk of the liberating actions were done by the Partisans.
David Binder

the only political organization working in all of the country's provinces and the only one to promote a "united Yugoslavia." This enhanced its image of patriotism, and carried it through the war with a prestige unequaled by any other communist party in Europe. It was a prestige that accrued also to Tito himself, who had been unknown to the world until 1943 and who was still called Walter, his Cominform code name, by the Russians at that time. (Tito was a code name he adopted in 1934 after release from prison for use in underground activity). When he traveled around eastern Europe in 1947 he was hailed by hundreds of thousands in Warsaw, Prague and Budapest, and by a crowd of half a million in Bucharest — welcomes that were noticed with mounting irritation by Stalin. Tito was infinitely more popular in what was becoming the "socialist camp" of east European "Peoples' Democracies" than those "Muscovites" like Germany's Walter Ulbricht and Wilhelm Pieck, Czechoslovakia's Klement Gottwald, Hungary's Matyas Rakosi and Bulgaria's Georgi Dimitrov, who had spent the war in safety behind the Russian lines. Popular at home, but also abroad, at least in the communist world, Tito presented more of a challenge to Stalin than any of the satellite leaders, representing incipiently what was later to be branded as "Titoism."

The split with the Soviet bloc ultimately boiled down to the question of who was to rule Yugoslavia — Tito or Stalin. That kind of question had already been resolved in the other European countries touched or gripped by the Soviet army. In the beginning it appeared to be moot in Yugoslavia because the Tito government (he was Premier) had rapidly recast the country's institutions in the Stalinist mold. Industry and banks had been nationalized, the property of the wealthy confiscated, large landowners expropriated, bourgeois politicians locked up. Farmland was rapidly collectivized and the panoply of traditional Soviet-style organizations spread across the country. Moreover, the new Yugoslavia dutifully formed joint Yugoslav-Soviet stock companies which rapidly took control of domestic aviation and Danube shipping. When the Yugoslavs found they had forfeited the lion's share of the profits in these joint-stock companies to the Russians, they stoutly resisted further proposals for an extension of the practice — which later brought the epithet of "English spy" upon the head of Tito's negotiator, Vladimir Velebit. There were similar attempts to penetrate not only the Yugoslav party apparatus, but also the security police which had been set up during the war by Aleksandr Rankovic. These penetrations were for the most part foiled, and only a handful of Tito's old comrades turned against him and worked for the Russians. Virtually all were apprehended and either arrested or shot while fleeing eastward. Just to make sure, after the full break, Rankovic's security service, the UDBA, rounded up more than 14,000 Yugoslavs suspected of pro-Soviet leanings.

Stalin accused the Yugoslavs of "anti-Soviet" attitudes, questioned the Marxist credentials of Tito's closest aides and suggested they might be Trotskyites, charged that the Yugoslav party lacked ideological purity and hinted that it was already infected with revisionism. Tito's reply on April

In Tito, Stalin found himself matched by a rugged individualist who had learned to fend for himself at an early age.

Tito enjoyed great popularity among the people of Eastern Europe. LEFT Tito with Jan Maseryk of Czechoslovakia in 1946 and BELOW with Rumanian party leaders in October 1956.

The most impressive quality of Josip Broz Tito to me was always his commanding presence, the presence of a man of almost regal bearing, a quality of leadership that he must have taught himself many years ago. He filled a room, he dominated everyone else around him, whether in a foreign setting or at home, and you had the feeling of his presence even when he was clowning. And of course he was the former drill sergeant who had made people obey him in the Austro-Hungarian army in World War One, and he carried this same quality of leadership into the communist party and into the partisan war where he was the commander-in-chief.
  David Binder

13 was defensive in tone and offered continuing "loyalty to the Soviet Union which has served and will continue to serve us as a great example." On May 4 Stalin responded with new accusations, charging "Comrades Tito and Kardelj" with accepting criticism "in a bourgeois manner" that was both "childish" and "laughable." He further charged Tito with having imperiled Soviet interests by challenging the West over Trieste. His deepest cut was to claim that not the Yugoslav partisans but the Soviet army "came to the aid of the Yugoslav people, crushed the German invader, liberated Belgrade and in this way created the conditions which were necessary for the CPY to achieve power." Still more serious was Stalin's warning that he intended to take the entire matter before the Cominform, which was the successor to the Comintern and had been established the previous October with headquarters in Belgrade.

There was one last letter from Tito dated May 17 voicing discouragement over the course of the exchange, but declaring: "We do not flee from criticism." The short note closed with yet another pledge of loyalty to Socialism, the Soviet Union and Stalin. At the same time, however, Tito and Kardelj refused to participate in a trial by the eight other members of the Cominform (the six east European and Italian and French communist parties). Until this time the entire correspondence had been kept secret and, except for scattered reports about the removal of Tito's portrait from public places in neighboring Rumania, few outside the closed communist world had an inkling of what was going on.

For Tito it was a crisis equal to his most dangerous moments of World War II, when he was wounded by German shrapnel in the battle of Sutjeska in 1943 and when he was nearly captured by German paratroopers at Drvar a year later. He had staked out his independence in his April 13 letter: "No matter how much each of us loves the land of Socialism, the USSR, he can in no case love his own country less." But later he would recall: "I have had to make many difficult decisions in my lifetime. But I think the hardest one was in 1948. The psychological strain was terrific. I had to fight an inner struggle between the disciplined communist in me and the conviction that profound injustice was being done."

The Cominform blow fell on June 28, 1948, St. Vitus Day, which is rich in south Slav historical connotations. On this day in 1389 the Serbian empire fought and lost to the Turkish empire; on the same day in 1914 a Bosnian youth shot and killed the Austrian archduke in Sarajevo, precipitating World War I. Meeting in Bucharest on Soviet orders the Cominform not only condemned the Yugoslav party for "hostility toward the Soviet Union" and the other crimes, but expelled it and called upon "healthy elements" in the Yugoslav Communist Party to "replace" the present leaders should they fail to bow and plead guilty.

Convening his own central committee the next day, Tito rejected point by point the Cominform charges, although retaining a reasonable tone. One month later, at a special party congress, Tito reiterated defiance of the Cominform resolution, but closed the extraordinary meeting with the cry: "Long live the great Soviet Union with the genius Stalin at its head!" At this time he was already being denounced in the Soviet bloc as the head of a "renegade clique."

How is it that little Yugoslavia could get away with defiance of the mighty Soviet Union? Many factors suggest themselves. For a time Stalin genuinely believed Tito would simply cave in, friendless as he was and now cut off from vital supplies of industrial goods and food from the Soviet bloc. Another reason may have been Stalin's innate caution and his desire in the initial stage not to provoke Western retaliation in a new sphere, being already engaged in the blockade of Berlin. He had warned the Yugoslavs against heightening the Trieste crisis and he was unhappy about Yugoslav support of the Greek communist guerrilla army, both signals that Stalin did not want a new test of power in the Balkans. He himself had agreed with Churchill at Yalta that Yugoslavia should be a country where Russia and the West ought to share influence "fifty-fifty" — a revelation that irked the Yugoslavs but also gave Tito a variety of options. He was also aware that Tito commanded an army of 300,000 that had learned how to fight even when outgunned. Finally, he lacked clients inside Yugoslavia — the "healthy elements" he sought never appeared as they did in East Berlin in 1953, in Budapest in 1956 and in Prague in 1968 when a pretext was needed to justify Soviet military intervention. In this respect Tito's example was a first and a last.

For his part Tito swiftly learned that his defense of Yugoslav independence had won him not only support but popularity among masses of citizens who had been either hostile or indifferent to his communist system. He also had the unwavering support of his inner circle with the exception of Sreten Zujovic. He had tested them in the first phase of the break, asking them if they wanted him to step down. In the same almost feudal fashion those whom Stalin had accused at first of betrayal asked Tito if he wanted them to step aside. Their mutual no's made an iron pact.

Tito had the satisfaction in 1955 of obtaining an abject apology from Stalin's successor, Nikita Khrushchev, coupled with acceptance of Yugoslavia's right to "different forms of Socialist development."

The logic of the break with Stalin inexorably dictated Tito's subsequent moves: his acceptance of American aid and arms in 1949 and 1950, his parallel authorization of pioneering ideological steps such as the introduction of "workers' self-management," his effort after the death of Stalin in 1953 to normalize relations with the Soviet Union, his move toward the practice of nonalignment in foreign policy and his pendulum swings from conservative to liberal domestic policies and back again. "We are dialecticians and we know that what is good today or necessary today becomes neither good nor as necessary tomorrow," he once said.

Tito's wish and his will to guard the fruits of his revolution kept him alive and active into very old age. Though occasionally slurred of speech, and halt, he maintained an incredible pace. At age 85 he still had the stamina to make two long trips to the Soviet Union and China and, early in 1978, to the United States. He was an uncrowned king, with palatial residences at his disposal in the Slovenian alps, on Brioni island, in the Vojvodina, in Bosnia, in Hercegovina and in Belgrade; and he dressed the role in superbly tailored suits and marshal's uniforms of sky blue and white. He believed it suited the temperament of his people to display finery, although it probably was a proclivity traceable to his peasant origins. Yet he was also shrewd enough to feed the appetites of Yugoslavs for luxuries, for freedom to travel, for access to Western goods and Western ideas.

Tito poses with hunting trophies.

Tito was an outstanding example of the power of resistance; resistance first to Comintern conformity in the 1930's and then to German-Italian invaders, and ultimately resistance to the domination of Stalin. Although he failed to achieve a dissolution of the great power blocs, he had at least a great deal of success in achieving balance between them. He met disappointment in his hopes to see Hungary follow Yugoslavia's path in 1956 and Czechoslovakia in 1968. Those were times when it appeared the Soviet Union might be tempted to crash into his own country, if it were not for the deterrent of his people's spirit of independence and his own personality.

His influence grew as many new states appeared at the United Nations and sought to preserve their independence through nonalignment. During this period any nation threatened with great power pressure was sure of Tito's support, whatever its ideological convictions. To no one was this support more welcome than to the volatile personality in whose power lay the strategic nerve-center of the Middle East. It was but a short trip across the Mediterranean from Yugoslavia to Egypt and it was one that Tito made many times, as a kind of mentor, to cultivate one of the most charismatic leaders of the third world whose power, like Tito's, extended far beyond the confines of his own country.

In economic development, the Russians and other communists, including Marshal Tito of Yugoslavia, influenced Nasser to undertake socialization measures, most of which caused grave disruptions and hardships and were to be repudiated after Nasser's death.

187

NASSER

I do not know why I always imagine that in this region in which we live there is a role wandering aimlessly about in search of a hero to play it. And I do not know why this role, tired of roaming about in this vast region, should at last settle down, exhausted and weary, on our frontiers beckoning us to move, to dress up for it as nobody else can do so.

Gamal Abdel Nasser

People's Pharaoh

by Raymond H. Anderson

Destiny seems to choose some leaders for brief heroic roles at times of revolutionary change, and then casts them aside.

Such a leader was Gamal Abdel Nasser of Egypt, who emerged from obscurity as a lieutenant colonel to become, for a short while, wildly acclaimed hero of the Arabs, deadly foe of waning colonial powers of the West and much-sought prize of the communist nations of the East. In the end, it turned out that he was not really a deadly foe of the West nor was he a prize for the communist East. He was not an enduring leader of the Arabs, and his own people, the Egyptians, turned their backs on his memory and ideas soon after his death.

In the 18 years after he and a handful of officers seized power in 1952 from the corrupt and corrupting King Farouk, Nasser turned Egypt's social, economic and political structure upside down. But the end effect was to spread poverty rather than his intent to spread wealth. He shattered the

PREVIOUS PAGES General Naguib, the nominal head of the revolution, acknowledges an ecstatic crowd in Cairo.

image of Egypt as a complaisant and compliant land by his defiance at one time or another of Britain, France, the United States and powerful Arab monarchs. But he almost delivered Egypt, unwittingly, into the ideological, economic and military sphere of the Soviet Union.

For a few years, Nasser was a virtual demigod to the masses of the Arab world, striving to recover their identity and self-respect after centuries under foreign domination. But after his death, the Arabs who proclaimed the ideals of Nasserism dwindled quickly. Seldom has the leader of a small country stirred up such a worldwide commotion, aroused such fear, hatred and adulation and then disappeared so quickly from the world scene along with his ideas.

Nasser aspired to revolution as a schoolboy of 13. Already at that age he was noted for patriotic fervor and hatred of the British, who still dominated Egypt.

"Egypt is in a state of hopeless despair," he wrote to a friend while in secondary school. "The government is based on corruption and favors. Who can cry halt to imperialism?"

Gamal, the son of a postal worker who had left the family village on the middle Nile for Alexandria and then Cairo, was active in student demonstrations and was listed by the police as a "dangerous agitator."

The path to revolutionary leadership for Gamal Abdel Nasser was via military service, as it was for so many others in the newly independent countries after World War II. Nasser had tried law school in Cairo but dropped out after a few months. Despite a police record for political protest, he managed to win admission to the military academy after impressing the general in charge with his seriously intense personality and qualities of leadership.

Nasser's point of no return in his commitment to revolution came on February 4, 1942, when the British sent tanks and troops to the Abdine Palace in Cairo to compel King Farouk to withdraw his appointment of a pro-German, Ali Maher, as prime minister and to name instead Nahas Pasha, head of the middle-class Wafd Party.

Former Egyptian premier Nahas Pasha (wearing fez), leader of the powerful Wafd party, gives his support to General Naguib.

Naguib, the figurehead of the revolution, broadcasts to the Egyptian people.

Nasser's resentment of Britain's dominance of Egypt increased after direct contact with British officers on duty with the Egyptian army. The English derisively called the Egyptians "wogs."

This public humiliation of Egypt prompted Nasser to form the organization of Free Officers, dedicated to revolution and expulsion of the British from Egypt. It took 10 years for the revolutionary conspiracy to achieve its goal. Before then Nasser and others in the Egyptian army were to experience further humiliation through the defeat of Egypt and other Arab countries in 1948 by the small and irregular forces of newly independent Israel.

"All the News That's Fit to Print"

The New York Times.

LATE CITY EDITION
Fair and warmer today and tomorrow.
Temperature range Today—Max., 65; Min., 48
Temperature Yesterday—Max., 53; Min., 46
Full Day's Weather Bureau Report, Page 11

Copyright, 1948, by The New York Times Company.

VOL. XCVII. No. 32,984.

Entered as Second-Class Matter, Postoffice, New York, N. Y.

NEW YORK, SATURDAY, MAY 15, 1948.

Times Square, New York 18, N. Y.
Telephone Lackawanna 4-1000.

THREE CENTS NEW YORK CITY

TEL AVIV IS BOMBED, EGYPT ORDERS INVASION

When the officer revolutionaries struck against King Farouk in the early hours of July 23, 1952, Nasser was to show another trait of his complex character — secrecy. Unwilling to stand at the forefront of the coup as the leader, Nasser arranged to have a respected army officer, Major General Mohammed Naguib, act as figurehead of the revolution. Nasser later explained his secrecy as a matter of concern that the Egyptian people might not accept him as revolutionary leader because he was only 34 years old. This explanation for the secrecy is not fully convincing, however, because the man Colonel Nasser was deposing, King Farouk, was even younger, only 32.

In the first years after the coup, Nasser was in effect a revolutionary in search of a program, an ideology. He had given little thought to what he would do after seizing power. He had expected the masses of Egypt to rise up in dignity and patriotism after the overthrow of King Farouk, he wrote later, and shape their own destiny. Instead, Nasser found dissension, petty bickering and calls for blood vengeance.

"Every man we questioned had nothing to recommend except to kill someone else," Nasser complained. "Every idea we listened to was nothing but an attack on some other idea. If we had gone along with everything we heard, we would have killed off all the people and torn down every idea."

In 1954, Nasser emerged from the shadows after a struggle with General Naguib, who had begun to act as if he was indeed the leader. The general was put under house arrest and Nasser took over the post of Prime Minister.

In 1955, Nasser found himself in the spotlight of world attention after disclosure of his weapons deal with the communists. He remained in the spotlight until his death 15 years later. And he was to enjoy the spotlight. Overcoming an initial diffidence, Nasser was to feel the thrill of sending audiences into virtual convulsions of applause and cheering. He was pleased and perhaps somewhat surprised by the devoted following he aroused in the Arab world. To some extent, it all went to his head and affected his judgment.

It was Nasser's decision to buy guns, planes, tanks and warships from the Soviet Union in 1955 — with Czechoslovakia acting as a front man — that first caused alarm in the West about the Cairo revolutionary.

Nasser kept as much out of
the picture as possible in the
early days of the officers'
revolutionary council. Later,
Naguib was put under house
arrest and Nasser himself
took the chair at council
meetings (BELOW).

In the first years after seizing power, Nasser and his fellow officers took some small steps toward land reform and social and economic improvements. But the progress was slight and Nasser focused his attention on a project for a high dam at Aswan, 500 miles up the Nile. Its purpose was to halt the annual flooding of the Nile, to store water for irrigation and to supply an abundance of electricity for industry and household needs.

The United States, Britain and the World Bank promised to help finance the billion-dollar project. But after Nasser turned to the Russians for guns, planes and tanks, serious doubts developed in Washington about the wisdom of aiding Nasser in the project. In a rather abrupt manner, John Foster Dulles, then Secretary of State, withdrew the United States offer. Britain and the World Bank did likewise. Nasser was enraged. He proclaimed during a speech in Alexandria on July 26 that Egypt was nationalizing the Suez Canal to use its revenues to pay for the Aswan high dam.

The world was stunned by his bold action. Arabs went wild with joy over this rebuff to the nations of the West. The West reacted with fright. And the Soviet Union stirred with pleasant anticipation, thinking that its time had come in the Middle East.

In October 1956, Britain, France and Israel cooperated in military action against Egypt to topple Nasser. A clandestine radio station set up in Cyprus called Nasser a "mad tyrant" whom the Egyptians should bring down. The French National Assembly adopted a resolution calling Nasser a "menace to peace."

The military intervention ended after the Russians hinted they would permit "volunteers" to go into the Middle East to fight on the side of the Egyptians, and the United States under Dwight D. Eisenhower condemned the British, French and Israeli action. The invaders withdrew in humiliation and the United Nations took up peace posts in Sinai. Anthony Eden, the British prime minister, resigned.

Nasser was at the peak of his power in the wake of the 1956 Suez fiasco. It appeared that he might rally the entire Arab world behind him in an alliance hostile to the West and friendly to the communist bloc. Nasser was revered by the nationalists in the Arab world, acclaimed by the third world and backed politically, economically and militarily by the Soviet Union.

One of the high points for Nasser after the Suez campaign of 1956 was the union of Egypt and Syria in 1958 into what was called the United Arab Republic. The door was open for other Arab countries to join the Nasser-led union, and the result was shock and apprehension in the West.

Nasser was reluctant, even afraid, according to his wife, to agree to the merger with Syria, but Syria's leaders pleaded with him, frightened that communists in the country might seize power. Nasser was correct in his apprehension of the merger with Syria. It was the merger that first exposed

Nasser reads about the West's reaction to the nationalization of the Suez Canal which led to the Anglo-French invasion on October 31, 1956.

Nasser was never again the same man after the exhilarating experience in 1956 of kicking the West in the seat of the pants and getting away with it, despite retaliatory military action.

weaknesses in his character and policies, including half-developed ideas about socialism and a tendency to resort to police repression against his critics.

High-handed Egyptian behavior in the Syrian region of the United Arab Republic soon led to unrest and then to uprising and withdrawal of Syria. Nasser was angered and humiliated by the Syrian secession and impulsively sent Egyptian paratroops to save the union. But within a few hours he reconsidered and canceled the military operation.

He decided to retain the name United Arab Republic, although Egypt now was united with no one. Ten years later, Anwar Sadat restored the proud name of Egypt.

After the Syrian secession, it was downhill for Nasser until his death. In the mid-1960's, Nasser foolishly involved Egypt in civil war in Yemen on the side of the republican forces against the royalists supported by Saudi Arabia. The intervention cost Egypt thousands of lives, vast amounts of money, and darkened Egypt's reputation in the world as a result of the use of poison gas by Egyptian troops.

The greatest disaster for Nasser came in 1967, when he blundered into war with Israel and alienated world opinion by bluster and threats. The war left Egypt's armed forces destroyed and the Israelis in occupation of the entire Sinai Peninsula, the West Bank of Jordan and the Golan Heights of Syria.

In humiliation and shame after the defeat, Nasser submitted his resignation during a broadcast speech. It remains a matter of dispute whether Nasser was sincere or was merely exploiting the emotionalism of the Egyptians. The result of his proclaimed resignation was an overwhelming flood of Egyptians into the streets, roaring their pleas to Nasser to stay on and lead Egypt at a time of unprecedented crisis.

Nasser yielded to the cry of the masses. But he was a different man from then until his death a little more than three years later. Still possessing a sense of historic mission but chastened and wiser, Nasser began to consider possibilities of settlement with Israel if a formula could be found that would preserve honor.

The 1967 defeat of the Arabs by Israel was a stinging defeat of the Soviet Union as well. There were observers who thought it meant the end of Soviet influence in the Arab world, where Russians were being spat upon in the streets in the weeks after the battlefield rout.

But as Nasser hung on, so did the Russians. They rearmed the Egyptians and Syrians. Then, early in 1969, they supported Nasser in what he called a "war of attrition" against the Israelis along the Suez Canal, involving artillery, air strikes and commando raids.

The war of attrition quickly escalated to a level of violence unintended by Nasser. Israeli fighter-bombers began attacking targets deep inside Egypt and Israeli commandos carried out bold forays aimed at humiliating and demoralizing the Egyptians. Moscow, using the Arab-Israeli conflict to its own military advantage, came to Egypt's rescue with fighter pilots, radar crews and anti-aircraft missiles, shielding Egypt's cities and industry from Israeli air power.

A major obstacle for Nasser in relieving Egypt of the

costly and endless struggle with Israel was pressure from
hard-line Arab countries like Algeria, Iraq and Libya, which
goaded the Egyptians to fight on and reviled any moves
toward political settlement. The farther from Israel they
were, the more militant they seemed to be.

As the war of attrition dragged on, with little effect except rising Egyptian casualties, Nasser sought to free himself of the constraints imposed by the Arab extremists. He
succeeded brilliantly. He arranged a summit conference of
the Arabs in Rabat, Morocco, in December 1969 to confront
the Arabs with a public demand to put up or shut up. To put
up meant contributions of men, weapons and money. Nasser,
in a splendid display of injured pride, walked out of the
conference hall at one point when the oil-producing Arab
nations resisted his demands for money, and the summit
disintegrated without even a final communiqué.

The highly publicized collapse of Arab unity untied Nasser's hands and opened the way for him to seek some kind of
Egyptian arrangement with Israel for cease-fire and settlement. After long periods of strain and uncertainty, the
turning point came on July 23, 1970, when Nasser accepted a
plan by Secretary of State William Rogers for a cease-fire in
the war of attrition and subsequent steps toward a settlement and peace.

Extremists in the Arab world exploded in anger over the
cease-fire, especially the Palestinian guerrillas. They
hijacked three western airliners to a desert field in Jordan
and blew them up along with a Pan American Boeing 747 on
the runway at Cairo. The guerrillas in Jordan held some of
the three airliners' passengers as hostages in refugee camps,
provoking a showdown battle with King Hussein's army of
Bedouin soldiers.

It was September 1970 and Nasser's life was running out.
In his few remaining days he was to play perhaps the most
noble role in his political life, using his authority and that of

*ABOVE Yasir Arafat, leader
of the Palestine Liberation
Organization. Defense
Minister Moyshe Dayan
(BELOW), in the black eye
patch, tours Israeli positions
in the Golan Heights.*

King Hussein of Jordan, (left) seals the agreement with Yasir Arafat.

Egypt to convene a meeting of Arab leaders in Cairo and work out an agreement between Jordan and the guerrillas.

Nasser had little stamina because of a heart attack he had suffered a year earlier, which had been kept secret. But he persisted through the tense talks, at which King Hussein and the guerrilla leader Yasir Arafat both wore pistols. On Sunday night, September 27, the Arab leaders announced a peace plan for the crisis in Jordan. It was a triumphant moment for Nasser.

The next day, while seeing off an Arab leader at the airport, Nasser fell ill. He was driven to his home, where he told his wife he felt tired and lay down to rest. Doctors were called. In a few hours he was dead. A grieving Anwar Sadat, the Vice President, announced the death on radio and television, just as 18 years earlier he had announced the seizure of power by Nasser and his fellow officers.

Sadat's grief seemed boundless that night but it did not last long. Within a few months after taking power as President, Sadat began to undo the policies and programs identified with Nasser. Within three months, Sadat moved to end the practice of seizing property of political opponents, a policy that was detested by most Egyptians. Within six months, Sadat made it known that he would sign a peace agreement with Israel.

Within eight months, Sadat outwitted pro-Soviet figures in the Egyptian leadership and purged them. He moved to curb Nasser's feared and hated secret police and he took part in a public burning of tapes from telephone taps and other listening devices.

Within two years, Sadat abruptly ordered Soviet military units to leave Egypt.

In October 1973, Sadat risked all with a military assault against Israeli forces east of the Suez Canal, attacking in cooperation with the Syrians. From the Arab point of view, it was a successful operation, in contrast with the military misadventures of Nasser.

The October war led to Israeli withdrawals in Sinai and to a reopening of the Suez Canal. The changed mood in the Middle East resulting from the war also made it possible for Sadat to make his historic and dramatic visit to Israel in November 1977, and opened the way to direct negotiations.

As time passed, Nasser began to come under criticism as a tyrant who had brought hardship and humiliation to Egypt. In 1978, Sadat announced that even the Arab Socialist Union, Nasser's political organization, would be abolished.

A decade after his death, Nasser, who had once sent Arabs into worshipful frenzy, was an ignored and virtually forgotten memory.

Power in the Middle East is a volatile commodity. Nasser was the first ethnic Egyptian to rule his country since the pharaohs; this fact alone should assure his place in history. But it was his fate that his moment of destiny coincided with that of another man with an even stronger sense of historic mission. The hope that one day their nation would be reborn kept the Jewish race alive after the suppression of their homeland by the Romans in the first century of the Christian era. The power of this idea was the driving force in the life of the man who became Israel's first Prime Minister and Nasser's most implacable foe.

In the days after the death of Nasser, Egyptians had vowed to raise colossal monuments to him. As the years passed, they thought better of it. The plans gathered dust and no monuments were raised.

BEN-GURION

*We are rebuilding the ruins of our
ancient land. We are building a state
which will serve, as I believe, as a model
to the peoples of the Middle East by its
social and spiritual values, its
democratic regime and its reverence for
the dignity of man.*
  David Ben-Gurion

One Place, One People

by Terence Smith

David Ben-Gurion's most striking characteristic was his almost frightening single-mindedness and determination. The creation of an independent Jewish state in Palestine was the central, galvanizing vision and goal of Ben-Gurion's life. Everything he did and everyone he knew was bent to that objective. He fought relentlessly against anyone who challenged the legitimacy and wisdom of statehood, be they Arab, Christian or Jew. Many of his most bitter battles, in fact, were with other Jewish leaders like Chaim Weizmann or Vladimir Jabotinsky, who questioned his tactics or challenged his authority.

Ben-Gurion's key decisions as a leader — cooperation with the British in World War II and the Suez campaign, restoration of relations with Germany — were predicated solely on the impact they would have on the creation and nurturing of the state of Israel. This is not to say that Ben-Gurion was a man without principles. On the contrary, he felt strongly about social democracy and the other crucial issues of his time. But one principle overrode the others. If

David Ben-Gurion, wearing a Turkish fez, as a law student in Constantinople.

Ben-Gurion with his family and his father, Avigdor Gruen. Ben-Gurion was a new name, apparently adopted from that of a noted Jewish freedom-fighter against the Romans.

there was ever a man with a central mission in life, it was David Ben-Gurion.

Ben-Gurion stalked political power and influence from his earliest days. Growing up in a Zionist household in czarist Poland, he developed a sense of his own destiny as a teenager. He never bothered to learn the Polish language, for example, because he knew his future lay elsewhere. He channeled his energies into the Paolei Zion party, the labor-Zionist vehicle that would carry him to Palestine and eventually to power. Later, when he studied Turkish law in Constantinople, it was not because he felt any loyalty to the crumbling Ottoman empire. Rather, he had his eye on the seat in the Turkish parliament reserved for a representative of the Jews of Palestine, which he saw as a route to power and prominence in his newly-adopted community.

The same motive guided his early efforts as a labor organizer and Zionist official — they were all moves to promote the creation of a Jewish state and insure a place for David Ben-Gurion in its leadership. He did not stumble into public life by accident; it was a goal from his earliest days.

But like many of the early Zionists, Ben-Gurion was blind to the growing force and aspirations of Arab nationalism. A genuine visionary in regard to Jewish nationalism, he was myopic about the other great political development that was going on simultaneously in Palestine at the time. None of Ben-Gurion's writings in the first 15 years after his arrival in Palestine in 1906 includes any mention of the indigenous Arab population or shows any understanding of the conflict that was to come. As late as 1915, Ben-Gurion wrote of Palestine as "a country without inhabitants, in the historical and moral sense."

The British royal commission in Palestine.

204

By 1920, Ben-Gurion had become the chief organizer for the Jewish labor movement in Palestine. He also founded the Histadrut, the General Federation of Labor, which was to grow into the single largest and most important economic entity in Israel. In addition, he helped forge the unified Labor Party, which was to become his base of power and stepping stone to political office. And later, he was crucial to the development of the Haganah, the Jewish defense force that was to become the nucleus of the Israeli Army. In this way, the first decade of the Mandate turned out to be the period when all the most important institutions of the future state of Israel were being formed.

At the same time, the third *Aliya,* or wave of immigrants started arriving from Poland and Rumania. This intensified immigration in turn alarmed the Palestinian Arabs, who stepped up their riots and demonstrations. The worst outbreak occurred in 1929, when religious Jews in Hebron and elsewhere were the special targets. The violence startled the British, who impaneled the Shaw Commission, which ruled that Jewish immigration must stop. This became the pattern of the Mandate period: a wave of Jewish immigration, followed by Arab riots, followed by British restrictions, followed by renewed Jewish pressure.

Arabs rioting in Jaffa in 1933.

ABOVE *Lord Balfour visiting Tel Aviv.* BELOW *Weizmann (extreme left) and Ben-Gurion (extreme right) at the Zionist Congress in 1939.*

The Zionist movement itself was also rent by major divisions. Its formal leader was the legendary Chaim Weizmann, a tall, urbane, aristocratic scientist who lived in London. Weizmann was convinced that Britain was the key to the future well-being of the Jews. While Ben-Gurion was arguing for nothing less than an independent state in Palestine, Weizmann thought the most that could be hoped for was some sort of protected status under British administration.

The differences between the two men went well beyond style and tactics. The short, inflammable, truculent Ben-Gurion was convinced that Israel would have to be built from the ground up. Hence, he lived and spent most of his time in Palestine, organizing the institutions that would someday be incorporated into the state. Weizmann, on the other hand, based in London, traveled widely through Europe and to the United States, meeting with presidents and prime ministers, and building diplomatic support for the notion of a national home for the Jews in Palestine — the phraseology of the Balfour declaration of 1917. This, of course, ran counter to Ben-Gurion's oft-quoted dictum: "What matters is what the Jews do, not what the *Goyim* [gentiles] say."

The two clashed repeatedly on how to deal with the British. Weizmann, the Anglophile, convinced that a close working relationship with London was vital, was prepared to negotiate restrictions on Jewish immigration in order to preserve it. Ben-Gurion flatly refused to agree to any curb in

the flow of Jews to Palestine, since he regarded unrestricted immigration as the key to eventual statehood.

Eventually, Ben-Gurion's views triumphed. In 1935, he was finally elected chairman of the Jewish Agency, the so-called "shadow government" of the incipient Jewish state. It was the first time that a Palestinian Jew was chosen to direct the work of the World Zionist Organization. The focus of world Jewry had moved to Palestine at last, nearly half a century after Herzl had begun promulgating the idea.

The benchmark crisis in relations between the Jews of Palestine and Britain came in 1939, after an especially severe round of Arab-Jewish rioting, when Whitehall produced a famous White Paper calling for a complete halt to Jewish immigration over a five year period and the creation of an Arab-dominated state in Palestine. Ben-Gurion and his colleagues were outraged, but World War II was beginning and they decided to postpone the confrontation. Instead, they threw their support behind the Allied war effort, eventually forming a Jewish Brigade to fight with the British army. But it was only a postponement of the dispute over immigration, not a capitulation. In a famous line, Ben-Gurion instructed his followers: "We shall fight the war as if there

I repeat again that His Majesty's Government has determined to base their policy on the assumption that they must lay down the Mandate under which they have sought for 25 years to discharge their obligations to fulfill the growth of the Jewish National Home and to protect the interests of the Arab population.

British address to the United Nations Assembly

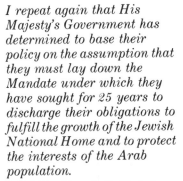

were no White Paper, and the White Paper as if there were no war."

Another important juncture in the gradual evolution of Zionist thinking came in May 1942, when the American Emergency Committee convened a conference of some 600 delegates at the Biltmore Hotel in New York. It was there that Ben-Gurion caused a sensation among Weizmann and the more moderate Zionists with a three point program that amounted to a virtual break with Britain. It called for unlimited Jewish immigration under Jewish Agency control; the creation of an independent Jewish army; and the establishment of a Jewish commonwealth in all Palestine. It was a direct refutation of the White Paper and a challenge to the authority of the mandatory government. Weizmann thought it madness, but in the end Ben-Gurion prevailed.

Immediately after Germany's surrender, Ben-Gurion set about building the Haganah into a credible fighting force. Clandestine training sessions were organized in Palestine and emissaries were dispatched to Europe and the United States to buy weapons, ammunition, artillery and even surplus aircraft.

Ben-Gurion sensed before anyone else that the day would come when the Jews of Palestine would have to defend themselves not only against hit-and-run attacks by Arab bands, but the organized forces of the regular Arab armies. His approach to the problem was fascinating. This man, who had been a deserter from the czarist army, chronically AWOL as a politically-active corporal in the Jewish Legion in World War I, and who had never seen combat, decided to educate himself in the principles of military strategy, tactics and armaments. He did it, as usual, with books. Beginning

British public opinion will permit no more expenditure of life and treasure. It will acquiesce no longer in the use of British forces and the squandering of British lives to impose a policy in Palestine which one or other of the parties is determined to resist. We have already used force enough in Palestine in the interest of our international obligations. It has brought to my government infinite anxiety and trouble; it has cost us dearly; it has brought down on our heads the execration of the Jews and the bitter resentment of the Arabs. It has made us the butt of malicious criticism throughout the world. We have played our part to the limit of our resources.
British spokesman at the U.N.

OPPOSITE PAGE Jewish terrorist explosion badly damages the King David Hotel in Jerusalem in July 1946. ABOVE The departure of British troops.

There should be one place in the world, in God's wide world, where we could live and express ourselves in accordance with our character, and make our contribution to civilization in our own way and through our own channels.
   Chaim Weizmann

with the Greek historian Thucydides, he read all he could get hold of on the subject of military matters. When the time came to act as leader of the new state in a formal war, he was ready. Also, when the time came to mold the Haganah, its elite striking force, the Palmach and the Irgun into one national fighting force, Ben-Gurion had the authority and knowledge of military organization to pull it off.

His decision to dissolve the different commands into one national army was perhaps the most important he made at the time of independence. Negotiations to that end began in early May and continued past the declaration on May 14. They were long and hard, and they involved several highly-sensitive egos. But Ben-Gurion persisted and the upshot of his firmness on this issue was to eliminate politics from Israel's defense forces and lay the groundwork for the single most effective and unifying institution in Israel today.

In his years as head of government, Ben-Gurion did more than guide the evolution of the state. He made most of the important military, political and economic decisions himself and then persuaded the others to come along. His role was so pervasive that he set the pattern for the next generation of Israeli leaders in everything from political technique to style of dress. His determinedly frumpy habitual costume — the open-necked white shirt outside the suit jacket — became a virtual Labor Party uniform.

One of Ben-Gurion's most controversial and politically volatile early decisions was to accept the reparations offered by German Chancellor Adenauer in September 1950. The

Ben-Gurion's greatest strength, like Churchill's, was that never in time of danger did he offer the easy solution. On May 15, 1948, for example, when other Israelis were delirious with the triumph of independence, Ben-Gurion was warning darkly and accurately of the fighting to come.

very notion of accepting financial payments as compensation for the suffering of the victims of the Holocaust was repugnant to many Israelis, especially Begin. When the issue finally came to a vote in the Knesset, a full-blown riot erupted outside the parliament building in Jerusalem. Jews fought Jews in the streets with clubs and paving stones and Ben-Gurion called in the army to restore order — an extraordinary act in a country as intimate as Israel. Begin sought to capitalize on the chaos to drive Ben-Gurion from office, but the Old Man stuck to his guns. He argued that reparations were vital to Israel's economic survival and that in any event they were being accepted not as compensation for the suffering of the victims, but as repayment for their property losses.

Ben-Gurion carried the ensuing vote of confidence by a narrow 61 votes to 50. Toward the end of 1953, the reparations began to flow into the country in the form of heavy industrial machinery, railroads and ships. The nation's future as an industrialized society capable of competing in the world was assured.

The most dramatic episode in Ben-Gurion's premiership was the 1956 Suez campaign. Because of the extreme secrecy the operation required, Ben-Gurion had no opportunity to take the decision to the Knesset or even ventilate it within the inner circle of his own party.

But he seems to have acted without hesitation, firmly convinced that the campaign was an irresistible opportunity for Israel to accomplish two important goals — the reopening of the Straits of Tiran, which gave access to Eilat on the Gulf of Aqaba and which Nasser had blocked, and stopping the guerrilla attacks from the Gaza strip. The short, quick war accomplished both, at least for a while.

The decision to withdraw from Sinai may have been even more difficult than deciding to join the campaign in the first place. Ben-Gurion, after all, was the same commander who had ordered in the 1948 war that not a single Jewish village, not a house, not a plow, should be conceded to the Arabs without a fight. But in 1956 pressure from the United States was too strong. Ben-Gurion, the pragmatist, recognized this. He negotiated the best terms he could, but capitulated in order to preserve the Israel-American connection that has proven so vital since.

Ben-Gurion firmly believed that the state of Israel was forged in its worst crises, such as the Nazi holocaust, British opposition to Jewish immigration to Palestine and the enmity of the Arabs. It was in moments like these, Ben-Gurion believed, that a people, his people, found the strength to rise above their own self-perceived limits.

Not surprisingly, he was a far less effective leader in quiet periods. When it came to economic planning, for instance, he proved to be an inattentive, indifferent administrator. And, since he tended to concentrate all the important power in his own hands, the other less vital ministries tended to be poorly run under Ben-Gurion.

Ben-Gurion first resigned in 1953 but soon returned to office. He resigned a second time in 1963. In 1965 he made an abortive comeback attempt but this time he was rejected even by his own party. He then receded into the desert he

loved so much and devoted himself to reading and writing at Sde Boker until his death on December 1, 1973. His small but comfortable prefabricated bungalow became an obligatory stop for all visitors. He was interviewed innumerable times by foreign journalists, but his fellow Israelis had stopped listening.

Nonetheless, Ben-Gurion's vision of the future had not failed him entirely. In 1967, for example, he was one of the few Israeli leaders who publicly called for the return of all the captured Arab territory, with the exception of Jerusalem, in exchange for real peace. Eleven years later, his old foe Menachem Begin agreed at Camp David to return all of Sinai to Egypt in exchange for a formal peace treaty. The Old Man, it seemed, was once again ahead of his time.

The formation of the state of Israel has been one of the foremost dramas of modern times. Many of the figures in this book played a part in it: Stalin's cynicism in the early years of the cold war as much as Hitler's anti-semitism; Churchill's colleagues who framed the Balfour Declaration in a desperate moment in the First World War, and his Labor Party opponents who had the difficult task of executing the Mandate after the Second; Truman, whose personal intervention against the advice of Marshall and the State Department was decisive; Adenauer in a moving scene of his own. There are scenes of unspeakable tragedy which will forever haunt the conscience of civilized men, and sub-plots like the abduction from Argentina of Adolf Eichmann and his trial in Israel. An ironic twist comes from the reflection that it was the Jews themselves who first introduced terrorism into Palestine as a political weapon against the established authorities. Nor can anyone predict what the final scene will be.

But when all has been said and written about this drama, the fact remains that it was through the will of one man that

In the years when I was Prime Minister of Israel I sought always to tell my people that in our lives, and in the society we wish to build in our regained homeland, we must make use of everything noble, useful, true and beautiful that we can find, both in the treasury of the past and in human accomplishment in our own day.

David Ben-Gurion

events happened as they did. Ben-Gurion himself acknowledged this. Describing the climactic hours in May 1948 when he had just finished his independence broadcast to the world and the first Egyptian bombs were falling outside the studio in Tel Aviv, he wrote: "This was our historic hour; if we did not live up to it, through fear or weakness of spirit, it might be generations or even centuries before our people were given another historic opportunity. However grave might be the repercussion of the decision to declare our independence, I knew that the future would be infinitely worse for my people if we did not do so." The fate of Israel, Ben-Gurion concluded, would not be decided on the material plane, but by a conflict of wills. "The stronger of the two wills wins." That Ben-Gurion himself was quarrelsome, always opinionated and not much liked by his colleagues was beside the point.

Power, in other words, is not to be measured on a physical scale. Ben-Gurion was supremely powerful, as powerful as any other figure in this book, because of the power of his will, which in turn took its strength from the power of an idea — the recovery of a Jewish national home.

What Ben-Gurion felt about his own people is true of every nation that values its past and is imbued with a sense of historic mission. De Gaulle and Churchill, even Hitler, had drawn upon that power. What of the Russians? Churchill described Stalin as an enigma wrapped in a mystery. There was not just an iron curtain of brute force, but an impenetrable veil drawn across the minds and souls of the Slavic people. What had Stalin done with Russia's past? Could his successors recover it? And what would they do with the power he bequeathed them, the power of fear?

KHRUSHCHEV

Had Stalin not died so propitiously on March 5, 1953, before he could carry out his last and most terrible Grand Guignol, a scenario which called for the execution of all of his old Politburo associates, Khrushchev would have perished in a cellar of the Lubiyanka prison.

The Bear's Embrace

by Harrison E. Salisbury

Khrushchev grew up in flint-hard poverty. Before he was five years old, as he told Richard Nixon in 1959, he was a barefoot cowherd who had to clear the dung from the farmyard. When Nixon said he had had to shovel horse manure out of the stables as a boy, Khrushchev rejoined fiercely: "You shoveled horse manure. Well, I also had to shovel human shit."

In the chilly twilight of an October Sunday in 1960 Nikita S. Khrushchev was chatting with American reporters at the Soviet U.N. Mission, Glen Cove, Long Island. He was talking about politics, a field to which he had devoted his adult life. One reporter repeated what was often said at that time: If Khrushchev had been born in the United States, he would have been just as successful a politician as he had been in the Soviet Union, possibly more.

The small pudgy man with the baggy trousers screwed up his country boy's raw face and answered very seriously: "Politics! You just don't know how hard it is to be a politician. You just don't know. It is the hardest job in the world."

Khrushchev was 68 years old. He had held the top leadership of the Soviet Union for a little more than four years, having grasped it from the uncertain hands of Georgi Malenkov, Josef Stalin's chosen successor in 1955. He had just four more years of power ahead of him, although no one could have guessed this at the time.

None who heard Khrushchev speak on that brisk autumn evening was likely to forget it. He spoke with such seriousness, such suppressed emotion that one could hear in his voice and see in his grim face the reflection of the terrible struggles of his climb to the top.

Khrushchev's grandfather had been a serf, his father a worker in pre-revolutionary Russia. Khrushchev himself learned to be a machinist. In 1918 he joined the Communist

Party and began to work his way up the party hierarchy, improving his education as he went along. Fortunate in the people he met, the most important being Stalin's wife, Khrushchev owed much of his success to his own energy and quick-wittedness. He showed himself to be tough, ambitious and a loyal party member. Stalin made him party chief of the Ukraine in the war. At the battle of Stalingrad Khrushchev served with distinction. After the war he became a member of the Politburo, an intimate of Stalin, and one of the contenders for power in the free-for-all which was bound to erupt as Stalin neared his end.

Stalin fell ill at his dacha in the countryside on Sunday, March 1, 1953; he had spent Saturday night with his Politburo associates. Khrushchev expected a call from Stalin all that day but it was not until evening that the telephone rang. It was Malenkov reporting that the police had called to say something was wrong and the Politburo had better come to Stalin's villa. They rushed to the house and found Stalin lying on the floor in his room. He had suffered a stroke and lain there all night and all day. No one had dared enter.

It was obvious that the end was near and Khrushchev and his fellows immediately began to try to decide how to line up when Stalin died. The man they were all afraid of was police chief Beria and with good reason. Stalin had hardly breathed his last before Beria set about to try with his police apparatus to take over the country.

Not all the details of what followed are known. Khrushchev first allied himself with Malenkov and others against Beria but they were too weak to throw him out. Then Malenkov was compelled to divide his powers with Khrushchev and Marshal Zhukov and the Red Army was brought in. In June of 1953 the army arrested Beria and his

By luck Khrushchev managed to miss participation in the worst of Stalin's purges, although he was well aware of what was going on.

Khrushchev with Russian troops at Stalingrad.

In Stalin's rough midnight carousings Khrushchev played the role of buffoon. Stalin would call on Khrushchev to dance the gopak, *a Ukrainian folk dance, and Khrushchev would squat down on his heels and dance and try to keep a pleasant expression on his face. As he once told his fellow Politburo member Anastas Mikoyan: "When Stalin says dance, a wise man dances."*

top aides. They were executed and the mighty stranglehold of the police was broken. Khrushchev steadily increased his power and by February 1955 managed to thrust Malenkov aside; he became both Party Secretary and prime mover in the government apparatus through his associate, Marshal Bulganin, whom he named Premier.

Khrushchev quickly eased the internal regime in the Soviet Union but reserved his most devastating blow against the Stalin era for what became known as his "secret speech" to the 20th Party Congress. Khrushchev's speech was delivered on the evening of February 25, 1956, at a closed session of the Congress from which foreign delegates had been barred. It comprised a long roster of Stalin's crimes, going back to the period before Lenin's death, recalling Lenin's long suppressed "last statement" which had warned against Stalin, making public Lenin's charge that Stalin had been rude and vulgar toward his wife, Nadezhda Krupskaya, and warned that he proposed to break off personal relations with him.

He followed this with a catalogue of Stalin's crimes against the Communist Party, his purge and execution on false charges of tens of thousands of party members, including most of the old Bolsheviks, the top leadership and almost all the officer cadre of the Red Army and the leadership cadres of many foreign communist parties. He revealed Stalin's ingrained anti-semitism, his execution of leading Jewish party members and intellectuals, his wiping out after World War II of the Leningrad party leadership, his collapse at the start of World War II, his failure to understand that the Nazis were about to attack and his enormous blunders during the war which cost Russia millions of lives.

The indictment read by Khrushchev not only destroyed

Stalin's reputation but, by implication, undermined the reputations of most of Khrushchev's associates in the Politburo, particularly the old Stalin guard which opposed his liberalizing policies.

A year later the old guard attempted a coup against Khrushchev but he thwarted it with the aid of the military headed by Marshal Zhukov and threw the "anti-party group," headed by Molotov, Malenkov and Kaganovich, out of the party. Now his power seemed secure. He entered into a world-wide campaign of personal diplomacy, visiting Marshal Tito to apologize for Soviet policy under Stalin. He went to India and England. After the sensation of the Soviet achievement in outer space with Sputnik, he came to the United States in 1959, had a whirlwind success and invited President Eisenhower to the Soviet Union on a return trip in 1960 which was supposed to translate the "spirit of Camp David" into permanent Soviet-American friendship.

Khrushchev made elaborate preparations for the Eisenhower visit. He had a golf course constructed for Eisenhower's use in the Crimea, built a lavish guest house for his stay at Lake Baikal in Siberia and even, it was reported, constructed a Russian Disneyland to rival the Disneyland he had not been able to see in California. However, the Soviet shooting down of an American U-2 reconnaissance plane over Russia on May 1, 1960, felled the Eisenhower trip. The invitation to Eisenhower was withdrawn amid angry recriminations. Khrushchev was later to tell a friend he never recovered the internal power in the Politburo which he possessed before the incident.

Spyros Skouras: My two brothers and I came here from one of the smallest villages of Greece and from a very poor family. In 1910 on coming here we worked as humble busboys. Because of the American system of equal opportunity, now I am fortunate to be president of Twentieth Century Fox, employing over ten thousand people.

Nikita Khrushchev: What you said about working since you were 12 certainly produced a very great impression. But you can't surprise me by that, because if you want to know who I am — I started working as soon as I learned how to walk. And I am the Prime Minister of the great Soviet State.

In September 1960 Khrushchev came back to the United States for the United Nations General Assembly and created more world headlines by taking off his shoe and pounding it on his desk at the U.N. as a sign of disapproval.

Two years later Khrushchev again moved against Stalin, revealing more of his crimes at the Party Congress. This caused Stalin's body to be moved out of the mausoleum which it had shared with that of Lenin since 1953 to a plain grave against the Kremlin wall.

His relations with the United States had turned tense with the advent of President Kennedy. The two men met at Vienna in the summer of 1961, did not get on well and soon a new Berlin crisis arose which finally simmered down after the construction of the Berlin wall. A second and more serious crisis arose the next year when Khrushchev permitted the shipment of missiles capable of carrying nuclear weapons to Fidel Castro in Cuba. The Cuban missile crisis

West Berliners at the
recently erected Berlin wall,
1961.

carried Kennedy and Khrushchev to the brink of nuclear warfare but Khrushchev pulled the missiles out. In the aftermath a new and increasingly warm atmosphere appeared in U.S.–U.S.S.R. relations.

Inside his own country Khrushchev had pursued an erratic course with his intellectuals, alternately giving them more freedom, then cracking down. He approved the publication of Alexander Solzhenitsyn's classic concentration camp novel, *One Day in the Life of Ivan Denisovich*, then harshly denounced a group of brilliant young artists, sculptors and poets at an exhibition in Moscow a few months later. Earlier he had stirred up a whirlwind against Boris Pasternak after the Nobel Prize committee honored him for *Doctor Zhivago*. Later in retirement Khrushchev read *Doctor Zhivago* and sadly told his friends there had been no need for the hullabaloo; the book should have been published, possibly with the change of a sentence or two.

Actually the twists and turns reflected internal politics and the waxing and waning of Khrushchev's power. He had succeeded in alienating most of his Politburo colleagues and the bureaucratic apparatus by his personal style of leadership. And the military was angered by his mass retirement of thousands of the officer corps.

223

Soviet bloc leaders gather for a pleasure cruise on an East Berlin lake in 1963.

After Marshal Zhukov had enabled him to survive the 1957 political crisis, Khrushchev took the prudent step of removing Zhukov from power. He did not want anyone more powerful than himself around. It was a wise precaution but in 1964 it did not serve to help Khrushchev. This time his Politburo associates, headed by his one-time protégé, Leonid Brezhnev, decided to take power into their own hands. As Khrushchev had before, they took the precaution of having the military, personified by Marshal Malinovsky, on their side. Khrushchev was vacationing in the Crimea when their plans came to a head. A Soviet space flight took off from the Baikonur launching pad about 10:30 A.M. on October 12. Khrushchev spoke with the astronauts by radio telephone and Mikoyan, who was with him, also did so; Khrushchev said to the television audience that Mikoyan was "literally tearing the receiver from my hands." The next day Khrushchev arrived back in Moscow where he was confronted with a united front by his erstwhile comrades. They had decided that he must go. This time there was no military to turn to. Khrushchev was out.

He spent his remaining years at his country house outside Moscow, returning to the city very occasionally, to vote in the elections or go to the theater or opera. He was permitted no foreign visitors and only rarely Soviet visitors. There was a guard detail on his doorstep. He passed his time restlessly, reading, working a bit in his garden. But his greatest passion were two foreign gadgets which his wife, Nina Petrovna, got for him. One was a Japanese 35 millimeter camera with which he amused himself, taking pictures of his family and scenes around the house. The other was a West German tape recorder. He set the tape machine beside him on a bench outside the house, probably to avoid the omnipresent electronic bugging apparatus, and there he talked by the hour about his life, about his friends, about his experiences, about his politics, about Stalin, about his boyhood and about his enemies.

Later on, by some complex intrigue which has never been fully explained, substantial excerpts from Khrushchev's tapes were taken out of the country, possibly with police collaboration. They were published throughout the West in two fat volumes, the second of which was entitled *The Last Testament*. In it he offered his ideas for the future of his country, good pragmatic advice about avoiding war and making life better and more fruitful: "I know people will say: 'Khrushchev is in a panic over the possibility of war.' I am not. What kind of panic would you expect from a man my

"All the News
That's Fit to Print"

The New York Times.

LATE CITY EDITION
Condemnation of U. S. Weather Bureau forecast:
Fair and mild today; seasonably
cool tonight. Fair tomorrow.
Temperature range today: 69—58.
Temperature range yesterday: 79.5—61.4.
Full U. S. Weather Bureau Report, Page 74.

© 1956, by The New York Times Company.

VOL. CVI—No. 36,068.   Entered as Second-Class Matter,
Post Office, New York, N. Y.   NEW YORK, WEDNESDAY, OCTOBER 24, 1956.   Times Square, New York, N. Y.
Telephone Lackawanna 4-1000   FIVE CENTS

HUNGARY ASKS SOVIET ARMY TO HELP PUT DOWN REVOLT

age? I'm nearly 77 years old. As they say, I'm no longer on my way to the fair. I started my journey home a long time ago."

A year later he died. He was buried in Novodevichy cemetery in Moscow under a simple monument designed by Ernest Neizvestny, one of the young sculptors he had so rudely castigated.

And yet his stocky figure still comes to life in the countless images of him which survive in newsreels and television recordings. No other Soviet leader has made such an impression on the public outside his own country. Perhaps this was because he was the first, together with Bulganin, to emerge from beneath the pall of terror that had hung over Stalin's Russia. Can anyone forget those early pictures of "B" and "K" bobbing and grinning their way around the world — two clowns, as they might have been, in a traveling circus? Khrushchev's personality always seemed to break through the barrier of language. The tilt of his hat, a quick smile, a frown, an expressive gesture with the hand, an enraged tirade — these characteristics needed no interpreter. Then

Champagne all round after the signing of the Test Ban treaty in Moscow in 1963.

there was his readiness to bandy words as he went along, words which never appeared to be entirely spoken in jest. And there was roughness also in his actions and the crudity of his threats which, after all, made it impossible to trust him. No more than trust a performing bear. Who can forget the brutality of Soviet intervention in Hungary in 1956?

Khrushchev's years at the top spanned the presidencies of Eisenhower and Kennedy. It was hard to believe he was the kind of man who would plunge the world into nuclear war, but neither president could be sure of that. If, after his disappointment with Eisenhower, Khrushchev felt he could intimidate the younger president, he grossly miscalculated the quality of toughness beneath his charisma which gave Kennedy the power to rally the free world behind him and call Khrushchev's nuclear bluff.

Nikita Khrushchev's grave in Moscow's Novodevichy cemetery.

KENNEDY

The men who create power make an indispensable contribution to the nation's greatness. But the men who question power make a contribution just as indispensable. Especially when that questioning is disinterested. For they determine whether we use power or power uses us. Our national strength matters, but the spirit which informs and controls our strength matters just as much.
John F. Kennedy

Years of Charisma

by Robert B. Semple Jr.

For four days in November 1963, an entire nation was invited, indeed compelled, by the power of television to share the misery of the family and intimate friends of a dead President of the United States as well as the splendid yet solemn pageantry that marked his passing.

There are few people over the age of 25 in the United States and Canada who cannot recall at least one scene in a panorama that is forever burned into our political and personal memories: the mad confusion of Dallas, Texas, where John Fitzgerald Kennedy had been assassinated by a sniper named Lee Harvey Oswald; the slim blue and white lines of the Presidential aircraft, Air Force One, as it touched down on the night of November 23 at Andrews Air Force Base in suburban Maryland bearing the coffin of the slain President, his wife, his aides and his successor, Lyndon B. Johnson, as different a man from Kennedy as night from day; the gathering of his friends and associates in the East Room of the White House where the coffin rested; the cortege with its top-hatted luminaries and its riderless horse; the solemn High Mass; the burial at Arlington Cemetery; the Eternal Flame.

These were moments at once sad and stirring. They were mesmeric too, and the country did little else over that long weekend but watch, and then watch some more. It also, quite understandably, suspended judgment for those four days and for a time thereafter on the man himself — who he was, what he represented and stood for, and what he had done and not done in his brief tenure.

This forbearance by the pundits and analysts seemed right and proper at the time; one does not rush to judge in

November 22, 1963. Dallas, Texas.

such circumstances. Yet the very manner of his passing clearly presented obstacles to a fair assessment of the man, an assessment that Kennedy himself might have wanted.

In his life he was popular, drew much praise, inspired deep affection and had as many critics as most politicians do. In death he became a hero. In life he was likable, charming and ambitious; by the circumstances of his death he became an instant legend, wrapped suddenly in mythology and sentimentality. There was a cultural center named for him, several highways, a major airport, countless streets and bridges and a piece of real estate in Florida, once known as Cape Canaveral, where the government shot rockets and men into space. The fact that he was only 46 when he died, that he was handsome, that he seemed to have another five years as Chief Executive ahead of him, did little to diminish the nation's sense of sorrow or its appetite for hasty canonization.

Such mythmaking defies calculated reappraisal. It was almost as if John Fitzgerald Kennedy had existed in amber, untouched by the currents of his age, unwilling to take real positions on real issues and speak his mind, sometimes profanely — almost as if he had never delivered a fiercely partisan address, which he did in abundance — with steel barons, with Governor George Wallace of Alabama, with his commitment of 16,000 American military men (then known innocently as "advisers") to South Vietnam. The mythmaking also turned minor successes and tentative steps into major achievements and large strides. He is remembered not as a Cold Warrior, which he was, but as the architect of the first important Test Ban Treaty, and thus a peacemaker. He is remembered as a friend of the common man, which in a sense he was, but his friends were anything but ordinary, and indeed were often and almost invariably clannish. No less regrettably the mythmaking produced an inevitable reaction *against* the myth that was equally unfair to his memory. Critics, gathering years later, would argue that Kennedy never really did anything in terms of concrete legislation, that his accomplishments were meager, that it required Lyndon Johnson to unleash the legislative cascade

Today, should total war ever break out again, no matter how, our two countries (Russia and America) will be the primary targets. It is an ironic but accurate fact that the two strongest powers are the two in the most danger of devastation. All we have built, all we have worked for, would be destroyed in the first 24 hours.

John F. Kennedy

known as The Great Society, to free the black man from the last remaining chains imposed by the post-Reconstruction South, to kick the economy onward and upward with creative legislation. Such criticism greatly understated Kennedy's capacity for innovation. The mythmaking, inevitable as it was, gave an exaggerated impression of greatness.

Among the things we quickly forget about Kennedy was that he was, at bottom, a shrewd and sometimes superbly artful politician. He was witty, ironic, well read, capable of viewing even his supporters and his success with a detached, wry irony, but he was by heritage and training a tough politician. Not since the days of the Roosevelts had so numerous, so vigorous and so political a family as the Kennedy's appeared on the American horizon. In energy, animal spirits and physical endurance the Kennedys displayed closer affinity to Theodore Roosevelt and his exaltation of "the strenuous life" than to the more commonly evoked images — images cultivated by some of Kennedy's own advisers — of the Franklin D. Roosevelt family.

This lust for political combat, true of Jack no less than his brothers Bobby and Teddy, sprang broadly from the Irish wards of old Boston, and more precisely from the union of two prominent Boston Irish political families — the Kennedys and the Fitzgeralds. Jack Kennedy's grandfather on his father's side, Patrick J. Kennedy, arrived in East Boston in the mid-19th century, started as a cooper, ran a saloon, acquired a coal company and a bank, and became prosperous. He was cool, reticent, an able and respected voice in backroom Boston politics. Jack Kennedy's maternal grandfather was a different fellow altogether. His nickname was Honey Fitz, and he was as raucous as Mr. Kennedy was retiring. He bounced around Boston like a rubber ball. He wore a *boutonnière* in his coat. He was merry and garrulous. His

What kind of a peace do we seek? Not a Pax Americana, enforced on the world with American weapons of war. Not the peace of the grave or the security of the slave. I am talking about genuine peace, the kind of peace that makes life on earth worth living, the kind that enables men and nations to grow and to hope and to build a better life for their children. Not merely peace for Americans, but peace for all men and women. Not merely peace in our time, but peace in all time.

  John F. Kennedy

eyes sparkled, and when he sang his campaign song, "Sweet Adeline," he rolled his eyes toward heaven.

The two men were co-workers in Boston politics. (Honey Fitz later became Boston's mayor.) But that was the extent of their fellowship. Mr. Kennedy found Honey Fitz insufferable. The feeling was apparently mutual.

There was a wonderful Irish inevitability, therefore, in what later happened. Political proximity brought Honey Fitz's daughter, Rose, into the general vicinity of Mr. Kennedy's eldest son, Joseph. The two offspring fell in love and married in 1914. Joe Kennedy temporarily set aside the ancestral political tradition, preferring instead to amass great quantities of money, a fortune estimated in 1960 to range between $200 million and $400 million. But he had fierce political ambitions for his sons, and when the eldest, Joseph P. Jr., died in a plane crash over Europe in World War II, he passed the political torch to Jack, who later shared it with Bobby and Ted. And all of the children of the union of Joseph and Rose were also the spiritual grandchildren of those quarrelling Irish grandfathers: competitive, questing, supremely self-confident like Patrick, ironic and merry and even a bit roguish like Honey Fitz.

Especially Jack Kennedy himself. One should not make too much of the influences of ancestry, but surely the competitive instincts of his Kennedy grandfather (and the competitive instincts of his father, whose slogan for his family was "Second Best is a Loser") had much to do with his bitter, tough, even threatening campaign against the steel companies in 1962, a match that Kennedy won decisively by forcing first United States Steel, then other industry giants, to roll back and rescind an increase in prices that seemed to be threatening price stability at home as well as America's competitive position abroad.

Kennedy and steel. The President talks to Roger Blough (left), Chairman of the Board of U.S. Steel Corp., and David J. McDonald, president of the AFL/CIO United Steel Workers.

Our problems are man-made. Therefore they can be solved by men. And man can be as big as he wants. No problem of human destiny is beyond human beings. Man's reason and spirit have often solved the seemingly unsolvable. And we believe they can do it again.

John F. Kennedy

After graduation from Harvard in June 1940, and after a wartime experience that included a narrow escape from death when the boat under his command, PT-109, was rammed and cut in two by a Japanese destroyer, Kennedy flirted with journalism, which he found "too passive" a life. He wished to be a participant, not a spectator, and thus set himself on a political course. His father took the credit. "I got Jack into politics," he was once quoted as saying. "I was the one. I told him Joe was dead and that it was therefore his responsibility to run for Congress. He didn't want to do it. He felt that he didn't have the ability. He still feels that way. But I told him he had to do it." Kennedy's own version is slightly different, but the death of his older brother Joe remains a constant in both accounts. "We all liked politics," he later recalled, "but Joe seemed a natural to run for office. Obviously, you can't have a whole mess of Kennedys asking for votes. So when Joe was denied his chance, I wanted to run and was glad I could."

Kennedy was elected to Congress in 1946 and to the Senate, against the Eisenhower landslide, in 1952. His years on Capitol Hill were spectacularly uneventful. Kennedy authored little important legislation, was widely viewed as having taken an ambitious stand on McCarthyism — he was, in fact, recuperating from back surgery when the Senate voted to censure Senator McCarthy — and was generally viewed as excessively diffident about the clublike atmosphere of the Senate.

What put Kennedy on the road to the White House were two events that, in truth, had very little to do with his Senate career. One was his unsuccessful try for the vice-presidential nomination in 1956. It cost him nothing and gave him increased visibility. The other was a project undertaken during his convalescence from one of several operations to correct his chronic and painful back ailments — a book ultimately known as *Profiles In Courage*. Just as surgeons fused the injured discs of his spine, so Kennedy fused his interest in history to produce a series of studies of notable examples of courage in American politics — from John Quincy Adams to Daniel Webster to George Norris and Robert A. Taft — a heady mixture of aristocrats, statesmen, populists, traditional conservatives. The book propelled Kennedy into an unusual category, a category of statesmanship and scholarship beyond the reach of most men in politics. The book won the Pulitzer Prize in 1957, but it served a more subtle political purpose as well. For in writing about brave men, most of them great men, Kennedy inevitably associated himself with these same qualities, taking on a stature that his own Congressional career hardly merited.

Those who would seek the special magic of John Kennedy, the personal qualities and political judgments that give a politician his distinctive cast, will be no less disappointed in the campaign of 1960 against Richard M. Nixon than those who seek marks of special distinction in his Congressional career. In truth, there was little to separate the two candidates on the issues of the day. Kennedy offered a somewhat more active, more embracing Federal role; Nixon offered a vision of Emersonian individualism. But the ideological differences were measured by degrees. Kennedy pledged to

get the country "moving again"; Nixon agreed that the recession of 1958 had been an error and pledged to correct it. Kennedy called Martin Luther King's wife while the black leader languished in a Southern jail; Nixon did not, and it cost him many thousands of black votes, but he cited instead the G.O.P.'s record on civil rights, which in fact was no worse than the Democrats'. Nixon said he would defend Quemoy and Matsu against communist assault; Kennedy created a fictitious "missile gap" which, he claimed, had developed under Eisenhower and which he pledged to eliminate in order to keep the Russian bear at bay. Judging by the campaign rhetoric (it is difficult to single out one speech as memorable) it is hard to see why Kennedy won. In reality, he won not for reasons having to do with political philosophy or practical solutions to national problems. He won because people were a little tired of the Eisenhower mode, a little impatient, a little suspicious of Mr. Nixon. The nation was restless and Kennedy touched that restlessness. The nation was well off and well educated. He promised to put education and wealth to work in a vaguely defined, higher cause.

"Second Best is a Loser." Senator John F. Kennedy (left) with his brother Robert during his campaign for the Democratic presidential nomination.

"Ask not what your country can do for you," he was to say in his Inaugural address, "but what you can do for your country." So the voters put him in office by the slimmest margin in history.

Yet the 1960 campaign cannot be wholly dismissed, if for one reason only: Jack Kennedy laid to rest the so-called religious issue in American politics. He had begun to attack the issue in his brutal struggle with Hubert Humphrey for the Democratic nomination, but it was not until September 12, 1960, before the Greater Houston Ministerial Association in Texas, that he delivered the speech that was to confront and subdue the historic suspicion that a Catholic could never be elected president because a Catholic would not automatically and instinctively protect the separation between Church and State. It may have been the one memorable speech of the campaign, and while it is still not clear whether it turned the tide in his favor (many Protestant counties, especially in the south, voted overwhelmingly against him), it did at least invite intelligent Protestants to treat him as an ordinary man.

> I am not the Catholic candidate for president . . . I am the Democratic Party's candidate for president, who happens also to be a Catholic. I do not speak for my church on public matters, and the church does not speak for me . . . If the time should ever come . . . when my office would require me to violate my conscience, or violate the national interest, then I would resign the office, and I hope that any other conscientious public servant would do likewise . . . If this election is decided on the basis that 40,000,000 Americans lost their chance of being president on the day they were baptized, then it is the whole nation that will be the loser.

There are two major reasons why it is difficult to make broad generalizations about Kennedy's period of presidential stewardship. One is that it was terribly brief. The other is that he found himself so preoccupied with events, with the exigencies of crisis management, that he had little time for philosophizing, for the construction of grand strategies that would content the New Frontier. "I don't have time for that," he once told a reporter who asked him to speculate about his visions of the future of his country. What kind of a world do you have in mind? another correspondent asked him not long after the infamous Bay of Pigs landing, and a month or so after his unsuccessful and tense meeting with Soviet Premier Khrushchev in Vienna. "I haven't had time to think about that yet," Kennedy replied with more than a touch of weariness and perhaps a touch of disillusionment. Indeed, the way most of us remember him and his presidency is in terms of snapshots, occasionally in moments of triumph and euphoria — the *Ich Bin Ein Berliner* speech to hundreds of thousands of German workers, for example. And more often in moments of urgent concern: threatening the steel bosses; admitting painfully that the Bay of Pigs had been a disastrous error, for which he accepted the blame; bending over his desk in the darkness of night as he wrestled with the possible responses he might make to the incredible discovery that the Soviet Union had placed missiles in Cuba, thereby threatening the entire balance of terror; exploiting

Fidel Castro and the Bay of Pigs affair.

The communist drive to impose their political and economic system on others is the primary cause of world tension today.
  John F. Kennedy

A slap in the face for the young President. Shortly after Kennedy's meeting in Vienna with Soviet premier Khrushchev, the Russians began erecting the Berlin wall.

television to vanquish George Wallace's attempt to bar black students from the University of Alabama and then to announce a major civil rights bill. He was not without his visions, one suspects. He had read too widely and too deeply of history not to have some coherent sense of national purpose. But to the end he seemed almost wholly controlled by events.

It is, however, possible to make a few general observations about the main strands of his foreign and domestic policies. As to foreign policy he gave little evidence, in the campaign and in office, that he was any less a Cold Warrior than Dwight Eisenhower, or Richard Nixon, or Hubert Humphrey, or Lyndon Johnson. The fact that American involvement in Southeast Asia reached calamitous proportions under Mr. Johnson and later, Mr. Nixon, has tended to

shield Kennedy from the consequences of that war, to put him in quite different company, to give his tenure a certain quality of innocence. It is also true that the Test Ban Treaty of 1963 was a major achievement, undertaken despite Khrushchev's repeated challenges to the fragile stability of Berlin and his bellicose ramblings at Vienna, and there were many thoughtful observers who lamented in post-assassination essays that Kennedy had been struck down just as he was seeking a new accommodation with the Soviet Union, and a new and more cooperative approach to world peace. Yet the strident language of his Inaugural address cannot be ignored in any assessment of his foreign policy views: "Let every nation know, whether it wishes us well or ill, that we shall pay any price, bear any burden, meet any hardships, support any friend, oppose any foe, to assure the survival and the success of liberty."

Similarly, the jury of historians is still out on the question of whether Kennedy would have escalated the war in Vietnam. There is internal evidence, in quotations by him and from his associates, that he intended to liquidate American involvement at the earliest possible opportunity and allow the South Vietnamese to defend themselves. But could he have acted quickly enough? Could he have resisted his own impulses to carry the fight to the aggressor? The world will never really know.

On domestic policy, too, his responses were largely conventional. He took the Eisenhower program on education, health and welfare and, in the tradition of Democratic liberals, added more money to them. But he did two things that showed, in the first instance, a capacity for innovation and an impatience with conventional thought, and in the second instance, a capacity for moral indignation.

The first was his extraordinary tax bill of 1962. Conventional Democratic Party wisdom dictated high spending and higher taxes to subsidize that spending and, simultaneously, keep the budget in line. Kennedy and his academic advisers threw the old ideology away, cutting taxes for rich and poor alike, doing nothing to increase the capital gains rate while giving business previously unheard-of incentives. The policy made a shambles of the old theory of a balanced budget, but it neutralized Kennedy's critics in conservative business circles, gave the economy a massive shot in the arm and provided Kennedy's own party with a fresh image.

The second was his Civil Rights Bill of 1963. Faced with growing black indignation, riots in Birmingham whose brutality was witnessed by millions every night on the television news, racial outbreaks in Maryland, Florida, Louisiana and Virginia, Kennedy determined that the time had come not just to preach about the black man's right to share the same toilet facilities with whites and eat at the same lunch counters, but to give the Federal government real tools to erase decades of discrimination and humiliation. It was not enough, as he had done, to federalize the Alabama National Guard to insure the right of black students to attend the University of Alabama. The rule of force was no substitute for the rule of law. Accordingly, in June 1963, he appeared on television to announce that he would shortly submit legislation forbidding discrimination in all public accommodations

The United States, as the world knows, will never start a war. We do not want a war, we do not now expect a war. This generation of Americans, has already had enough, more than enough of war, and hate, and oppression.

We shall be prepared, if others wish it. We shall be alert to try to stop it. But we shall also do our part to build a world of peace where the weak are safe and the strong are just. We are not helpless before that task. Or hopeless of its success. Confident and unafraid, we must labor on. Not towards a strategy of annihilation, but towards a strategy of peace.

John F. Kennedy

239

and services, whether publicly or privately owned, giving the Department of Justice the power to bring suits and the Federal government power to withhold funds from any state, town, jurisdiction or county in which such discrimination occurred. Henceforth blacks could not be excluded from schools, colleges, hotels, motels, restaurants, theaters, whether managed by governments or private individuals. The proposal represented a massive step forward, and while it was true that Kennedy was being severely pushed by a liberal coalition of Republicans and Democrats, it was also true that he was being propelled forward by events that no president could easily have ignored, and true, finally, that the bill was not enacted into law until after his death, but it was he who took the overdue and fateful step that ushered in nearly a decade of massive civil rights activity.

At the end of the day, the image of the Kennedy administration and the achievements of his era are not likely to be measured by specific programs or legislative gestures. Something less definable and more evanescent may, oddly, tarry longer in the minds of those who knew and watched him. It has something to do with style. He said in his Inaugural that "the torch has been passed to a new generation of Americans," and he brought some of that new generation to Washington, and instilled in millions more a sense that public service was service at its noblest. He stressed excellence, extolled "vigor," celebrated the active life. He said that public service could be not only rewarding, but fun, and while some of the people around him took themselves very seriously, and the image of Camelot was contrived from the

I look forward to a great future for America, a future in which our country will match its military strength with our moral restraint, its wealth with our wisdom, its power with our purposes. I look forward to an America which will not be afraid of grace and beauty, which will protect the beauty of our natural environment, which will preserve the great old American houses and squares and parks of our national past, and which will build handsome and balanced cities for our future. I look forward to an America which will reward achievement in the arts, as we reward achievement in business or state craft. I look forward to an America which will steadily raise the standards of our artistic accomplishment and which will steadily enlarge our cultural opportunities for all of our citizens.

conceits of sentimentalists, Kennedy himself could not resist the deflating gesture, the ironic touch, even at his own expense. Facing the White House correspondents after returning from an Easter holiday at his plush Florida retreat, he said he had been "back in touch with my constituents and seeing how they felt. And frankly, I've come back to Washington from Palm Beach, and I'm against my entire program."

Combative, competitive and self-assured though his family and his associates might have been, there was something vulnerable about John Kennedy himself, something in him that seemed to want to defuse the passions of the age. He detested violence, at home and abroad, but neither he nor anyone else could have lived or served long enough to completely eliminate the dark side of human nature, and in the end it was this dark side which brought him down.

And I look forward to an America which commands respect throughout the world, not only for its strength, but for its civilization as well. And I look forward to a world which will be safe, not only for democracy, and diversity, but also for personal distinction.

John F. Kennedy

ELIZABETH II

*It is my resolve that under God I shall not only rule
but serve. That is not only the tradition of my family.
It describes, I believe, the modern character of the
British crown.*
  Queen Elizabeth II

The Winds of Change

by Drew Middleton

Many sympathized with the Queen's concern over Princess Margaret and her love affairs. For there are few families in the kingdom that do not have a loved but wayward member. Princess Margaret's affair with Peter Townsend, her marriage to and separation from Lord Snowdon — these were the sort of problems faced by many British families.

The state coach rolls slowly between lines of rigid Guards. The Household Cavalry, providing a sovereign's escort, clatters by, resplendent in cuirass and helmet. Bands play. Guns boom. Elizabeth II, "By the Grace of God, Queen," is at Westminster opening a new session of Parliament.

The Guards' rifles snap to the salute. Swords flash. A small crowned figure in a full-skirted gown descends from the coach. A cheer and handclaps from the crowd. Big Ben tolls the hour.

A state opening of Parliament is one of those state occasions in which Queen Elizabeth epitomizes power. But, theoretically at least, she is only a symbol of power. Yet there is a twilight zone between theory and practice. Few will estimate the extent of the influence, which is a form of power, that the Queen exercises after more than a quarter of a century on the throne. Nothing in politics is as difficult to measure as influence.

The limitations of a modern British monarch's power are well defined. If power is considered as executive action, then the Queen has precious little. The monarch may be consulted by governments, may advise prime ministers and may warn.

Constitutionally the power resides in "the monarch in Parliament" and of the two, Parliament is clearly the more powerful.

But, as Sir William Anson explained in *The Law and Custom in the Constitution,* the power of the sovereign "is not to be estimated by his legal or his actual powers as the executive of the State."

"The King or Queen for the time being," Sir William wrote, "is not a mere piece of mechanism, but a human being carefully trained under circumstances which afford exceptional chances of learning the business of politics."

The pertinent, and by the nature of the situation, the unanswerable question is: how much influence does an intelligent and industrious woman exert after more than two and a half decades at the center of British politics? And how much will she exert ten or twenty years from now?

Royal power has declined over the last 150 years. The decline, already evident, was accelerated when, after the death of her consort, Prince Albert, Queen Victoria withdrew into seclusion. Her virtual retirement from most state duties coincided with the arrival on the British political

scene of a series of masterful prime ministers, respectful, even obsequious, to the throne but jealous of the accumulating power of Cabinet and Parliament: Disraeli, Gladstone, Salisbury.

Victoria's heir, Edward VII, accepted the loss of executive power but managed to exert extraordinary influence, particularly in foreign affairs. Extensive travel, intimate family relationships with half the crowned heads of Europe — in a day when royalty meant far more than it has since 1918 — a good command of languages and an undoubted flair for negotiation were the bases for that influence.

Edward VII was singularly and surprisingly successful with the republican French. His function, which he fulfilled with skill, was to create the atmosphere in which Britain and France, two old rivals, could establish the alliance that withstood the shocks of World War I. The King's influence also induced Nicholas II of Russia to take a more realistic view of the deteriorating situation in Europe resulting from the rise of the German empire and to accept, eventually, an alliance with France, a country which, to a Russian aristocrat, was the symbol of anti-monarchical republicanism.

Both George V and George VI are considered model constitutional monarchs whose conscientious devotion to duty

"All the News That's Fit to Print."

The New York Times.

LATE CITY EDITION
Cloudy, mild, with occasional rain to-day; clearing, colder tonight. Tomorrow colder.
Temperature Yesterday—Max., 45; Min., 33

Copyright, 1936, by The New York Times Company.

VOL. LXXXVI.....No. 28,811.   Entered as Second-Class Matter, Postoffice, New York, N. Y.   NEW YORK, FRIDAY, DECEMBER 11, 1936.   P   TWO CENTS In New York City. | THREE CENTS Within 200 Miles. | FOUR CENTS Elsewhere Except in 7th and 8th Postal Zones.

EDWARD VIII RENOUNCES BRITISH CROWN; YORK WILL SUCCEED HIM AS GEORGE VI; PARLIAMENT IS SPEEDING ABDICATION ACT

made it possible for the institution of monarchy to survive the crisis in which George VI's older brother, the uncrowned king Edward VIII, was forced to abdicate. Yet George V was seldom backward in expressing opinions contrary to those of his ministers. He told them, for example, that the conduct of the 1914-18 war in France should be left to military "experts," by which he meant to Sir Douglas Haig and his staff, rather than to politicians. There were many, including Lloyd George, the prime minister of the day, who wished to interfere with Haig's power or, if possible, dismiss him. Haig stayed.

George V twice used his discretionary power in choosing from alternative candidates the man he believed best suited to be prime minister. Of course, in each case, the candidate chosen had to have the support of his party in the House of Commons.

George VI, a more diffident monarch, made one such decision that profoundly affected not only the future of Britain but of the world. In May 1940 the King was faced with a choice between Winston Churchill and Lord Halifax as prime minister of a coalition government. Although there is some evidence that the King favored Halifax, he chose Churchill, aware that the Labor Party would not serve in a government led by the former.

British attitudes toward the Queen and the institution of monarchy range from indifference through toleration to admiration. But it is fair to say that even among those who

Returning a Queen. The historic moment when Elizabeth II returns to Britain from Kenya where the news reached her of the death of her father George VI. Winston Churchill stands bare-headed to greet her at the bottom of the steps.

At my coronation next June, I shall dedicate myself anew to your service. But I want to ask you all, whatever your religion may be, to pray for me on that day, to pray that God may give me wisdom and strength to carry out the solemn promises I shall be making. And that I may faithfully serve Him and you all the days of my life.

Queen Elizabeth II

admire the Queen and the institution most, there would be a public outcry if it became known that her influence was being exerted in politics. This is the main reason why the Queen's influence is never discussed in public and only very cautiously in private by those who have had the opportunity of measuring it.

How popular are the Queen and the monarchy? When the tumult and the shouting associated with the Queen's jubilee in 1977 died, British social scientists assessed the popularity of the monarchy. There seemed to be no change in the 40 turbulent years between Elizabeth's jubilee and that of her grandfather, George V. Support for a republican form of government was under one percent of those questioned; support for the Crown ranged from enthusiasm to acceptance.

One perhaps significant aspect of the polling was that many of those who supported the monarchy advanced the reason that constitutional monarchy was a defense against dictatorship. Is there, in this sentiment, a residue of the old, half-forgotten feeling that by some undisclosed means the monarch remains the protector of the people? The monarchy is the one institution that, in war and in peace, in good times and in bad, has endured in Britain. The Queen and the monarchy symbolize stability, continuity and Britain's endurance.

By the time of her silver jubilee Queen Elizabeth had seen seven prime ministers preside over her country's changing fortunes, drawn from both the Conservative and the Labor parties. It was on the behalf of Her Majesty that Anthony Eden made Britain's last attempt to wield imperial power at Suez; led by Harold Macmillan Her Majesty's Government, bowing before the wind of change, then initiated the rapid decolonization of Britain's far-flung possessions. In the case of Harold Wilson, it was Her Majesty's Government again which proved unable to bring the rebel Rhodesian colony under Ian Smith to heel, while it was once again on behalf of Her Majesty that Edward Heath successfully negotiated Britain's entry into the European Common Market. And whatever voters might think of these actions, they would always cheer the small, attractive figure of Her Majesty herself as she was drawn in state to Parliament to announce her ministers' forthcoming program of legislation. Though Britain's constitution treats the crown as a legal fiction, the monarch herself is a very real focus of loyalty for ordinary people.

Familiarity and 25 painful and precarious years in the life of Britain have dissipated the euphoric enthusiasm for the

Madam, in this hall of fame and antiquity, a long story has been unfolded of the conflicts of the Crown versus Parliament, and I suppose we are most of us at this moment within a hundred yards of a statue of Oliver Cromwell. But Madam, those days are done; it is no longer a case of Crown versus Parliament but of Crown and Parliament. In our island, by trial and error and by perseverance, across the centuries, we have found out a very good plan. Here it is: The Queen can do no wrong.
Winston Churchill

Queen that marked her coronation. Since that enthusiasm was ill fitted to the realities of life in postwar Britain, this change in attitude was a psychological gain. The illusions about "a new Elizabethan age" have been replaced by a more realistic and practical approach to the monarchy's role.

As a business people, the British realize that the monarchy is good business for Britain. The Queen's jubilee in 1977 brought to London tens of thousands of visitors who otherwise might have holidayed in France or Spain or Italy. Some went to see the Houses of Parliament. But the vast majority stood gaping around Buckingham Palace. Tourists from the continent, from the Commonwealth and from the United States have money in their pockets and they spend it on hotels, restaurants, and on a wide range of souvenirs, many of which bear the royal cipher or a picture of the Queen.

State visits by the Queen overseas have a double impact. British imports usually increase in lands visited by the monarch. But there is a political impact as well. The Queen's visit to the United States soon after the dispute between Washington and London over Suez undoubtedly created the atmosphere in which old ties were at least partially restored. Similarly, the first state visit to West Germany was a striking success in that country where it proved to many Germans that all was forgiven, if not forgotten, after two world wars.

Queen Elizabeth, then, is a symbol of national unity, a focus of patriotism, an example of continuity and a living link with what remains of the Commonwealth and the Empire. The basis for the acceptance of this by a hard-headed people is a psychological mystery. It may be that, in each of us, there is an unacknowledged love for the pageantry and glamor of royalty. Or the subconscious may seek instinctively some person, some institution that is above the murky clamor of politics, that symbolizes continuity in a rapidly changing world.

The popular assumption in Britain and elsewhere is that the Queen has no power beyond those advisory powers of consultation, advice and warning. This assumption begs the question of influence. After a quarter of a century on the throne the Queen is far more experienced in national or international affairs than any contemporary or future prime minister is likely to be. She sees all state papers and is punctilious in discussing important items with her prime minister, who confers with her each week. She has reached a position in which her warnings and advice should have an impact.

As a strong-minded, experienced monarch, the Queen often holds ideas on national and international affairs that differ from those of her ministers. Wide travel in the Commonwealth has given her a knowledge of affairs in Canada or Australia or New Zealand not equalled by cabinet ministers. She is not shy about giving her opinion when a question arises about British policy in one of these countries. After all, as she has reminded more than one minister, she is Queen of that country as well as of the United Kingdom.

To the fund of information gained from personal observation the Queen has added information derived from direct contact with Commonwealth leaders. During his visits to

London the then Prime Minister of India, Jawaharlal Nehru, invariably sought a private audience of the Queen. In these meetings he passed along intelligence on Indian and Asian affairs, much of it of high importance, that he had not seen fit to impart to the British cabinet.

Since her accession in 1952, the Queen has discussed British and world affairs with men as varied as Winston Churchill and Harold Wilson, Alec Douglas-Home and James Callaghan. She has accumulated a fund of information about the workings of "her" government and of international affairs. She has, one former prime minister confided, "an acute sense of the possible and this, after all, is the basic wisdom of politics." He believed that to this vast store of information the Queen adds acute judgment. (And in the summer of 1979, for the first time in Britain's history, the Queen called on a woman to be her prime minister.)

Does the Queen use these advantages to exert her influence in meetings with her prime ministers? It strains credibility to assume that today, and as she grows older, she will not. What is certain is that, through her devotion to her duties, Queen Elizabeth has shown that constitutional monarchy is not an anachronism in the second half of the 20th century. A well-loved sovereign standing above party politics has enabled Britain to weather the winds of change that have torn at the fabric of British society. Centuries-old traditions surrounding the Queen have given stability to a people experiencing all kinds of upheavals at home on top of the sudden loss of power and prestige abroad. The Emperor Hirohito of Japan has likewise proved the value of monarchy in providing continuity through times of violent change.

The Queen with her Commonwealth prime ministers at a dinner party at Buckingham Palace.

Cummings

By Appointment to the Prime Minister

Countries without such traditions, like Italy, seem fated to suffer chronic disorder. In 1958, France's Fourth Republic collapsed in conditions of near civil war, which enabled de Gaulle to forge a new and more powerful presidential system of government. But who can say how long the Fifth Republic will last? Spain, on the other hand, has reverted to a form of constitutional monarchy after 40 years of Franco's rule. Even in the oldest republic in the world, Kennedy's brief occupancy of the White House suggested an imitation style of royalty which added to his charisma, and so to his power.

In Britain, Queen Elizabeth, in her person and in her office, brings charisma to the processes of government. Ministers of the crown know that, because of its mystique, a constitutional monarchy is a most effective source of power. In contrast, monarchies which have no constitutional tradition seem to lack charisma and often, as in Iran, prove short-lived.

SHAH of IRAN

There is a very dangerous situation developing in Iran. The Russians are refusing to take their troops out . . . and this may lead to war.
Truman to Harriman, 1946

The Politics of Oil

by Harrison E. Salisbury

The afternoon of February 4, 1949, was cold in Tehran. Snow covered the jagged mountains of the Elburz range to the north and the city that sprawls over a 4,000-foot plateau sparkled in the thin air under a blue sky and brilliant sunshine.

Shah Mohammed Reza, 29 years old, slim, tall, dark-haired, dark-eyed, handsome in a gray military uniform with shoulderboards and golden epaulets, arrived at the University of Tehran in his black bullet-proof Rolls just after 3 P.M. and started up the steps of the law school.

At this moment a young man named Fakhr Arai drew a 6.35 millimeter Belgian automatic out of a camera case and opened fire. He fired three times, each bullet penetrating the Shah's visored military cap without even grazing his scalp. Before the Shah could take another step the gunman fired a fourth time, the bullet striking the Shah's right cheek. Blood pouring from his face, the Shah stared at his assailant. Not one bodyguard intervened.

"In 25 years we will be the fifth largest world power."

"My would-be assassin," the Shah later recollected, "was within six feet of me. He was now aiming his revolver at my heart. At such point-blank range how could he miss?"

There were two more bullets in the gun. What could the Shah do? If he rushed the assailant he feared he would be killed before he could close in. Suddenly, the Shah began to dance — one step this way, one step that, dodging as he moved. The young man fired a fifth time. The bullet struck the Shah in the shoulder and twisted him toward the ground. But even as he stumbled the Shah ducked. He knew there was one more bullet in the chamber. For the sixth time the assassin pulled the trigger. A click — the gun misfired. In an instant the Shah's bodyguard leaped into action and killed the assassin in a fusillade of shots.

The Shah was rushed to a hospital. His wounds proved superficial and that evening he broadcast to his people and set in motion a reign of terror in which hundreds of students and suspected radicals were arrested. The left-wing Tudeh Party was largely liquidated and severe restrictions were placed on press and parliament. After these harsh repressions the Shah relaxed, decreed clemency for most of those arrested, announced a program of social reform and turned to the United States for economic, technical and financial aid. It was a pattern of response the Shah was often to repeat.

In 1925 Mohammed Reza's father, Reza Khan, had made himself dynastic head of one of the world's oldest states. In imitation of his political idol, the nationalist leader of Turkey, Kemel Pasha, Shah Pahlavi set about to transform Persia into a modern society and to raise his son, Mohammed, born in 1919, to be Emperor in his footsteps.

The old Shah was intent on shoving, bullying, pushing Persia into the modern world. He ordered his ministers to abandon Persian dress and shave their beards. Women were ordered to give up the *chador,* the long heavy black veil that covered them from head to ankles. He brought his wife and daughter to official receptions unveiled; when an *imam* preached against the Queen's dress the Shah burst into the mosque and beat the priest until he bent his steel-tipped cane. He seized enormous quantities of Persian land, some of it public and unclaimed, some of it belonging to the thousand wealthy families in whose hands almost all of Persia's wealth was concentrated.

What young Mohammed thought of his father's conduct can only be conjectured. For years the Shah has spoken of his father in terms of veneration, carefully building up the legend of a patriarchal nationalist who laid the foundation for modern Iran. That much of the picture is true. Reza Shah was a flaming nationalist in a pattern familiar in today's era of emerging nations in Asia and Africa. He was also violent, unprincipled, voracious, a tyrant with no limit to casual cruelty and no rein to his absolutism.

When Mohammed Reza was 12 his father shipped him off to Switzerland to enter Le Rosey, an exclusive, expensive private school in Rolle, where he spent four years and became a passionate football fan.

In 1936, now 17, the Shah was summoned back by his father. It was time, Reza Shah told his son, to bring academic

Reza Khan had sprung from the Persian deserts. Not much has ever been known of his origins but by the age of five he was a donkey driver. Illiterate, living by his wits, strong, tough and quick-witted, he had huge shoulders, a sturdy body, a flaming temper and iron fists. He was six feet six, a massive figure in his fur cossack shapka, *and mounted on a powerful cavalry steed.*

studies and schoolboy sports to an end and learn to be a soldier. Mohammed was put into cadet school; by the time he was 19 he had been brevetted a lieutenant. He also had become the fastest young man in town. Almost all his free hours were spent in racing cars, on horseback or with one of a succession of attractive young women.

The Shah was not pleased. After a bit of diplomatic negotiation he won approval from King Farouk of Egypt for his beautiful 17-year-old sister Fawzia as a bride for his son. On March 1, 1939, the Shah showed his son a photograph of the girl and told him he was leaving the next day for Cairo to marry her.

The marriage was celebrated on March 15. When the young couple arrived back in Tehran the Shah gave them a reception such as Persia had not seen since the day of Shah Abbas the Great, 300 years before. The great celebration was designed to make known to the world the grandeur of the new Persia and to provide a platform from which to launch into the world the Shah's son and heir.

As World War II approached the old Shah followed the traditional policy of a weak state confronted with powerful neighbors, that is to rely as much as possible on a third more distant power, Germany. He brought in German technicians, German educators, German advisers, German military instructors. And when he constructed his great Trans-Persian railroad with its 800 tunnels, he took the precaution to begin it some distance inland from the British-owned oil installations at Abadan and the sea coast, and he halted the tracks short of the Soviet-Iranian frontier in the north. He did not want the Russians or the British to employ his new creation to invade his country.

It was, as it turned out, a naive precaution. The Shah's balancing policy worked until June 22, 1941, when Hitler attacked the Soviet Union. Then it came to an abrupt end. The British and the Russians regarded the Shah as high-handed, pro-German and treacherous. In their life-and-death struggle they had no time for the niceties of diplomacy. The Shah was confronted with a series of ultimatums and on September 15, 1941, was compelled to abdicate in favor of his 21-year-old son; within a few days he was on his way to exile on the island of Mauritius, never to see his son again. He died in 1944 in Johannesburg.

Seldom could a rule have begun more precariously than that of Mohammed Reza Pahlavi. That he occupied the Peacock Throne at all was an accident of great power politics. The British and the Russians had decided to run Persia for their mutual interest and it seemed marginally better, in their judgment, to keep the dynasty as a figurehead rather than brush it aside and encourage more unrest and revolt among the powerful Persian tribes. But they had no intention of letting young Pahlavi rule.

Within weeks Pearl Harbor brought the Americans into the war. They moved to join the Russians and the British in the great supply operation which had as its mission the provision of millions of tons of guns and food for the Soviet Red Army. Persia was carved into three zones: the north, Soviet; the south, British; and Tehran, where all three powers ruled. Soon the Americans were running the rail and truck supply routes, leaving the politics of Persia to the British and the Russians.

The young Shah, as anyone who tarried in Tehran quickly saw, was a pitiful figure. Not only was he not consulted by

OPPOSITE PAGE Mohammed Reza Pahlavi arrives in Cairo, Egypt, to meet his seventeen-year-old bride, Princess Fawzia, sister of King Farouk.

Wartime aid to Soviet Russia flows through Iranian ports.

the great powers; they hardly bothered to inform him of what they were doing. When Roosevelt, Stalin and Churchill decided to meet in Tehran in November 1943 for the first Big Three conference, security was so tight the Shah was not even officially advised until the very eve.

All three leaders had courtesy meetings with the Shah but, contrary to protocol, the Shah had to call on both Churchill and Roosevelt. Stalin, however, visited the Shah, gave him a bear hug and offered to provide him with bombing planes and tanks. It was not an offer which the Shah was in a position to accept. And the Shah had no sign whether the Big Three intended that Persia would survive or be carved up.

There was no way in which young Pahlavi could influence the situation. He had no more power than a printed king on a deck of cards. He did engage in desultory correspondence with Roosevelt. In this he was following the basic line of his father's policy: If a weak country is to thwart powerful neighbors it must win the sympathy of a distant power. The Shah's son had little choice — it was the American gambit or nothing.

Whether Mohammed Reza knew it or not, his first major political decision was a winning move and with the end of war the young Shah needed every trick he could take. He was untried, a political amateur. He had powerful enemies, many of them inherited from his father — the Qajar dynasty which Reza Shah had overthrown, powerful tribal forces, ambitious military men, native fascist groups, the strong left-wing Tudeh Party with vocal and fiscal encouragement from the Russians, the charismatic leader Mohammed Mossadegh and others. There were breakaway movements in the north even before the end of World War II, centering around Azerbajani nationalists.

The Americans made plain their determination to abide by the three-power agreement and evacuate Persia. The British demonstrated a certain reluctance but went along. The Russians showed little desire to leave. They pulled out of Tehran but hung on in the north where Soviet-sponsored separatist movements overthrew the weak forces of the Shah.

The Iranian case erupted into the first postwar confrontation of the United States and Moscow. The Shah appealed to the United States for aid. President Truman (whom the young Shah feared had no interest in Iran) gave Stalin an ultimatum. If he did not pull his forces out, American troops would land in the Persian Gulf. Stalin yielded and the Russians withdrew on May 9, 1946. By the end of 1946 the Shah had saved his country from partition and his throne as well. But at a price. He was now firmly in the U.S. camp, an American satellite, his enemies claimed, with a powerful American ambassador at his right hand, American military advisers to train his army, the former New Jersey state police director, Colonel Schwartzkopf, to establish his internal police force or gendarmerie, and the first $26 million of United States arms grants whose total ultimately was to run into the high billions.

But if his throne was temporarily secure and his country whole, the Shah's personal life had come apart. He and the

We cannot allow a conflict in the Middle East to spread. Our survival as a nation depends on oil and nearly three quarters of our oil comes from that part of the world. Chaos in the Middle East could permanently lower our standard of life here in this country, in Europe, as well as in many poorer countries in the world.

Anthony Eden

beauteous Fawzia had broken up, in part because Fawzia did not produce a male heir, in part due to the intrigues of the Shah's highly politicized twin sister, Ashraf. It may not have been true that Ashraf was running Iran in these years but this was the gossip. The Shah's preoccupations seemed to be extremely expensive young women who were flown in from Paris for him, high stakes gambling (bridge and poker), sports cars and airplanes. He bought a B-17 bomber and flew it like a World War II Spitfire. Fawzia returned to Egypt in 1948 and the Shah had no consort. It was in this period that the events of February 4, 1949, occurred. The assassination attempt provided the first run-through of the new secret police apparatus, SAVAK, constructed for the Shah by his American advisers.

On February 12, 1951, the Shah married a second time. His bride was the beautiful Soraya Esfandiary (who later was to go on to a movie career of sorts), daughter of a leader of the Bakhtiari tribe, the most powerful in Iran. The wedding occurred against a background of political crisis. The Shah had won his A from the United States — a steady flow of aid funds, advisers, military supporters, guides in building SAVAK. Now the new American C.I.A. was at his service with its underground methods, gadgetry and piles of dollars. Agitation rose against the British-owned Anglo-Iranian Oil Company, growing demands for its nationalization which spread xenophobia and violence in the streets. Premier Razmara was assassinated. The man of the hour was Dr.

The Shah returns to Tehran after his brief exile following the C.I.A.-inspired coup d'etat against the nationalist government of Mossadegh.

Mossadegh whom the old Shah had confined to prison, releasing him only at the urging of his son. In the political turmoil the Shah turned to Mossadegh. Before his honeymoon with Soraya ended he had named the aging nationalist and veteran rabblerouser to the post of prime minister.

With the Shah's backing the oilfields were nationalized. The British responded with a display of force — the cruiser Mauritius to Abadan and troops airlifted to Cyprus. They took their case to the international court at The Hague and pulled their 2,500 employees out. Production dropped to a trickle, from a high of nearly 32,000,000 tons of oil in 1950 to one million.

Mossadegh began to move forward on his own. He refused to follow the Shah's suggestion that the United States mediate the oil dispute. After an appearance at the United Nations in New York he became *Time* magazine's Man of the Year; now he wanted to become Defense Minister, giving him control of the army. The Shah fired him but had to call him back after four days of explosive rioting.

Now the Shah was learning the price of his gamble. Mossadegh made himself Defense Minister, purged the army, took over the Shah's personal budget and exiled the Queen Mother, the Shah's older sister Shams, the meddlesome twin, Ashraf, and the Shah's brother Ali Reza. He broke diplomatic relations with England but he could not break the international oil blockade which kept Iran's supplies stopped up in the Abadan tanks.

The crisis deepened. It was Mossadegh or the Shah. For a time in 1953 it seemed Mossadegh would win. In August, the Shah and his wife fled to Baghdad and then to Rome. But by now the United States had decided Mossadegh was a security risk. Elements loyal to the Shah were supported by the C.I.A. acting on President Eisenhower's orders. Mobs were encouraged to demonstrate for the Shah on the streets.

By August 19 it was over. Mossadegh fled. The military

garrisons declared for the Shah. It was the C.I.A.'s first and most successful coup. The Shah returned to his capital on August 22, flying at the controls of his Beechcraft. He wore his air marshal's uniform. It had been flown from Tehran to Baghdad especially. Five days later Mossadegh surrendered, was tried, convicted of treason, sentenced to death, but amnestied by the Shah to die a natural death of cancer in 1967 at the age of 87.

The Shah was back on his throne but he knew better than anyone (the full revelations of C.I.A. involvement were not made for some years) that it had been the Americans who had saved his neck. What he may not have known was that the C.I.A. was not certain he could retain power. For a time the C.I.A. contemplated putting him aside and setting up in his place a democratic parliamentary alternative.

In 1953 as in 1949 the Shah ordered savage repressions, thousands of arrests, torture by SAVAK. Then, he amnestied many of those arrested, launched a grandiose program for giving land to the peasants, invited David Lilienthal of TVA fame to launch a great program of dam building, water power, irrigation and land conservation and himself visited the United States to lobby for more aid.

And, as before, he had a problem with the succession. Soraya had borne no children. In 1958 at the age of 26 after seven years of marriage she packed her bags and went to Rome. In settlement she was said to have received a

Mossadegh kisses the Shah's boots.

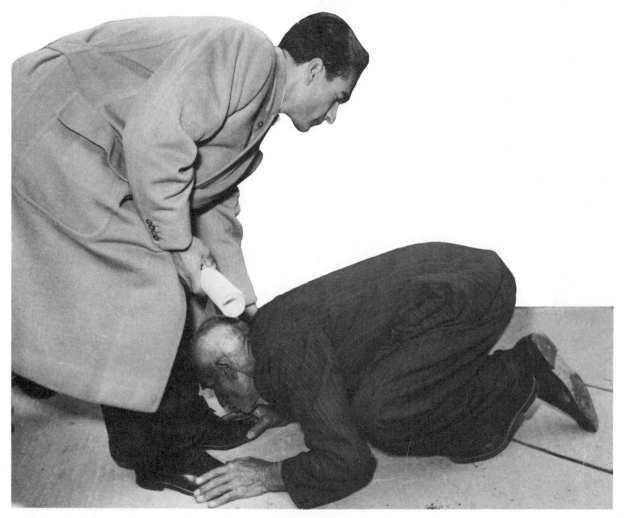

$1,000,000 cash payment and a guarantee of $4,000 a month. The Shah quickly found a new wife, Farah Diba, daughter of a well-to-do Tehran family. They were married on December 21, 1959, and on October 31, 1960, she gave birth to a son and heir to the throne.

The 1960's proved auspicious for the Shah. Oil revenues flowed in. The Shah pursued what he called a "white revolution," distributing parcels of land each year to peasants, drawing on the enormous reserves of land acquired by his father and putting pressure on Persia's enormously rich landowners to follow suit. International contractors built dams, put up highways, extended the railroad, built airports. Tehran underwent a population and territorial explosion like that of Los Angeles in the 1920's.

By 1967 Iran's oil revenues topped $700,000,000 a year and the Shah claimed that 75 percent of this was going into his "white revolution" which he asserted had freed half of the country's peasants from the sway of the landlords. That was

On a visit to Britain the Shah inspects the Folland Gnat, Britain's smallest and lightest fighter.

the year he conducted his own coronation — a ritual that had been skipped in the tricky days of his father's abdication. With his own hands he placed on his head his father's jewel-encrusted crown. There were those who thought the ceremony was one more act in the Shah's endless ritual of legitimization. By this time he had carried out more sweeping reforms — abolition of the right of Iranian men to take concubines, limitation of the number of wives to two (the Koran allows four), abolition of public hanging and prohibition of *droit de seigneur* — the right of the landlord to spend the first night with a peasant's bride. Iran's per capita income was now estimated at $250 a year.

But if the 1967 coronation was designed to satisfy the Shah's inner psychic needs, it was as nothing compared with the extravaganza he staged in 1971, a dazzling $100,000,000 celebration of what was officially called the 2,500th anniversary of Persia's putative birth under Cyrus the Great.

In 1973 the Shah led the Organization of Petroleum Exporting States into a boycott which drove up oil prices so rapidly that Iran's oil income quintupled from 1973 to 1975 to a level of $25,000,000,000. With that move the Shah put Iran into a position of power she had not had since the days of Cyrus and Darius. She became a major world factor.

By 1975 the Shah had become the world's leading arms importer. He bought KC-135 tanker planes, F-4 fighters, helicopters by the hundreds, Chieftain tanks by the hundreds, C-130 troop transports, more supersonic fighters than any NATO power except the United States. Tehran was the hub of countless entrepreneurial schemes. Salesmen from all over the world filled its hotels. Iranian businessmen,

The Shah bought arms like a child buys gumdrops, two or three billion dollars a year of the most sophisticated American weapons, guided laser bombs, advanced weapons systems not always regular issue in the United States.

particularly representatives of the royal family and the so-called Pahlavi Foundation, were buying and building everywhere. Iran now owned 25 percent of the great Krupp steel combine in Germany, a skyscraper on Fifth Avenue and banks in California. Soviet engineers built the Shah a great steel mill at ancient Isfahan.

Within 25 years, the Shah assured visitors, Iran would be the world's Number 5 power with a population of 65 million. There could be no doubt that the Shah had created a new and vibrant Iran although the contrast between the wheeler-dealer atmosphere of Tehran and subsistence poverty in the deserts to the south was spectacular.

The Shah in 1978 was still an absolute monarch — a dangerous role if he should not escape another assassin's bullet or if power eroded in a sudden popular uprising. His country was rated the worst in the world for human rights by Amnesty International with an estimated 25,000 to 50,000 political prisoners. SAVAK had become a world acronym for torture and repression and yet, even with the vast police and military powers at the Shah's command, the last months of 1978 saw Iran swept by disorder, revolt and uprisings such as had not been seen since the time of Mossadegh a quarter century previously. It was an unrest triggered by religious leaders but drawing in its train the other social and political elements which had long opposed the Shah's imperial power.

"All the News That's Fit to Print"

The New York Times

LATE CITY EDITION

Weather: Snow likely and cold today; snow changing to sleet or rain tonight. Temperature range: today 28-35; yesterday 25-41. Details on page B9.

VOL.CXXVIII... No.44,100   Copyright © 1979 The New York Times   NEW YORK, WEDNESDAY, JANUARY 17, 1979   20 CENTS

SHAH LEAVES IRAN FOR INDEFINITE STAY; CROWDS EXULT, MANY EXPECT LONG EXILE

New York City Gets Passing Grade On $100 Million Notes It Will Sell

By ANNA QUINDLEN

The city prepared to go ahead this month with its proposed $100 million note sale after the notes received a passing, but not superior, grade yesterday. The note sale will be the city's first foray into the public borrowing market in nearly four years.

The fiscal rating is expected to be one piece of evidence of economic recovery Mayor Koch takes with him when he testifies before the Senate Banking Committee. The committee's chairman, William Proxmire, announced yesterday that he would hold hearings Feb. 7 on the city's financial condition.

The MIG-3 rating given to the notes by

New York State to Try New Negotiation Plan

By RICHARD J. MEISLIN
Special to The New York Times

Moody's Investor Service yesterday was lower than city officials had hoped for, but it was still an improvement over its last investment grade, the lowest ranked MIG-4. That rating quashed a scheduled note sale in November 1977. Moody's noted in a statement that while repayment of the short-term notes seemed secure, the "chronic financial weakness" of the city made a higher rating impossible at this time.

Moody's defines MIG-3 as an investment of "favorable quality, but lacking the undeniable strength" of the two higher classifications. The letters MIG stand for Moody's Investment Grade.

'A Climate of Uncertainty'

"Reliability of pledged revenues from the quality of the mechanism to assure payment of notes provides basic security," Moody's said in issuing its grade.

"The chronic financial weakness of the issuer (continual budget balancing efforts, persistent revenue shortages, mag-

United Press International
Shah Mohammed Riza Pahlevi and his wife, Empress Farah, as they prepared to leave Teheran yesterday

RULER GOES TO EGYPT

He Voices Hope Bakhtiar's Government Can Make Amends for Past

By NICHOLAS GAGE
Special to The New York Times

TEHERAN, Iran, Jan. 16 — Shah Mohammed Riza Pahlevi left Iran today, driven from the country he has ruled for 37 years by a popular upheaval that gathered force until it undermined his throne.

A year of demonstrations and crippling strikes culminated in a brief farewell ceremony near the imperial pavilion at Mahrabad Airport, before the Shah's departure for Aswan, Egypt, where he was to be a guest of President Anwar el-Sadat. Tears appeared to be welling in the ruler's eyes.

"I hope the Government will be able to make amends for the past and also succeed in laying the foundation for the fu-

---

This time the United States was unable or unwilling to bail the Shah out of trouble. In early 1979 huge popular demonstrations swept him out of the country and overwhelmed his army, many of his generals being barbarously executed to satisfy the mob. All the Shah's high-powered weaponry proved useless to safeguard his throne. The politics of oil had given the Pahlavi dynasty its moment of gilded

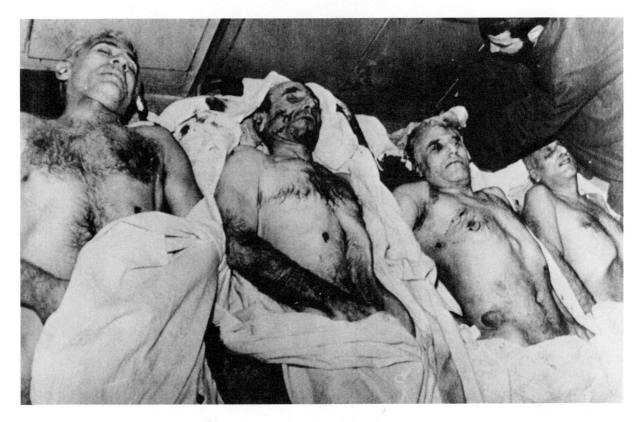

power but, like a genie escaping from a bottle, they also produced a situation which no one seemed able to control. When Mohammed Reza's father seized power Iran was a miserable central Asian country whose territory was disputed by the great powers of the day. Under the Pahlavis, Iran herself became once again a power in the world and history will no doubt be more generous to the Shahs, father and son, than will their vengeful countrymen.

But if uncertainty hangs over Iran's future, it is dwarfed by the question mark that hangs over the world's most populous state. With a civilization twice the age of Persia's two and a half thousand years of history, China at the beginning of the 20th century was in an even worse plight. No new dynasty could transform her wretched society, nor any outside power, nor any sudden acquisition of wealth. The force required had to come from within China herself and it had to operate on a scale that defies the imagination.

The Ayatollah's revenge. Four of the Shah's generals, executed by the revolutionary firing squads.

MAO

The lever by which Mao intended to move China was the power of her peasant masses. The force behind the lever was the power of hatred. Hatred of the landlord and the money lender; hatred, organized and controlled for specific ends; hatred which would be allowed to spend itself in killings so that the force behind the hatred could be turned to productive communal labor.

Long March to Power

by Harrison E. Salisbury

Mao Tse-tung understood power better than almost any contemporary statesman. He understood it in realistic terms. Power for him was on a scale that is almost inconceivable for any Westerner to understand because it meant the leadership and movement of an enormous tide of people.

In 1927, when he was no more than an obscure Chinese agitator, he wrote:

> In a short time, several hundred million peasants will rise like a tornado — a force so extraordinary, swift and violent that no power, however great, will be able to suppress it. They will send all imperialists, warlords, corrupt officials, local bullies and evil gentry to their graves. All revolutionary comrades will stand before them to be tested.

Mao Tse-tung, center, with Chou En-lai on his right.

Eventually Mao found a way to harness the power of China's peasant millions to make himself the ruler of a quarter of the world's population.

Mao summed up his philosophy, typically for a Chinese, in a poem.

> *So many deeds cry out to be done*
> *And always urgently.*
> *The world rolls on*
> *Time presses*
> *Ten thousand years are too long*
> *Seize the day — seize the hour*
> *The four seas boil — clouds and water rage*
> *The five continents rock in the wind and roaring thun-*
> *der*
> *Away with all pests! Our force is irresistible!*

Mao then said something about what he was going to do with his power — something about killing.

> *The head of a man does not grow like a leek*
> *And once it is cut another will not come out*
> *If a head is wrongly cut there would be no way to correct*
> *the mistake.*

He was going to kill. But he was going to kill selectively.

According to Mao, his father had once been a poor peasant who by hard work and good business sense rose to be a rich peasant. Rich enough, at least, to give Mao a start in life. Without help of this kind, Mao could never have emerged from the anonymity of China's peasant class. He would have remained only a statistic — the kind of statistic concerning China which in terms of numbers, poverty and suffering defies the imagination. Instead, Mao took whatever it was his father was able to give him and found his way through self-education and revolution to absolute power.

In 1893, when Mao was born, China was still ruled by the Manchu dynasty. China's exotic appearance and ancient civilization made her an object of wonder to outsiders, but no one could see how her terrible problems could be solved or her vast territory effectively governed. Eight thousand years of civilization lay heavily on China's back and seemed to have drained all the strength out of her. She was a museum piece among the powers of the world, a dinosaur that had somehow survived into the wrong age.

The struggle for power in China began with a Nationalist revolution against the old regime led by Dr. Sun Yat Sen. Two young men joined this movement, each representing a different way in which China could move forward into the 20th century. One of them was Chiang Kai-shek, a man from the cities, able, ruthless, well-favored. Chiang was a graduate of China's leading military academy. He studied military affairs also in Tokyo and Moscow but he would always look to the West; the other was Mao Tse-tung, an unknown from the country, self-willed and pragmatic, who would look to China's own best resource — her manpower.

Mao was one of the 12 men who founded China's Communist Party in July 1921. He considered himself a Marxist and held a variety of posts within the communist movement.

In the 1920's under orders from Moscow, the communists

Mao first learned about power in childhood quarrels with his father. And he learned that defiance paid off, and that his father would compromise, and he could almost have his own way. Later, he studied a German philosopher named Polsen, who believed that there was power in every individual, that if you could release that human power, you could move a nation.

Almost the only source of material about Mao's early life has come from interviews he gave at Yenan. Mao had learned in those tranquil years that one of the secrets of power is the ability to create one's own image.

collaborated with the Nationalists in the struggle to turn China into a modern state. Both drew their support mostly from the cities. Mao concerned himself more with the peasants, starting with those of his own province of Hunan. When Chiang Kai-shek turned on the communists in the cities and killed them by the thousands, Mao was in the countryside forming the nucleus of a peasant army which would eventually carry him to supreme power.

As the danger of war loomed in Europe, China was left wide open to the depredations of the Japanese. Chiang succeeded in maintaining control over his own forces; Mao and his fellow communists were on the point of collapse.

By following his own line and not the one dictated by Stalin, Mao was virtually cut off from communist headquarters. Chiang retained Russian support and chose to deal with Mao's peasant stronghold before meeting the outside aggressor.

The most legendary and costly event in Mao's rise to power came to be known as the Long March. He started out from his Kiangsi base on October 16, 1934, with a column of 100,000 supporters, 85,000 of them soldiers and only 35 women, among whom was Mao's second wife, Ho Shih-chen, already advanced in pregnancy. Some 20,000 wounded were left behind with a rearguard. (A rearguard leader was Mao Tse-Tan, Mao's brother, who was killed by the Nationalists.)

The Long March covered 6,000 miles. Of the total number, hardly a third survived. Their destination was northwest

Floods in Mao's home province of Hunan. The period flooding of the Yellow River was known as China's sorrow.

China and the first halt was the town of Pao-an. Later they moved to Yenan, staying there until the spring of 1947 when it was briefly abandoned to Chiang Kai-shek in one of the quick chessboard moves which soon led to Chiang's defeat and expulsion from mainland China.

If Hunan was the key to Mao's rise as a peasant communist, if his early collisions with his father taught him the basic tactics of power, 10 years of comparative peace and safety in this remote base of Yenan gave Mao a chance to refine his philosophy. From past experiences he fused together liberal quantities of pure rebelliousness, a strain of anarchy, a strong foundation in peasant China, traditional Chinese beliefs including Confucianism, a powerful nationalism, a harsh (but sometimes concealed) anti-Russian anti-Sovietism, an abiding didacticism combined with a hatred of Chinese scholarly bureaucratism, and a decidedly puritanical streak.

The puritanical streak did not necessarily affect Mao's private life. He lived in spartan quarters, in a hillside cave like his associates. He dressed in the simplest clothes; he ate the simplest peasant foods. He had no privileges not shared with his comrades. However, his second wife, Ho Shih-chen, brought charges in 1937 that Lily Wu, an interpreter, had alienated Mao's affections. Later that year Mao divorced her and she went to the Soviet Union. Although she bore Mao five children, none appear to have survived to adulthood.

And in 1938 in Yenan occurred an event which was to prove climactic in Mao's life, and in the revolution he was to make. He began to live with a 24-year-old actress, Lan Ping. Much later she would become known to the world as Chiang Ching, his most intimate political associate, mainspring of the Great Proletarian Cultural Revolution and eventually deposed and arrested after Mao's death as a member of the Gang of Four.

Mao employed the years of the Long March and the Yenan interlude to demonstrate to Chinese peasants that his army, the PLA, was different from all other Chinese armies. Instead of being a gang of organized brigands who ravaged, pillaged and raped, his soldiers were kind, well-behaved, paid for what they needed and helped the peasants. It was wonderful propaganda. Soon peasants were flocking to Mao's cause. Communist cadres taught them to read and write, gave them medical assistance, advice with their agricultural problems and urged them to take the land from the landlords and farm it on their own — a call that fell melodiously on the ears of harassed and often starving farm laborers.

Mao's relations with the Russian communists did not improve. Stalin was buttressing a United Front policy against Germany, Italy and Japan. He sent aid and assistance to Chiang Kai-shek, not Mao, and when Chiang was kidnapped at Sian in a bizarre incident in 1936, Moscow insisted that he be released. Mao wanted him tried and executed.

World War II further cemented Stalin's relations with Chiang. This may have given impetus to Mao's steadily broadening relations with the Americans. In the first outward sign of this, in 1936, he chose American Edgar Snow, a Peking school teacher, to write the story of the communist movement. *Red Star Over China* gave the world its first picture of Mao and his associates. And Mao showed constant preference for American sympathizers over other foreigners. With World War II and the common cause against Japan, Mao began to receive American correspondents in Yenan. Under the wartime "truce" between Mao and Chiang Kai-shek, Chou En-lai was stationed in Chungking as liaison with the foreign — largely American — diplomatic and journalistic community; by 1944 an official American diplomatic and military mission was stationed in Yenan with easy access to Mao and the other leaders.

Mao made no secret of his desire for postwar collaboration

In 1943, Roosevelt and Churchill invited Chiang to join them in drawing up a declaration of Allied war objectives in the Far East. Probably no one was more surprised than Chiang himself at the dignity that was being conferred upon him.

To the Chinese mind, Russians and Americans were both barbarians, whether you called them communists or capitalists.

with the United States. He saw no other source for the aid which China needed. He deeply distrusted the Russians — particularly Stalin — and the feeling was cordially reciprocated. Mao let it be known that if he and his communists came to power they would hope to see industrialization of China carried out by private entrepreneurs and they looked to the United States for aid and an alliance. Twice Mao suggested that he and Chou En-lai were ready to come to Washington to meet with Franklin D. Roosevelt. But in the complex maneuverings of American policy Mao's initiatives came to nothing.

Mao's feelings toward Moscow were hardly enhanced during World War II. The Chinese were not real communists, Stalin and Molotov repeatedly asserted. "Margarine" communists was the phrase that most often trickled from the lips of the Russians. And when the war ended Stalin made it official. He signed a treaty of friendship and alliance with Chiang Kai-shek. He told Mao to enter a coalition government with Chiang and dissolve his army. There was, Stalin said, no hope that the Chinese Reds could overcome the Nationalists in a civil war.

Mao was no more interested in this advice from Stalin than he had been in that of the Soviet advisers to the Chinese communists in 1927. He went ahead with the civil war. In less than three years he drove Chiang Kai-shek off the mainland

China's growing military power made her a dangerous neighbor to Russia, especially after she had exploded her first atomic device and so became the world's fifth nuclear power.

to his sanctuary in Formosa, despite American aid to Chiang and the efforts of George Marshall to mediate on behalf of the United States.

It did not escape Mao's notice that the Soviet ambassador was the last to leave Chiang's entourage. Nor that in the summer of 1949, shortly before the final Nationalist collapse, Chiang's lieutenants and Moscow engaged in a still-mysterious negotiation. Its objective seemed to be either the creation of an independent Soviet-aligned protectorate in westernmost Sinkiang province or the turning over of that vast area to Moscow.

Mao proclaimed the establishment of the new People's Republic of China on October 1, 1949, having completed the conquest of the mainland. His regime was almost immediately recognized by most of the major powers with the significant exception of the United States. He then went off to Moscow in December to try to settle up matters with Stalin. By now he had despaired of depending on the United States for the assistance he needed to build up the new China. His talks with Stalin were far from satisfactory. He spent nearly two months in the Soviet capital. Later he told his comrades that Stalin neither trusted him nor wanted to deal with him. Finally, however, a treaty of friendship and alliance was signed on February 13, 1950. Mao had been forced to make enormous concessions. He granted the Soviet

The Chinese have a word — Luan. It means chaos, anarchy. Mao Tse-tung, absolute ruler of China's millions, believed in Luan. But he saw it as a positive force, a force which, paradoxically, could be organized to produce order. The greater the chaos, the greater the order. In the Cultural Revolution Mao Tse-tung plunged his country into chaos, assuming that out of it would come the greatest order which China had ever seen.

Union privileges in mining, extraction of oil and air transport, not unlike the old comprador concessions of Imperial China to the European powers. The Soviet Union was to have control of the mixed companies exploiting China's resources and Mao had to agree to Russia maintaining special bases and privileges in Manchuria. In return he got aid loans worth a trivial $60 million a year for five years.

It was hardly an auspicious start for relations between the two communist giants. There were many signs that Mao and Stalin would have split apart had it not been for the sudden eruption of the Korean War. The circumstances under which that conflict started in June 1950 have never been entirely explained. There is a substantial body of opinion in China that Stalin launched it deliberately, hoping to solidify a stranglehold on Peking. (He already had his positions in Manchuria as well as a secret agreement with Kao Kang, the Chinese communist ruler of Manchuria; he dominated outer Mongolia and may have felt that if he secured all of Korea he could bend Mao to his will.)

Whatever the causes and motivation, China was quickly drawn into the Korean struggle when American and south Korean forces swept across the 38th parallel and up to China's Yalu river border. It became a Chinese-U.S. conflict which was to sow intense hostility between communist China and the United States for 20 years.

After the Korean War Mao turned inward to the task of building up his country and found himself increasingly in disagreement with some of his associates. He wanted to try out ad hoc experiments. In 1956 he launched a drive called "Let 100 Flowers Bloom" in which all of China was invited to speak out frankly and critically about the regime. But when the criticism turned out to be extremely sharp Mao promptly chopped off the flowers, that is, he had the most vocal critics repressed.

He tried to start a movement for Chinese self-sufficiency in which all of China was invited to set up small model industries, such as backyard steel mills and the like. This proved a disaster. It set back production more than furthered it, and was ridiculed by the Russians and by some of Mao's associates.

Relations steadily worsened between the Soviet Union and the People's Republic. The death of Stalin brought a brief respite. Premier Khrushchev launched an enormous aid program for China — the construction of more than 1400 factories and other large scale enterprises. But when Mao and Khrushchev fell out over policy toward the United States and nuclear arms, Khrushchev suddenly in 1960 pulled all 40,000 Soviet technicians out of China, taking their blueprints with them and leaving industrial enterprises all over the country half finished. Many were not completed for 10 or 15 years.

As hostility rose in China toward Moscow, Mao seemed to be gradually assuming the aspect of an elder statesman. Direction of the country was in younger hands. He spent more and more time in the picturesque watering place of Hangchow and in Shanghai, home base of his wife, Chiang Ching. Up to now Chiang Ching had played virtually no role in Chinese politics. She had been ill much of the time, twice undergoing treatment in the Soviet Union. She had borne Mao one daughter.

Now all of this was to change. In the autumn of 1965 Mao spent most of his time in Shanghai. From there, with the aid of his wife and several Shanghai political associates, Mao launched what became known as the Great Proletarian Cultural Revolution — almost four years of turmoil, anarchy and occasional civil war in some of the cities, factories and most of the universities.

Even today not all of Mao's objectives are entirely clear. Probably thousands lost their lives violently, particularly in colleges and factories. For years the nation was in such an uproar that production in factories dropped to low levels. Only the peasant masses and the army were more or less immune from the struggle.

Long before it was over Mao himself conceded he had not expected to stir up such a storm although he repeated his basic belief in what the Chinese call *luan*, or chaos. He had always preached that out of chaos came order. If so, a mighty order should have ensued from the chaos which he created.

After a time the country began to simmer down. The army directed the expulsion to the countryside of hundreds of thousands of Red Guards whom Mao had personally addressed in million-member mass rallies in Peking's Tien an-men Square. But the trouble was by no means over.

Lin Piao, Defense Minister, Mao's right-hand man in the Cultural Revolution and his constitutionally designated successor, suddenly fled to the country. He crashed to his death with his wife and several close associates in his plane in Outer Mongolia. He was said to have been plotting the assassination of Chairman Mao.

After the death of Lin Piao the country quieted. This was the period of the great rapprochement between the United States and China, engineered by President Nixon, Henry Kissinger, Mao and Chou En-lai. It grew out of the intense antagonism between Russia and China which had escalated in the late summer of 1969 almost to the point of a Soviet nuclear strike against China.

Then came the visit of President Nixon to Peking. It was an event which warmed Mao's old heart, so closely did it resemble the customs of ancient China in which the barbarians were compelled to come to Peking to pay their tribute. It seemed that Mao at last had directed his country along a firm, secure and tidy path which it would follow at least through the last years of his life and, he hoped, the period thereafter.

In 1972 Mao was 79. At his side stood Chou En-lai, a spritely, energetic 73. Chiang Ching had receded once more into the background.

But Mao's career was not to end so benignly. Within 18 months a stormy political war began to rage just under the surface in Peking. Chiang Ching and her close associates of the Cultural Revolution had launched a drive to take power when Mao died. The principal obstacle in their way was Chou En-lai, now in the first stages of terminal cancer. What did Mao make of this? It is not entirely clear, but when Chou finally died in January 1976 Mao did not attend the funeral.

By that time Mao's health was erratic. He was not always in command of himself but he took one step which was to prove decisive. He named an obscure agricultural specialist from his native Hunan, Hua Kuo-feng, to the post of first deputy chairman, a move which was to place Hua at the head of contenders for authority in the event of Mao's death. Soon thereafter Mao acquiesced in the ouster of Teng Shao-ping who had been Chou En-lai's choice as successor.

From the death of Chou in January to that of Mao on September 9, 1976, Peking was the scene of feverish intrigue and struggle. Much of the time, it is now said, Mao was unable to comprehend what was happening. At 83 his mind functioned erratically. Were there moments when he consciously hoped to see his ambitious third wife, Chiang Ching, ascend the heights as a latter day Dowager Empress? No one today can say for certain although a hundred stories flourish in Peking of Chiang Ching's caprices, of her trying on the gowns of the old Dowager, of her preparations for supreme power. Throughout this period she was at Mao's side. But what the aging ruler of China knew of her actions cannot be determined.

When Mao finally died all China halted to honor and revere the career of the man. Whatever his eccentricities and complex personality, he had given his nation unity. As the lowliest peasant would say, he had enabled all of China to stand up.

Many scholars of China feel that the Mao revolution and his concept of where he wanted to move the Chinese people is probably the greatest social change that has ever been attempted in this oldest of all our social organizations.

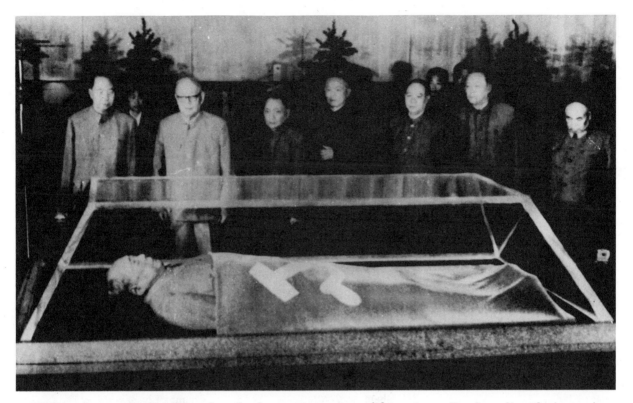

Within the month Hua Kuo-feng had come to power with the aid of China's military chiefs. Chiang Ching and her close associates were under arrest. The members of what now began to be called the Gang of Four were charged with all manner of crime and corruption. And in the shadows of the *hutangs* and even out in the villages there were discreet whispers that it was not a Gang of Four, but indeed a Gang of Five, with the Chairman at its head.

But of this there was no public notice. Instead, in Tien an-men Square a simple classic structure was erected and on the first anniversary of his death the Mao Memorial Hall was opened to the public with Mao himself inside, his body preserved within a crystal block.

Dead or alive, the image is the power.

Index

This index was prepared by
Glynis E.C. Barnes.

Acknowledgments

Although every effort has been made to insure that permission for all
material was obtained, those sources not formally acknowledged will be
included in all future editions of this book.

Associated Press *142 & 143, 145, 161, 171, 173, 188 & 189, 191, 197* (above),
198, 216 & 217, 237 (below), *254 & 255, 267.* British official photo (Crown
Copyright) *174 & 175, 179, 180.* Consulate General of Israel *202, 203, 215.* E.
E. Cummings, Allen & Unwin *253.* Eastfoto *279.* Courtesy of George M. Elsey
94. Gamma *256.* Keystone Press *242 & 243, 245, 247, 248, 250, 251, 252.*
National Archives *26, 27, 29, 31, 36, 37* (below), *39 44* (below), *44 & 45, 69, 70 &
71, 84, 88, 92 & 93, 95, 96, 98, 99, 102, 104 & 105, 110* (below), *114, 115, 120*
(above), *120 & 121, 123, 124, 125, 127, 128, 130, 132 & 133, 137, 149, 150, 152 &
153, 154* (below), *154 & 155, 155, 156* (above), *156 & 157, 159, 169, 194, 200 &
201, 204* (above), *204 & 205, 208, 209, 210, 214, 244, 246, 249, 258* (below), *259,
261, 275.* The New York Times *64 & 65, 72, 146 & 147, 148.* United Press
International *75, 76 & 77, 131* (above right). Wide World *22, 23, 32, 34 & 35, 37*
(above), *40 & 41, 42, 43, 46, 47, 48 & 49, 50, 51, 52, 54, 56, 57, 58 & 59, 59, 60*
(above), *60 & 61, 63, 66, 67, 73, 79, 86, 87, 90* (below), *90 & 91, 100, 103, 106, 107,
108, 109, 110* (above), *112 & 113, 116, 188 & 119, 129, 131* (left), *134, 136, 138,
141, 142* (above), *144, 162 & 163, 165, 166, 167, 168, 176, 177, 178, 180 & 181,
183, 185, 186, 187, 190, 193, 195, 197* (below), *206 & 207, 211, 213, 218, 219, 220,
221, 223, 224, 225, 226, 227, 228 & 229, 230, 231, 232, 233, 235, 237* (above), *238,
240, 241, 258* (above), *262, 263, 264, 265, 273, 274, 281.* Zionist Archives and
Library *206* (above).

PORTRAITS OF POWER is based on a 26-part television film series entitled
"Portraits of Power: Those Who Shaped the Twentieth Century,"
narrated by Henry Fonda. The television series was developed by
executive producers Sam Summerlin and Pat Ferns, was produced by
Nielsen-Ferns International Ltd. and New York Times Productions, and
is available through Learning Systems Corporation of America.

JEREMY MURRAY-BROWN was born in 1932 in the Northwest Frontier Province of India. He was educated at Winchester College and New College, Oxford, where he took a first class honors degree in Modern History. From 1955 to 1962 he worked for B.B.C. television, mainly as a producer on the public affairs program, Panorama. He left the B.B.C. in 1962 to concentrate on his freelance activities as an author and filmmaker. His films, among them a number of important historical documentaries, have appeared on television both in Britain and North America. Mr. Murray-Brown has compiled the essays included in this book and is the story consultant and director for the companion television film series.

RAYMOND H. ANDERSON joined *The New York Times* in July 1960 as a copy editor specializing in the Soviet Union and eastern Europe and almost six years later became a *Times* correspondent in Moscow. In 1969 he moved to the Cairo bureau and then in 1972 was appointed to Yugoslavia with responsibility for eastern Europe. At present Mr. Anderson holds the post of copy editor on the foreign desk, his special interest being the Middle East.

DAVID BINDER was born in London, England, the son of a newspaper family. He was educated in the United States, graduating from Harvard College in 1953; in the following year he studied at Cologne University as a Fulbright scholar. In 1956 he received a fellowship from the Institute of Current World Affairs to carry out a study of East and West Germany and, as a result of his research, wrote a series of 50 reports. Mr. Binder was appointed Berlin correspondent of the London *Daily Mail* in the spring of 1959. As the Berlin crisis ebbed, he turned his attention to East Bloc affairs and joined *The New York Times* foreign news desk in 1961.

TURNER CATLEDGE can be said to have been a newspaperman for over half a century, having spent most of those years with *The New York Times*. He grew up in Mississippi and at 14 started work setting type for a local weekly. He first joined *The Times* in 1929; in 1943 and 1944 he covered the European battlefronts and the South Pacific. Mr. Catledge scored a world reporting exclusive in May 1957 with his interview with Russian premier Nikita Khrushchev. He resigned as a vice president of *The Times* in 1970. He is the author, with Joseph W. Alsop, Jr., of *The 168 Days*, a study of President Roosevelt's unsuccessful effort to expand the Supreme Court, and is also the author of *My Life and The Times*, a volume of memoirs of his career, which was published in 1971.

RICHARD EDER is the chief drama critic of *The New York Times*, succeeding Clive Barnes in the post at the end of 1976. Mr. Eder was born in Washington D.C., but grew up in Buenos Aires, and graduated from Harvard College in 1954. His first foreign posting with *The Times* was to Bogota, where he spent three years. He returned to the United States as a member of the Washington bureau and early in 1967 was appointed correspondent in Belgrade. From Yugoslavia he moved to the Madrid bureau where he served for four years before joining *The Times* London bureau in June 1972.

PAUL GRIMES was born in New York City and graduated in 1948 from Cornell University. His first foreign assignment was in 1959 as *The Times* chief correspondent to South Asia, based in New Delhi. Three years later he returned to New York to become assistant to the foreign news editor, a job he held until 1966 when he left the newspaper to join *The Philadelphia Bulletin*. In 1973 he was the only reporter to cover the Yom Kippur War from both the Israeli and Egyptian sides. In all he has made nine reporting trips to Israel and Arab countries. In 1974 Mr. Grimes returned to the foreign desk at *The New York Times* and now holds the post of assistant business/financial editor.

DREW MIDDLETON was appointed military correspondent for *The New York Times* in May 1970. In 1939 he had gone to London to cover sports for the *Associated Press* and found himself covering a war instead. At 25 he was the youngest reporter with the British Expeditionary Force; from 1944 to 1946 he reported from Britain, French North Africa, Germany, France and Belgium and won many awards for his work, including the U.S. Navy Certificate of Merit, the U.S. Medal of Freedom and the Order of the British Empire, military division. From 1946 to 1965 Mr. Middleton served as *The Times* chief correspondent in Moscow, Germany, London and Paris. He was then appointed head of the United Nations bureau in New York and four years later, in 1969, was posted to Brussels as European affairs correspondent.

HARRISON E. SALISBURY retired on January 1, 1974, as associate editor of *The New York Times*. He joined the staff of *The Times* in 1949 as Moscow correspondent. In 1944 he had been head of *United Press's* Moscow bureau and during eight months in Russia had traveled 25,000 miles. From 1945 to 1948 Mr. Salisbury held the post of foreign news editor of *U.P.*, and covered the founding of the United Nations. He won the Pulitzer Prize in 1955 for his reporting from Russia, and has received many other journalistic awards, particularly for his unique reporting from Hanoi at the height of the Vietnam War. In 1972 Mr. Salisbury visited China and became the first Western correspondent in many years to visit North Korea. He is the author of more than a dozen books, including *The 900 Days: The Siege of Leningrad* and *To Peking and Beyond*.

ROBERT B. SEMPLE JR. was appointed foreign news editor of *The New York Times* in December 1976, returning from London where he had been chief of *The Times* bureau since May 1975. In 1959 Mr. Semple graduated from Yale with honors in history, spent the next year on a Carnegie Teaching Fellowship teaching European history at Yale, and during 1960-61 attended the University of California at Berkeley under a Woodrow Wilson Fellowship to obtain his M.A. degree in American history. In 1961 Mr. Semple worked at *The Wall Street Journal* and was subsequently on the staff of *The National Observer*, before joining *The New York Times*.

TERENCE SMITH became *The New York Times* White House correspondent in January 1978, and is based in Washington. Mr. Smith joined *The New York Herald Tribune* in 1962 and moved to *The New York Times* in 1965. He went to Israel for *The Times* in June 1967 and from 1968 to 1969 headed the Bangkok bureau. He spent 18 months as bureau chief in Saigon before being assigned to Washington where he specialized in foreign affairs. He returned to Israel as bureau chief in 1972, remaining there until 1976. Mr. Smith has contributed articles on subjects as varied as sports, politics and foreign affairs to *The New York Times Magazine*, *Esquire*, *Harper's*, *The New Republic* and *Saturday Review*.

ROBERT TRUMBULL is based in Honolulu, having served as chief of the Ottawa bureau of *The New York Times* from 1974 to 1978, although he had previously spent more than three decades in Asia and the Pacific. Born in Chicago, he became Honolulu correspondent for *The Times* shortly after the attack on Pearl Harbor. Covering the war for the newspaper, Mr. Trumbull was aboard the *Missouri* for the ceremonies marking Japan's surrender. After the war, he headed the bureaus in Singapore, New Delhi, Tokyo and Hong Kong, culminating in a roving assignment in Australia, New Zealand and the South Pacific islands. His interviews have covered the full spectrum, ranging from Ho Chi Minh to Mahatma Gandhi. Robert Trumbull is the author of several books, among them *The Scrutable East*, a personal account of events in Southeast Asia, and chosen by the Overseas Press Club of America as the "Best Book on Foreign Affairs in 1964."